Village of Immigrants

Rivergate Regionals

Rivergate Regionals is a collection of books published by Rutgers University Press focusing on New Jersey and the surrounding area. Since its founding in 1936, Rutgers University Press has been devoted to serving the people of New Jersey and this collection solidifies that tradition. The books in the Rivergate Regionals Collection explore history, politics, nature and the environment, recreation, sports, health and medicine, and the arts. By incorporating the collection within the larger Rutgers University Press editorial program, the Rivergate Regionals Collection enhances our commitment to publishing the best books about our great state and the surrounding region.

Village of Immigrants

Latinos in an Emerging America

Diana R. Gordon

RUTGERS UNIVERSITY PRESS

NEW BRUNSWICK, NEW JERSEY, AND LONDON

Library of Congress Cataloging-in-Publication Data
Gordon, Diana R.
    Village of immigrants : Latinos in an emerging America / Diana R. Gordon.
        pages cm. — (Rivergate regionals)
    Includes bibliographical references and index.
    ISBN 978–0–8135–7590–2 (hardcover : alkaline paper) — ISBN 978–0–8135–7591–9 (ePub)
— ISBN 978–0–8135–7592–6 (Web PDF)
    1. Hispanic Americans—New York (State)—Greenport—Social conditions. 2.
Immigrants—New York (State)—Greenport—Social conditions. 3. Working class—New
York (State)—Greenport—Social conditions. 4. Hispanic Americans—New York (State)—
Greenport—Biography. 5. Immigrants—New York (State)—Greenport—Biography.
6. Working class—New York (State)—Greenport—Biography. 7. Social change—New
York (State)—Greenport. 8. Greenport (N.Y.)—Ethnic relations. 9. Greenport (N.Y.)—
Biography. 10. Greenport (N.Y.)—Economic conditions. I. Title.
    F129.G714G67 2015
    305.9'069120974721—dc23
    2015002824

A British Cataloging-in-Publication record for this book is available from the British Library.

Visit our website: http://rutgerspress.rutgers.edu

Manufactured in the United States of America

CONTENTS

PREFACE

This book is the result of both personal interest and professional discomfort.

It was not until *after* I had taught a doctoral course on American immigration policy—twice—that I realized I knew almost nothing about how that policy affected the everyday lives of both recent immigrants and the native-born. What did it mean to empower a million new citizens each year and yet leave many times that number of eager and anxious migrants in vulnerable limbo because they had dared to cross our borders illegally or overstay their visas in search of better and freer lives? How were recent arrivals, whether documented or not, coping with the hardships of settlement—opportunities for work and education that were often thwarted, a "path to citizenship" that wound through a bureaucratic bog or was blocked from the start, communities that were ambivalent at best about their presence? And how were those communities, lacking both resources and coherent guidance from the federal government, handling the demands—social and political as well as material—of a new and needy population? I could not illuminate for my students the daily details that would have turned the history and theory of my classes into rich reality.

Then I moved to Greenport, New York, a village of three thousand people (including about eight hundred second-home owners) on the North Fork of Long Island, ninety miles from New York City. I had known Greenport in another life, but it was then a dilapidated, drug-infested stopover on the way to lovely, nearby Shelter Island. Now, however, it was lively and attractive, worthy of being included in a *Forbes* feature on "America's Prettiest Towns" in 2011. Although I had noticed a Hispanic presence in the supermarket and behind the counter at the pharmacy, I was surprised to discover that Latinos made up a third of the full-time residents in 2010. What were these immigrants doing in a small town, far from the urban hurly-burly that absorbed most European immigrants of the past? Were they part of the renaissance of the village? With few exceptions, they had arrived from Latin American countries since the 1990s and tucked themselves into available rental housing with very little fuss. Most were undocumented and worked in low-wage jobs—often seasonal, as Greenport is a much busier place when the attractions of boating and beaches bring urban visitors—while sending their children to local schools. Several small businesses owned or managed by Latino immigrants had sprung up and were surviving, perhaps even thriving.

A few months after I became a Greenporter, a terrible thing happened. A group of boys from Patchogue and Medford, small adjoining towns west of Greenport, killed an Ecuadorean man who had lived and worked in the United States for many years. They did not know Marcelo Lucero; he was simply a target, game in the sport of attacking "beaners," poor brown-skinned men assumed to be immigrants. This was not the first violent crime committed against a Latino in the area; in fact, Suffolk County had a decade-long history of harassment and worse, spurred by anti-immigrant groups and antagonistic politicians.

Greenport is not far from towns where hostility to recent arrivals is the norm. By contrast, however, it is relatively peaceful. I decided to channel my general curiosity into a particular investigation: how twenty-first-century immigrants in this village were faring in the ambiguous atmosphere of current immigration policy. What interested me most was the ecology of a small town undergoing demographic transformation, the interplay of lives and their surroundings. This meant poking my nose into the business of the institutions that interact with the newcomers—education, health care, housing, law enforcement, work—as well as discovering how the immigrants were handling both obstacles and opportunities they would never have known at home (or in a larger community, perhaps). The results of both kinds of inquiry are on display in the following pages.

◆ ◆ ◆

Although I was an academic for twenty-five years, this is not a scholarly work. My method is not rigorous and my conclusions, though based on interviews with almost a hundred Greenport residents between 2011 and 2014, are very personal. As I came to know members of the immigrant community in the village, hanging out became more important than structured conversations. I do not pretend to be objective about the contributions that Latino immigrants have made to the revitalization of Greenport; as the former mayor David Kapell says, "They've saved this town." The rescue may not, however, be permanent; the cautious tolerance of the migrants by typical native-born Greenporters is a fragile adaptation to the globalizing demographics of twenty-first-century America. As a professor, I would have wanted my work to lead to generalizable findings. But this book is a tale of a town, giving glimpses of individuals' lives and the forces that shape their trajectories. Perhaps Greenport has something to offer other small towns confronting new and sometimes threatening population shifts; it's a situation that many are sharing. I have found both the unique and the universal in the experiences of both immigrants and the native-born. The warp and woof of village life yields patterns as well as irregularities.

A note about confidentiality: It is always difficult to write about living people and particularly when some are not in the country legally. I have changed many names, most often because of immigration status but sometimes because people wished to protect their privacy. Disguising employers who defy the law by employing workers without papers was necessary. I have also occasionally changed identifying details—a child's age or the location of an event—for similar reasons. But the events themselves are always rendered with the greatest truth I can bring to them, and the quotes are always taken from my interviews.

And notes about nomenclature: Recent debate about how to refer to immigrants whose presence in the country is not legalized by citizenship or permit (visa, green card, or employment authorization document [EAD]) has not led to resolution. Immigrants' supporters have reacted with indignation to their identification as aliens or "illegals"—two recent books about immigration enforcement are titled *No One Is Illegal*—but the *New York Times* abandoned the term "illegal immigrants" only in 2013 and only in part. I don't wish to reduce human beings to mere bearers of legal status, but identifying people by that characteristic is necessary in a book about the consequences of immigration; so I use a variety of labels, most frequently "undocumented immigrants" or "unauthorized migrants" and occasionally "people *sin papeles*." At least these tags leave room in an individual's identity for other, less stigmatizing attributes. I also use "Hispanic" and "Latino" interchangeably.

◆ ◆ ◆

I have incurred many debts in working on this book. Discussing immigration as a set of policy questions is difficult enough, but talking about individual experiences—whether of harrowing border crossings or employers' exploitation of undocumented workers—is even more emotionally charged. Both immigrants and native Greenporters have given me multiple interviews, sometimes reviving very painful memories. I am deeply grateful for the generosity with which people have helped me with this project.

As with other books I've written, libraries have been of great value, even in this time when books and documents are so often in electronic form. The staff of the Floyd Memorial Library in Greenport was of great assistance, and the Live-Brary access to the Suffolk County public library system made much of what I needed available within forty-eight hours. For academic journals, I depended on the databases and physical collections of the Mina Rees Library at the Graduate Center of the City University of New York. The history chapters could not have been written without the help of Dan McCarthy (especially) and Melissa Andruski at the Southold Free Library; the resources they shared, from the Whitaker Collection of the Southold Free Library and the Southold Historical Society, were invaluable. Antonia Booth and Joe Townsend read history chapter drafts and gave me very useful suggestions.

Special thanks go to Sister Margaret Smyth, who heads the North Fork Spanish Apostolate, and to former Greenport mayor David Kapell, who provided both his time and his wisdom to launch me on the project. They gave me many interviews, suggested others to speak with, and generally supported my interest in telling Greenport's story. I also profited enormously from conversations with Greenport mayor David Nyce. I am most grateful to Sandra Dunn of the Hagedorn Foundation, not only for the two-year grant I received but also for counsel and expertise beyond her duties as program director. It will be a great loss to Long Island and to issues of immigrant integration and civic engagement when Hagedorn closes its doors at the end of 2017.

I am delighted that Marlie Wasserman at Rutgers has believed in my work for the second time. Thanks to her and her team for their competence and support.

Every writer needs a live-in editor, supporter, and occasional scold. Michael Keating has been mine, and I couldn't ask for a better one. My women friends have read drafts and urged me on when I panicked: thanks especially to Marge, who gave equal attention to fine points and big ideas. But my deepest gratitude goes to the people embedded in these chapters and in my heart, many of whom still cannot be named.

PART I

A Village Transformed

CHAPTER 1

Hola, Greenport

If you were to arrive in Greenport, on the east end of Long Island, on a summer weekend afternoon, knowing next to nothing about its past or present, you might be surprised to see the crowds strolling in its tiny center. After all, it's just a knuckle on the finger of the North Fork—population 2,190 in the 2010 federal census, an incorporated village within the town of Southold, bordered by fields and vineyards on the west, bays and coves to the south and east, and the rocky shoreline of Long Island Sound to the north. To be sure, some sizable boats—yachts both bulbous and graceful—are moored at the public marina on Greenport Harbor just beyond the grassy expanse of Mitchell Park. The painted horses of the carousel promise at least momentary thrills for small children. And several fine restaurants lure a number of visitors to the L-shaped downtown—nothing more than the perpendicular arms of Front and Main Streets.

But the attraction of Greenport goes beyond watery views, boutiques full of items that no one really needs, and historically interesting residential architecture. For day-trippers from farther west on Long Island and weekend vacationers from the New York metropolitan area, the draw of Greenport is that it is more than the sum of its parts. Or, more precisely, each of its parts exceeds what is generally expected. The fancy marina gives way to more democratic activities—a daylong fishing expedition on the *Peconic Star* or a forty-five-minute putter in a graceful thirty-foot launch among the yards and small boats of people who are lucky (or foolish) enough to live in some of Greenport's coves. And Mitchell Park has more exotic charms than the carousel. For people interested in optics, devices used in the creation of

Renaissance art, or spying on your neighbor, the camera obscura housed in a bunker-like digitally constructed building (and one of only five in the country) is compelling. For music lovers of a certain kind, the venerable Greenport Band (founded in the late nineteenth century as the Greenport Cornet Band) offers a chance to both listen and participate on Friday evenings on the green. And the dense land use of the village gives it a real downtown, a feature that many visitors crave.

What the casual summer guest doesn't see—at least not right away—is the full assortment of Greenport residents. Better to arrive on a weekday afternoon in the fall or spring when school is getting out and African American, Latino, and white teenagers are walking home or hanging out downtown; retirees are visiting the supermarket and the post office; commercial fishermen are tying up at the railroad dock; and artists are emerging from the South Street Gallery life-drawing workshop. To get a glimpse of the class and ethnic diversity of the place, one needs to wander the side streets as well as the thoroughfares. Behind some of the handsome nineteenth-century facades are multiple dwellings housing several families in cramped spaces. North of downtown on the edge of the Sound (technically outside Greenport Village, which is barely one square mile in area) are recently built McMansions with commanding water views; but closer in are blocks where small, dark houses in various stages of disrepair are reminders that the average family income here is much lower than in surrounding communities.

In recent decades Greenport has been transformed in many ways. A model of nineteenth-century enterprise and innovation, it suffered extreme economic and demographic decline after World War II and staggered through the era of sex, drugs, and rock and roll without enjoying the associated excesses. Then its fortunes began to change. The efforts of a succession of progressive mayors and committed citizens began to pay off—first with the cleanup of neglected and abandoned structures, then with a visionary plan for a revived downtown, promptly aided and executed by government and private support. At the turn of the millennium the renewed village had become became a magnet—for the visitors who now throng its streets for the annual Maritime Festival and also for recent retirees and second-home owners who have joined North Fork natives in repairing and restoring its lovely old houses.

Middle-class whites seeking the attractions of the rural were not the only people who arrived in Greenport. David Kapell, the savvy and energetic former mayor responsible for many of Greenport's amenities, discovered a less visible population when he attended a Spanish-language mass on Christmas Eve in 2005. "I found the church packed to the rafters with Latino families," he said a few years later. The metaphor of Greenport as a magnet was relevant for them, too. What was, in 1990, a predominantly working-class village of about two thousand primarily non-Hispanic whites with a small African American community attracted an unprecedented number of Latinos over the next twenty years. The magnetic field was wide, extending beyond Mexico to Central American countries—El Salvador, Guatemala, and Honduras—with a few South American migrants from Ecuador and Colombia. While the force of the magnet—its nature, its origins—is somewhat mysterious, it operated with extraordinary speed, attracting young families as well as single men looking for work, benefiting from available rental housing, and building on itself as word spread. By 2010, Latinos made up about one-third of the full-time village population. Largely undocumented immigrants, they found work not only in Greenport but also on the surrounding farms and vineyards and in all the hamlets—Southold, Cutchogue, Mattituck, and the town of Shelter Island—of the North Fork. Their labor shaped and sustained the new economy of the village—building and cleaning houses, repairing roads, working in restaurant kitchens, and landscaping gardens. Their mostly American-born children were now a majority of pupils in the lower grades of the local school; they found medical services at the low-cost community health center (and Eastern Long Island Hospital, in emergencies); and they started small businesses. Most were poor and poorly educated (nationally, 51 percent of workers without a high school degree are immigrants, though the percentage is only half that in New York State), and they took on work that was often both menial and seasonal. Some had arrived with more debts than assets; the families they came to join had paid for their migration and now expected to be paid back. Despite these problems most immigrants liked Greenport and felt safe there.

The combination of economic development that has built on Greenport's charms—the sparkling bay, a vibrant downtown, beautiful parks and beaches—and a fortuitous bulge in the working population has attracted notice from many quarters. It doesn't come just from *Forbes* and the *New York Times*, which reminded New York City foodies that the trek to the North Fork would be a memorable treat for children as well as for the parents focused on farm stands and the local fish and fowl. Latinos outside the village have taken note also. A Colombian businessman who has lived in another hamlet on the North Fork since the 1980s says, "Fifteen years ago Greenport was just an old-fashioned town, with no one on the streets. Now it's very busy, and we go there all the time."

Quite inadvertently, Greenport has become an exemplar of a national trend—immigrants spreading beyond the coastal states and big cities, the traditional destinations of Europeans settling in the United States in earlier eras. Hispanics—many of them recent arrivals—are driving much of rural population growth nationally. In Minnesota, immigrants are "reversing the currents of rural decline," which spurs new employment possibilities for the native-born as well as for the immigrants.[1] Hispanic immigrants— documented and undocumented—are milking cows and starting farms, now that young Americans who find dairy work unrewarding at best and backbreaking at worst have decamped to the cities. In Iowa, where most counties lost population in the first decade of the new century, the mayor of West Liberty, a town about the size of Greenport, says, "I think if we didn't have the Hispanic community here we'd have a lot more empty businesses downtown."[2] The trend may be most visible in the Midwest, where mechanization and globalization have battered agriculture, but it's also observable in other regions. Independence, Oregon, with a population of 8,650 in 2012—35 percent Hispanic, mostly Mexicans, both citizens and not—reversed its decline so successfully that it was awarded an All-America City designation in 2014. Dalton, Georgia, has maintained its boast of being "the carpet capital of the world" with a heavily Hispanic workforce. All over the country, immigrant labor—from Asians and sub-Saharan Africans as well as Latinos—adds to the tax base of small communities. Where new arrivals settle down and form families, immigrants' children prevent the decline in the school-age population that characterizes many rural areas.[3]

Greenport's immigrants don't see themselves at the prow of a movement. The people whose stories are told in these pages are too busy trying to survive and thrive to see how they fit into the big picture. But they are participating in a national experience that may help to arrest the "hollowing out" of the American small town.

◆ ◆ ◆

It would be a mistake to portray relations between the immigrants and the native-born as tension-free. Discomfort over cultural and linguistic differences rumbles below a superficially tranquil surface, and racist remarks uttered behind closed doors are not uncommon. Competition for scarce resources, particularly in the area of housing, occasionally produces heated dispute in public meetings. But the native- and foreign-born live side by side without conflict most of the time on most village streets. Immigrants need not fear violence or overt hostility from the native-born as they manage their lives.

Greenport's tranquility is not the norm in Suffolk County. Part suburban sprawl, part rural outpost, part chic summer resort, the county is beyond the reach of the daily commute to New York City. With a population that grew 500 percent in the second half of the twentieth century, it appealed to postwar arrivals as an alternative—or complement, for the part-time residents—to the Big Apple. It was quiet and green and affordable; for many, it seemed a haven of white exurbia. Until the mid-1990s the ten towns of the county and the villages and hamlets within them were mostly non-Hispanic white and often residentially segregated. But by 2000 some communities had attracted substantial proportions of racial and ethnic minorities, and ten years later, a handful of those minorities had become majorities. The 2010 census reported that during the previous decade, while the number of whites in the county had declined slightly and the number of blacks had grown by 9 percent, the number of Asians had increased by 46 percent, and the number of Hispanics jumped by a staggering 65 percent. "These trends are expected to continue," announced the county's comprehensive plan.[4]

Not everyone celebrates that prospect. The arrival of a substantial Latino population in Riverhead, the county seat, and communities like Brentwood (population 60,664 in 2010), fifteen miles east of the county line, where some sections were more than 60 percent Hispanic, did not by itself spawn antagonism. It took human agency to do that. In Farmingville, a hamlet of about fifteen thousand people in the town of Brookhaven, young people influenced by the protests of an anti-immigrant group began attacking Latinos in 1999. The following year a murderous beating in nearby Shirley landed the two perpetrators in prison for long terms and led to intervention by the federal Department of Justice Community Relations Service. Violent episodes in many other communities in the county continued through the first decade of the twenty-first century, and in 2014 Ku Klux Klan recruiters attempted to mobilize anti-immigrant activism.[5] Attacks occurred in the affluent Hamptons as well as in working-class towns to the west and not necessarily in the communities with the highest prevalence of recent immigrants. They were sometimes met with official indifference. When a group of boys who called themselves the Caucasian Crew fatally stabbed an Ecuadorean in what turned out to be the latest instance of a regular game of "beaner-hopping" (harassing and attacking Latino men presumed to be immigrants), the anti-immigrant County Executive Steve Levy bemoaned the national coverage of the boys' crimes; the murder should have been a "one-day story," he told reporters. Responding to many complaints, the Civil Rights Division of the US Department of Justice opened an investigation of police discrimination against Latinos and indifference to crimes committed against them. No wonder the Southern Poverty Law Center titled its 2009 report on anti-immigrant violence in Suffolk County "Climate of Fear."[6]

The county is hardly the only locus of violence and hostility against Latinos and immigrants in general. Vigilantes have shot people crossing the Mexican border, laborers have been beaten in the Midwest, and a Mexican father of two was murdered in a small Pennsylvania town. Nationally, more than five hundred hate crimes based on anti-Hispanic bias were reported to the Federal Bureau of Investigation (FBI) in 2011; while this is surely an undercount of what actually occurred—many police departments don't collect data—we cannot know which of those crimes targeted immigrants.[7] A nativist network of well-funded anti-immigrant groups and prominent media figures on the political right has fanned the flames. The nationally syndicated radio talk show host Michael Savage, for example, said of protesters on a hunger strike—DREAMers, students brought to this country too young to have come by choice—"Let them fast until they starve to death, then that solves the problem."[8]

The problem, as extremists like Savage and Fox's Lou Dobbs (and Suffolk County's former county executive) see it, is that the country is being overrun by immigrants. From this perspective, the undocumented are criminals and, whether they are legally present or not, immigrants are polluters of American culture. More mainstream critics of the wave of immigration in the past generation express concern about the increased demand on schools and health care services, the prospect of increased crime, and the possibility that newcomers are taking jobs away from Americans. Some of the native-born are uncomfortable with the image of a majority-minority nation in just a few decades. They worry that the social and cultural identity of their communities—or American identity more generally—is threatened.

◆ ◆ ◆

Traditionally, immigration has been seen as a federal matter. More than a century ago the Supreme Court announced that the regulation of foreigners entering the country "has been confided to Congress by the Constitution."[9] But it also left open the possibility that states could enact laws that would protect them against those who were "paupers, vagrants, criminals, and diseased persons" as long as they didn't undermine federal law. In the grip of nativist fervor or under the pressure of increased demands on public services (or both), states and localities have been stretching this loophole in recent decades. The best known among current restrictions is the 2010 Arizona law with its "papers, please" provision permitting police to check a person's immigration status. In Suffolk County, which includes Greenport, local legislators introduced (but failed to pass) bills to penalize businesses that hired undocumented workers, prohibit loitering (i.e., "walking while brown") on county roads, and limit the number of tenants in rental units.

The ambiguity about when federal authority preempts state action has propelled local effects that both repress and support immigrants. On the one hand, national labor laws that theoretically protect everyone, whether legally present in the country or not, are widely ignored. On the other, a dozen states now grant driver's licenses to undocumented residents who pay taxes, have lived in the state for more than a year, and can pass a driving test and prove that they have insurance. Several states—New York among them— now charge regular in-state tuition for all residents to attend public colleges.

Although there are still some Americans who feel that the best immigration policy is one that deports undocumented immigrants and admits only highly qualified professionals, their ranks are shrinking. The country needs manual labor of the kind that Greenport immigrants do for the growing tourism and hospitality and health care sectors, just as it needs technical skills for innovation in the STEM—science, technology, engineering, and mathematics—industries. And Americans think of themselves as compassionate people, sympathetic to those who have fled threats of homelessness or repression. Polls find that a majority support "a path to citizenship" for immigrants illegally in the country, provided that they learn English, work and pay taxes, and have demonstrated a commitment to American society.[10]

President Barack Obama's record in moving forward with immigration policy reform is mixed. Although his administration has deported a record number of people, it has also propounded temporary deferrals that enable some undocumented immigrants to emerge at least partway from the shadow of illegality. But congressional intransigence, strengthened by the Republican sweep in the elections of 2014, seems, at this writing, to block further action. Prior political experience, when it took a decade for immigration reform to become law in 1986 (the Immigration Reform and Control Act), should remind us that change in this area can be a lumbering beast.

◆ ◆ ◆

As the president and Congress struggle with the complexities of immigration policy and politics, Hispanic immigrants in Greenport go about the daily business of fitting themselves into a small community where the language, the culture, the educational system, and the social life are all new. Beyond the economic contributions they make through the work they do, the money they spend, and the new citizens they are sending into Greenport's classrooms— most immigrants' children were born in the United States—they are not well incorporated into village life. Those who are Catholic attend a special Spanish-language Saturday evening service at Saint Agnes, the largest church in town. The men get their hair cut at Comb and Cut, where the barbers are also Latino, rather than at Anton's Salon, where the native-born are shorn by the descendant of earlier Italian immigrants. Few Anglos eat at Rinconcito Hispano, which serves lunch to Latino workers and offers *pupusas*, the Salvadoran national dish, for takeout. At the more elegant restaurants frequented by longer-term residents, Latinos are usually found in the kitchen chopping vegetables or washing dishes and only occasionally work in the dining room busing or waiting on tables. Relegated to low-wage jobs with little upward mobility, few immigrants work with native-born colleagues who could help them advance. As for political involvement, during the monthly meetings of the Village Board of Trustees, not a whisper of Spanish is heard—nor is there a Spanish surname represented on the board and only rarely in the audience. And the threat of removal, however unlikely, that immigration policy brings to every household with undocumented residents cannot be disguised or countered, no matter how comfortable the living situation or how welcoming the school system.

Although "Americanos" and Latinos move in separate spheres, their mutual need supports continuing prosperity for a community only recently rescued from the shrinkage and blight that afflicts much of small-town America. Hiring undocumented workers for relatively low pay is exploitation, of course, in the sense that employers are receiving more material benefit from their laborers than if they were citizens and, therefore, freer agents. But North Fork bosses are not living by the philosophy of plunder—they are opportunists, rather than victimizers—and few of their workers complain about starting wages of $15 to $20 an hour for laying tile and planting hydrangeas.

How to understand Greenport's success at absorbing immigrants in relative tranquility at a time and in a territory where conflict over immigration is the norm? Village history provides some clues. Greenport flourished under other waves of immigration dating back to the 1840s and extending through the early twentieth century. Municipal leadership has played a role as well, rising above the politics of hate evident elsewhere in the county. The immigrants themselves share some of the credit as they participate in a process of shared adaptation, where needs and interests reinforce one another. A force that holds the community together is Sister Margaret Smyth, a Dominican nun who provides service and succor to thousands of Latinos up and down the small communities of the North Fork. Through the North Fork Spanish Apostolate, which she heads, she provides counseling and sometimes cash, advocates for people applying for all manner of benefits, and works with local attorneys to protect workers who are victims of wage theft. A former school principal in Brooklyn, Sister Margaret is tireless in her support of children and families. Former mayor Kapell describes her as "a powerful leadership example for her entire community in her commitment to practical and humane treatment of the new Hispanic community on the East End."[11]

Most important, Greenport accepts its immigrants because employers need them so badly. As a 2010 editorial in the *Suffolk Times* noted, "Immigrant workers . . . are the backbone of our agricultural economy."[12] And the modest growth of village tourism and associated amenities—good restaurants, nearby sources of organic chickens and pigs, vineyards, residential renovation, and landscaping—depends on low-wage workers no longer available among the native-born. It's an old story. Immigration has always appealed to entrepreneurs as a matter of increasing profits and reducing costs. Alexander Hamilton, who promoted manufacturing to supplement the country's agrarian economy, told Congress in 1791 that immigration was to be supported as a means of confronting "the dearness of labor."[13] And a century later

Andrew Carnegie, a steel magnate—at one point probably the richest man in the world—saw immigrants as "the golden stream which flows into the country each year."[14] It was a self-interested perspective—a stream that fed the vast ocean of his profits. Carnegie put a value (in 1886 dollars) on each immigrant of $1,500 a year. But he probably had other kinds of value in mind, too. As a philanthropist, Carnegie made an impact nearly equal to his capitalist might; he gave away most of his holdings—tens of billions' worth if calculated today—before his death in 1919. An immigrant himself—he arrived, at age thirteen, in steerage with his family—he funded thousands of public libraries, supported African American education, and considered himself a "friend of labor" (though he was a ruthless strikebreaker).[15] And he believed that American hospitality in bestowing citizenship was a defining national attribute. He surely would have seen Greenport's "golden stream" at the turn of the millennium as more than a low-wage labor pool of quantifiable value. He would have shared an understanding with Greenport's employers that the Hispanic residents of the village are a fount of energy and industry that enriches a country soon to become majority-minority.

Will that wellspring of sweat and enterprise be enough to sustain Greenport's success as the multicultural hub of the North Fork? Will the tensions simmering below the surface erupt as housing costs rise and Hispanic students become the majority of high school graduates? Immigration reform that would liberate and incorporate the Latino community seems likely to be gradual and spasmodic. Without the development of an economic base that fully engages the working-age population of whatever ethnicity—and housing to accommodate it—the balance of interests in the village will remain delicate. So far, Greenport's acceptance of its immigrant population has enabled it to thrive without the gentrification typical of many East Coast waterfront towns. The future challenges are intertwined: to preserve the recent rise in the fortunes of the village and to incorporate its new population into that success. Meeting both of them will be necessary for Greenport to become a beacon of accomplishment for other small towns to emulate.

◆ ◆ ◆

Since this book is organized in a somewhat unusual way, it may help readers to have a road map. The structure is intended to present a kind of ecology of demographic change. Instead of biological organisms relating to their physical environments, we have people relating to institutions. Interdependence is at the heart, not only of the experiences of immigrants and their hosts, but also of the method of the book. So most chapters are of two kinds, interwoven to help the reader absorb the institutional along with the personal. Even this chapter has its companion profile, of Javier, who has experienced rejection and recovery—a poignant reminder of how many undocumented immigrants arrive as lost children—but who has nonetheless found solace and dignity in the limited resources available to him in a small town.

Before I present the remainder of the profiles and institutions chapters, some background may help provide context. One of the reasons that Greenport has received its immigrants with relative ease—not quite tranquility, but at least an absence of overt hostility—is that it has such a rich history of European immigration and internal migration by African Americans. Older Greenporters who have lived here all their lives often have vivid memories of a grandfather who could still swear in the Italian his father had used, or the aunt who had come north to pick potatoes as part of the Great Migration of southern blacks in the mid-twentieth century. Even when there is no specific recollection, an institutional memory of earlier changes hovers over the identity of the village. It's as though, embedded somewhere in at least some residents' consciousness, is an awareness of common features of then and now. For this reason, this book includes three historical chapters that take the reader from the first immigrants—English colonists—to the Europeans who shaped the energetic village of the nineteenth and early twentieth century and finally to the Hispanics of the present. A focus on African Americans' internal immigration, first as slaves and then as laborers arriving from the South, is an important part of that historical picture.

Following the presentation of earlier immigration in Greenport and a brief foray into the present demographics of the town, descriptions of daily encounters that confront current immigrants at school, in the health center, in court, at work, and among their neighbors introduce all but the final division of the book, while the accompanying profile chapters tell individual stories that relate to the chapters that precede them. The institutional chapter about Greenport's schools and how they deal with immigrant students, for example, is followed by the chapter about Edgar, a bright boy who arrived from El Salvador with some knowledge of English, eager to learn but confounded by the limitation on New York State's obligation to educate him. The chapter about law enforcement is followed by the chapter about Conchita, whose life has been defined by various kinds of legal violations—by others and by herself—but who has emerged as a law-abiding exponent of the rewards to society and to young immigrants when immigration restrictions are lifted. Some profiles relate more directly than others to the institutional chapters that precede them. Pointed inquiry into one facet of life may give way to the need to draw a fuller picture; the complicated background of Sofia's life with her children is crucial to an understanding of her quest for a permanent home but departs somewhat from the issues discussed in the housing chapter. And in every profile, the immigrants' real and imagined encounters with immigration policy and practice are a part of the story.

The interweaving of institutional descriptions and portraits is a simple way to understand what immigration means for different populations. It's a bit like alternating narrators in a novel. The concluding chapter, however, takes an omniscient perspective, positing a future ecology in which small towns incorporate their immigrants but also warning of economic and political uncertainties.

Lost and Found

The boy who came for help from Sister Margaret in late 2009 was forlorn indeed. As if the hangdog look and nervous shuffle weren't enough, he began to weep, silently but copiously. Short and muscular, he could have been fifteen or twenty-five—except that the torrent of tears gave him away. He was sixteen and had just come from Guatemala, walking with six strangers for ten days through the desert on both sides of the Mexican border. He planned to join his father, whom he had not seen for many years, but by the time he arrived in Greenport his father had taken off for points unknown—he thought Florida, but maybe Atlanta. "I don't want to talk about him," he said, looking at the floor.

At that time, Javier was living with his Aunt Rosa in a basement apartment that flooded every time there was a heavy rain. Perhaps he could have tolerated the physical discomfort. But it soon became clear that the aunt didn't want him. Now it was she who came to see Sister Margaret. Javier leaves water on the floor after taking a shower and walks around the house bare-chested, she complained. Initially, he was "humble," but no longer. After only a few months in America, he was staying out until ten or eleven at night. For his part, Javier was frustrated. He wanted to go to school and learn English, he said, but his aunt was resistant. She said she doesn't have time to register him, and even if she did, she didn't want to draw attention to herself. These reasons, however, seemed to be disguises for what she really wanted, which was that Javier go to work to help her pay her rent.

No child can avoid school if Sister Margaret is involved, so in January 2010 Javier enrolled at Greenport High School in the ninth grade. It was not a placement based on his abilities or educational background, as those were unknown quantities. He couldn't be put in a lower grade, because he would stick out as a much older student, and if he were at least formally in high school, he would be in the appropriate English as a Second Language (ESL) class. There were other recent arrivals in the class, and the teacher, Elzbieta Kulon, herself an immigrant (from Poland), spoke a little Spanish and was prepared to give him lots of individual attention. At first Javier said he had two years of secondary school, then he confessed that it wasn't "a regular school" but, rather, evening classes for young boys who worked during the day. With five brothers and sisters, a few half-siblings, and a single mother, he had gone to work at the age of eight or nine. School was only an occasional experience.

Such poor and chaotic young lives are not uncommon in Guatemala. Almost twenty years after peace accords ended thirty-six years of civil war, the country still feels its effects. Widespread corruption and unremitting gang violence make it one of the most violent places in the world. Labor laws are loose and often unenforced. Legally, a child under the age of fourteen is not permitted to work, but exceptions are allowed for families in poverty, as most are. "Child labor keeps children out of school," noted the UNICEF representative in Guatemala in 2007. "The numbers are very high and there's a social acceptance in this country that child labor is O.K."[1] Although six years of primary school are mandatory, many children don't attend regularly, and only 37 percent go on to secondary school—the lowest share, except for Honduras, in the Latin American and Caribbean region—according to a UNESCO report.[2] Education is not a high priority for the government; in 2012 only 3 percent of GDP was spent on it on it, about half of what Costa Rica spent.[3]

So it was not surprising that Javier did not fit easily into an American high school. The classes were too advanced, and homework (virtually unknown in many Guatemalan schools) was formidable. Although he was literate, Ms. Kulon noted that he had "poorly developed reading fluency" in Spanish and, of course, none at all in English. In addition to ESL he took global history, algebra, and biology, all of which he failed. He shone, however, in the cooking class, where he was interested in the subject and could flirt with the Latino girls who made up most of the students. "A pleasure to have in class," wrote that teacher on his final report card—recognizing, perhaps for the first time in Javier's life, the charm that was to emerge as he matured.

He was not a pleasure to have in the three class hours of ESL. Although it was obvious that he was bright, he was also disruptive, saying rude things to other students, listening to music on headphones during class, and ignoring the teacher's comments. "I have to listen and listen until I get a headache," he said, frustrated. Ms. Kulon saw that he was angry and couldn't concentrate; "He is often on another planet," she sighed. He had dreamed of learning English and getting a high school diploma that would qualify him to go to university at home and become a bilingual guide for tourists there. He had underestimated the difficulties of this project, and he hadn't realized that he would have to meet academic expectations in other subjects.

It wasn't just schoolwork that frustrated him. His quarrels with Aunt Rosa had escalated, and now no resolution was possible. Another aunt offered a corner of her living room, but that presented other problems. There, Javier would sleep on a mattress on the floor, but the aunt shared the space with three single men who also lived in the house. Javier was a proud boy who wanted to be independent, so he found a room in the home of one of his classmates. For a while this seemed a felicitous solution; his friend's family included a mother, a toddler, and two boys who provided some help with homework. He even enjoyed moments of fun, romping with their fuzzy dog. But the landlord had been clear that the small house could contain only four people, and Javier was the fifth. So the family was constantly trying to hide his presence, an uncomfortable situation for all. For his second year of American school, his registration recorded him as being homeless.

Repeating the ninth grade was no more successful than his first try. He was still distracted and angry, and he couldn't understand enough of the reading for his content courses (everything except ESL) to absorb the material. Outside of school, however, he was beginning to acclimate to his new surroundings. For one thing, he made friends—with other young Hispanic males and with an American boy who helped him improve his English. He was good-looking and had a sense of style, and soon he sported a spiky hairstyle and fashionable sneakers, aided by volunteers working with Sister Margaret. But school was hopeless. When an American friend tried to help him with his homework, he became so distraught that they couldn't continue: "A couple of tears trickled down his cheeks and into my heart," said the friend. Within a few months, he dropped out.

◆ ◆ ◆

If getting an education was not an option, at least jobs were plentiful, though hardly rewarding. At a restaurant in nearby Shelter Island, Javier washed dishes with a team of South Americans who could tell him what to do in Spanish, but they sometimes kept him so late at night that he missed the ferry back to Greenport and twice had to sleep on the bench at the ferry house until morning. At a different restaurant near the village, the boss (an American this time) yelled at him, he said, and did not pay him for all his hours in the kitchen. When he worked at a greenhouse, the temperature was over 100 degrees, and a job with the biggest landscaping business in the area (again with a Hispanic crew) was only part-time and irregular at that. In another restaurant, he moved up from dishwashing to vegetable chopping, which he enjoyed, but for that job he had to be on hand at all times and ready to work on a moment's notice. Even more irregular were pickup jobs weeding and watering for American homeowners. Although he was a competent and conscientious worker, he was defined occupationally by his lack of education and his immigration status.

Despite what seemed like insurmountable obstacles to living a productive and gratifying life in the United States, Javier did not want to go back to his home country. His mother moved around a lot, he said, which suggested she was homeless. He wasn't in touch with most of his siblings who were still in Guatemala, including the one who gave him money to make the trek north. If there was nothing for him in his country of origin, there was at least safety and friendship in Greenport. In 2012 President Obama announced that some unauthorized young people who had immigrated as children would be temporarily spared the threat of deportation and receive work permits, a program called Deferred Action for Childhood Arrivals (DACA). Javier immediately inquired as to whether he was eligible. (He wasn't, since his sixteenth birthday had passed by the time he arrived and he hadn't been in the United States for five years.) He began to think about developing new skills; perhaps he would learn to play the guitar and become the American version of Ricardo Arjona, the Guatemalan super-star singer-songwriter.

Most important, he finally found work that he liked and was good at. An older half-brother whom he barely knew had preceded him to New York and was working in Riverhead, the Suffolk County seat twenty-five miles to the west. He was cutting hair at a barbershop and beauty salon—"Our special services include modern haircuts for men, women, and children, colors, spiral perms, manicure and pedicure, waxing, makeup"—and doing well. Comb and Cut was actually a mini-chain, with additional storefronts in towns farther west on Long Island. In 2012, alert to business develop-ment in areas with many potential Hispanic customers, the owner opened a branch in Greenport and hired Javier's brother as the barber.

Here was real opportunity for Javier, who became initially his broth-er's apprentice and later his coequal. Always fastidious, he learned new skills—cleaning and fixing the barber's equipment as well as cutting hair. The barbershop has become a fixture on Front Street, and Javier has flourished along with it. Although most customers are Hispanic, he notes that it now serves *americanos*, too, including the police chief of Shelter Island. He feels confident about his haircutting ability; one client recently told him his work was "an art." It's the old story of an ethnic enclave—the term used by sociologists to refer to economic pockets dominated by particular national groups that hire and protect their members—coming to the rescue. The connection with family and countrymen has served him well. Although he reflects nervousness about his illegal presence in the country—"I don't feel free," he says—he knows that the network of entrepreneurial Central Americans has given him a modicum of security, both personal and occupational, that he could not have imagined in the dark days when he was out of school, without a home or a regular job.

But his situation has its limits, too. After five years in the United States, Javier is no longer the lost boy but a serious young man with ambitions for independence and advancement. Although he has tried, on his own and with good results, to improve his English—he now uses the progressive present and simple past tenses with ease—he needs formal language instruction and preparatory courses to help him pass the GED test to compensate for the education he has missed. He has applied to New York State's cooperative educational program but does not know how he will be able to afford the $4,500 cost. He finally has a comfortable room in a family home but wishes for an apartment with more privacy. He is not paid well, he says, but adds quickly, "I don't complain. I like the work." What he would really like is his own barbershop.

Becoming a licensed barber, however, is almost certainly out of his reach. He might be able to get away with not having a high school diploma—there appears to be no formal state requirement—but the licensing process would require a Social Security number. Barber schools are regulated by the state and likely to be vigilant about the legal status of their students, so using a fraudulent document is out of the question—and Javier is too honest to commit such an offense. For the foreseeable future, the protected employment of Comb and Cut is his only option. So although he is generally content with his life, the restrictions of immigration policy and the unlikelihood of moving outside the ethnic enclave with so little education have combined to lock him into a very limited future.

PART II

Absorbing Immigrants since 1840

CHAPTER 2

The European Legacy

At the entrance to the public meeting room of Greenport's Fire Station No. 1 sits an 1880 fire bell that, rung by hand, was for many years the primary means of rousting firefighters and alerting villagers to a conflagration. The names of the men who restored the bell in 1974—Giorgi, Skrezec, Heaney, Carlozzi, Jaeger, and Sycz, along with Biggs, Bumble, and Andrews—are testimonials to the richness of Greenport's history. They serve as reminders that, for more than a hundred years before the current immigrant influx, the village was an exception to the general rule that immigrant assimilation was an urban experience.

Greenport's history is a classic American tale of discovery, development, and assimilation. Looking closely at it provides an opportunity to understand how local character develops, what constitutes political leadership, and why small economies decline or thrive. Understanding the process by which newcomers became neighbors, associates, and citizens in the past can illuminate the transforming of the United States into a majority-minority nation in the present. A sense of history, even (or especially) as it relates to such a small community, can put contemporary immigration in perspective. Without it, Americans are doomed to be outsiders as globalization creates a world without natives.

What follows is selective. It doesn't detail the full range of countries that Greenport residents of the past came from, nor does it provide comprehensive information on the work that the immigrants did. It does not deal in large part with reactions of the native-born to the new arrivals, mainly because such information is unavailable. There are, of course, hints of suspicion and bias directed at immigrants. Mike Zukas, born in Southold in

1915 to immigrant Lithuanian parents, remembered in a 1997 oral history that when he was small, he heard his family denigrated as "dumb immigrants." That attitude changed, however, when his father bought a farm; he then became "Mr. Zukas." There are also suggestions of a welcoming spirit, as when DeWitt Clinton Sage built cottages for his brick workers who had families. What seems important to record is the organic contribution that waves of immigrants, starting with the colonists, have made to the vibrant community that Greenport is today.

◆ ◆ ◆

The North Fork was not uninhabited when the first immigrants—British settlers—arrived. The natives on the North Fork were the peaceful Corchaugs (a European mangling of a word in the local language, perhaps meaning "principal place"), one of thirteen Long Island tribes. They grew corn, beans, and squash and ate deer and shellfish. Local history suggests that they had been in residence for at least twenty-five hundred years; elsewhere on Long Island, Indians may have been present as long as ten to twelve thousand years ago. Elaborate burial rituals, with goods and artifacts thrown into the pits and on the fires that surrounded them, were common. One writer speculates that "much high drama occurred on these windswept hills of eastern Long Island 3,000 years ago."[1]

But the arrival of the first European immigrants to the North Fork in the 1630s and 1640s appears to have occurred without major drama. The Corchaugs traded with the settlers and showed them how to bury the local bunker fish *under* corn plants to fertilize the already-rich loam. (The fish were also called menhaden, an oily scavenger that was an important source of income for Greenporters until the middle of the twentieth century.) Their construction of a seventeenth-century fort—a rectangular log building in a wooded area near Peconic Bay—was intended to protect against other tribes, not against the Europeans. The Corchaugs deeded to the settlers the town of Southold—not once but twice, as the jurisdiction shifted in 1665 from the New Haven colony to that of Connecticut.

The utilitarian bond of Native Americans and colonists should not be overstated. It was hardly the equivalent of the modern expectation that immigrants will integrate or assimilate into the culture of a receiving country. The Corchaugs had no written language, no sophisticated weapons, and were themselves under threat of attack from other tribes—not a dominant culture into which the English were likely to blend. The newcomers seem to have been more occupiers than immigrants; a nineteenth-century historian asserts that "when it became convenient, they purchased the Indian title to the land which they had already occupied."[2] Deeding away their property probably seemed to the Corchaugs like granting a sort of license, rather than conveying individual ownership as the English presumed.

The Indians put up with abuse of other kinds, too. In addition to being afflicted by the plague and smallpox brought by the newcomers, some were enslaved. Antonia Booth, the town historian of Southold, reports that in 1648 James Pearsall of Southold sold to John Parker of Southampton for sixteen pounds an eight-year-old Indian girl, "becoming the property of Parker and his heirs 'during her natural life.'"[3] And there was sometimes a fine line between indenture and slavery. In 1678 a local Indian named Jerred, ill with tuberculosis and "not expecting to recover," gave his six-year-old son to Captain John Youngs (a son of the founder of Southold) "to serve with him the said Youngs his heirs or assigns as an apprentes until he shall have attained to the age of twenty one years."[4] So accommodation by the Corchaugs came at a steep price.

Some of the first European arrivals in Southold (and what would become Greenport) apparently had purely commercial motives and did not intend to stay there. They came to turn the oaks into timber or the pines into turpentine ("sperrits resin from ye trees in ye greate swamp," as described in a contemporary document).[5] Or they were advance men for settlers to come. The carpenter Richard Jackson, who probably came to Hashamomuck (now at the western edge of Greenport) with a group of adventurers from Antigua in the late 1630s, might be considered the town's first speculator. He bought his land on August 15, 1640, built a house on it, promptly sold it, and disappeared from the historical record.[6]

He probably would not have fit in with the colonists that settled nearby just as he left. The founding legend of Southold holds that thirteen men with their families and provisions crossed Long Island Sound from the New Haven colony in the fall of 1640, led by the Reverend John Youngs. Although a nineteenth-century historian called into question this account of the journey and the identities of the group, there is no doubt that Youngs and those who joined his congregation intended to create a community that embodied their Puritan zeal.[7]

Youngs was apparently a hard man with, however, a sentimental side. Born and raised on the outskirts of Southwold on the North Sea coast of England, he reached back to childhood associations and named the new town for his birthplace (though he left out the "w"). He shaped his new community as a village theocracy where he was in charge of administrative matters as well as moral discipline. The Ten Commandments became town law, as elsewhere in the New Haven colony, and at least one of Youngs's critics was whipped, branded with an "H" (for "heretic"), and banished for his effrontery. Booth notes that "temporal and religious authority was vested in the church and only white freemen who were also full church members could take an active part in governing."[8] The English immigrants very quickly acquired the power to exclude even their own—Episcopalian and Methodist settlers, as well as the truculent Quakers.

The colonists, like immigrants in many eras and environments, were often called on to wear many hats. Barnabas Horton, generally considered the most economically substantial of Reverend Youngs's followers, was a baker by trade but also had skills that gave him economic and political power. During the 1650s he served as a constable and court official for the New Haven colony and helped to regulate the hard-drinking settlers as "receiver of customs and excise on wines and spirits for the town of Southold," according to town records. He built a house large enough for his family of ten children, a local landmark that his descendants occupied for almost two hundred years after his death in 1680. As of 2013, there were eighteen Hortons listed in the local telephone directory.

The town of Southold eventually included the village of Greenport, though in the early decades of settlement the area to the east was simply called "the Farms." The second John Youngs, son of the pastor, owned most of it but seems not to have developed it substantially. What is now downtown Greenport—a few blocks of stores around a T-junction—took much longer to evolve; the 1838 history of the area announces that the village "has arisen as if by magic. Eight years ago there was but one small house in the place; now it contains about 100 buildings and 400 inhabitants."[9] It had already undergone several name changes—from Winter Harbor, because in that location the bay rarely froze; to Stirling; to Greenhill, named for a prominent topographical feature; and finally to Greenport, after the eponymous hill had been leveled in favor of filling in the marsh near the center of the village. Its waters and wharves had already given Greenport a whaling industry. And thence came the next immigrants.

◆ ◆ ◆

The longstanding local dispute about which town was settled first—Southold or Southampton, across the bay on the South Fork of Long Island—has not been resolved. Both claim to be the earliest town settled by whites in New York, and no definitive victor is likely ever to be declared. But one thing is clear: the first whaling fishery in the American colonies, established by settlers in 1640, was on Long Island in Southampton. Whaling began in the seventeenth century, not as an opportunity for expanding British power on the high seas but as the harvest of a subsistence resource from which all residents could benefit. The immense animals that washed up on the beach provided light (oil for candles and lamps), food, and soap. They must have seemed like gifts from the Almighty, a boon that didn't have to be cultivated or hunted—or even deserved. As a community enterprise, the early whale fishery was a smelly one, and rules were soon imposed. A local law imposed a fine on those who brought their unrendered whale fat within "25 poles from Main Street," since "the trying of oyle so near the streets and houses is so extreme noysome to all passers by, especially to those not accustomed to the sent thereof."[10] By the 1650s the colonists of Southampton were no longer willing to leave the discovery and exploitation of whales to chance. Shore whaling—men venturing out in boats with harpoons to kill whales at sea—turned the communal activity into a business that eventually sponsored longer trips and larger vessels.[11]

Greenport entered the whaling business somewhat later and was not an important whaling center. But, like New Bedford, Massachusetts, which had a fleet of 329 whalers in 1857, the village had a deep harbor as well as close proximity to Sag Harbor, where the government customs house registered every voyage.[12] And shipbuilding, along with the related trades of cooperage, sail making, and the construction of rigging, was already established in the early nineteenth century. So whalers could be both built and outfitted in Greenport. According to local records, the first whaler left the harbor in 1829 and the last in 1858. By 1834 the local diarist Augustus Griffin spotted "8 or 9 whale ships" in Greenport Harbor and declared the village "a port for ships and merchandise."[13] A decade later he commented that Greenport "has grown up nearly as suddenly as a mushroom."[14] The reference was presumably to conditions resulting from the whaling boom, as the railroad—an even greater cause of economic development, as it turned out—was only just arriving on the North Fork. Between 1830 and 1860, ninety-three whaling voyages departed from Greenport.[15] Although this activity was dwarfed by the more than four thousand voyages in the same period that left from New Bedford, the whaling capital of the country, it was at least more significant than the mere nine voyages that departed the neighboring hamlet of New Suffolk.

The captains and owners of Greenport's ships did very well for themselves. David Gelston Floyd, the richest man in Greenport in 1860, is estimated to have made $300,000 from the voyages of just one of his three ships, the *Italy*. No wonder the 1860 census records the value of his wife's jewelry as $30,000! He and his colleagues were among the local elite who never had to put a toe in the water, but the whalemen—the "blubberhunters"—were, by and large, a rough lot. Like the crew of the *Pequod* in *Moby-Dick*, they hailed from many parts of the world, "a polyglot mixture of white and black Americans, Pacific Islanders, Portuguese, Azoreans, Creoles, Cape Verdeans, Peruvians, New Zealanders, West Indians, Colombians, and a smattering of Europeans."[16] Perhaps 30 percent of mid-nineteenth-century whalemen were of African descent.

A whaling voyage could yield great financial reward for its sponsors and adventure on the high seas for its crew. That adventure, however, was fraught with danger and unlikely to enhance the worldly prospects of a young whale-man, since he was generally paid very little if anything. Conditions aboard the whalers were grim. The food was often terrible. There was little light and space in the forecastle where the whalemen slept—one study reports that it was common to have four bunks for six members of the crew—and the long voyages (sometimes lasting for several years) fostered loneliness and sexual frustration. And then there was the constant danger of being thrown into the sea and becoming a snack for its occupants. It is hardly surprising that on completing a voyage in an American port, an otherwise rootless young man could decide to stay put for a while, perhaps even settling down with a local girl in the New World. That's how Greenport got its most important Portuguese citizen.

Manuel Claudio embodied the mythology of the successful nineteenth-century immigrant. One of fifteen children born in 1839 to a Portuguese customs agent on the island of Faial in the Azores, he was hired as a twelve-year-old cabin boy on the Greenport-built whaler *Neva* in the early 1850s. In the town of Horta, where Claudio was born, life choices were probably limited once early schooling was complete, and whaling would have been an opportunity—for adventure, if not for much economic reward—for local youth. So when the *Neva*, in its long and roundabout journey from the Arctic to south of the equator, stopped at Faial for supplies, Claudio joined the crew. He first arrived in Greenport in June 1854, but not to stay. After a few more whaling voyages to the Arctic, he jumped ship in 1870 in favor of an American life. Perhaps he gave up whaling because he knew from his own miserable experience that whales were increasingly scarce and that their oil was no longer an efficient source of heat and light. Perhaps he was just sick of the dangers, the weather, the shipboard conditions, and the lousy (or nonexistent) pay. He must have been a confident young man; he married Ellen Heaney, a local widow nine years older than he—an Irishwoman with four sons—and soon had two sons with her.

He was ambitious, too. Starting in business as a liquor dealer, he then opened Claudio's Tavern, expanded it into a restaurant (which still exists), and even operated a short-lived hotel, the Star. By 1900 he had become a citizen and owned a house on Main Street, where he lived with his large family and a servant. And fifty years after he left Faial, his nephew, born as Francisco but Americanized as Frank, also came to make his fortune in Greenport. Benefiting from a small but powerful migration network, the second member of the Portuguese Claudios to earn local distinction could take advantage of the reduced risks and costs of immigration that scholars say provide incentives for migrants to follow the first adventurous family member. Once settled in Greenport, he worked in the family business, married young (to another immigrant, from Austria), and moved in next door to his prosperous uncle. When he died at the age of eighty, Manuel had outlived both his sons, but he had launched his nephew in the business that remains a mainstay of the Greenport economy.

Family migration from the Azores ended with the second generation. At forty-three, Frank Claudio, described in his obituary as "a generous, affectionate parent," took his two sons to New York City to shop just before Christmas in 1929 and died of a heart attack in his hotel room, leaving three children. William, the oldest, had to leave school after the eighth grade to help support the family and, ultimately, to run the restaurant. Through the Depression, the downturn after World War II, and the doldrums of Greenport in the 1970s and 1980s, he kept it going. The fourth generation of Claudios has taken up where William left off, and the business is now a small empire, with a large restaurant, a clam bar that attracts crowds of revelers for weekend dances, and a seafood shack that attracts the attention of adoring reviewers on Yelp.

For East Coast whaling, the Golden Age lasted about fifty years. By the time Manuel Claudio made his fortune in providing food and drink to the riffraff of Greenport (including other Portuguese and waves of immigrants from elsewhere), the industry was a shadow of its former self, dogged by many problems. Whales were harder and harder to find in the Atlantic Ocean, necessitating higher business costs just as demand for whale products faltered. Other sources of illumination—first gas from coal and kerosene, then crude oil, which was discovered in 1859 in Pennsylvania—were brighter and cleaner than whale oil; cheap kerosene flooded the lighting market and fueled American industrialization. During the Civil War, Confederate ships and privateers attacked the slower, heavier whalers, some of which met an undignified end, sunk at the mouth of harbors to deter hostile entry. And whalebone stays—made of baleen, a hairy, flexible plate found in the mouth of the whale—fell victim to the vagaries of fashion, as women no longer wanted the look of the corseted hourglass figure.

◆ ◆ ◆

The first European settlers arriving on the North Fork of Long Island in the 1630s and 1640s brought with them most of the skills and experience they would need to survive in the New World. In addition to the carpenter Richard Jackson, the group that came from the West Indies included a smith, a miller, a planter, a weaver, and farmers. We know this from a deposition taken much later in a property dispute by one of their number, Thomas Osman, who identified himself as a brickmaker.[17]

Even in seventeenth-century rural America, brickmaking would have been a valuable skill. Although most houses were wood frame structures, brick was used for chimneys and hearths. Osman took quick advantage of his skills. According to town records, by 1656 he owned a two-acre brickyard at the western edge of Greenport.[18] Like his contemporaries who were discovering fine clay deposits in New England and along the Hudson River in New York, Osman must have been pleased with the quality of the brick he could produce. He prospered, and when he finally sold his house and lands in 1684 he reserved to himself "the privilege to make brick on that two acres of upland during my own life."[19]

Privilege it was for the boss, but it was also hard labor—digging the densely packed clay from the pit, loading it on to a horse cart to be taken to another pit, where it was mixed with sand and water and sometimes coal dust and lime, then pressed into molds. The molded clay was loaded onto wheelbarrows or carts and set to dry before being lifted into the kiln shed, where it was fired. Working in the brickyards was also dangerous. Heating the heavy clay mixtures, building the kiln and maintaining it, the workers sometimes suffered fatal accidents. But the growth of the industry was unstoppable; the local brick was turning out to be as good as anything that might be imported, at great cost, from England or Holland. And in 1882 local records note that for 220 years "the tramp of the moulder and the smoke of the kiln have borne witness to the immense amount of labor performed" in making bricks at Greenport's pits.[20]

By then American growth as an industrial power was a "pull factor" for European laborers with few opportunities at home and the willingness to do jobs like extracting clay and sand for bricks. Between 1880 and 1910 the United States admitted more than seventeen million foreigners as immigrants, most of them arriving with the expectation of doing manual labor, at least at first.[21] That period was the apotheosis of brickmaking in Greenport. In 1882 the Graham brothers from Canada bought a small brickyard from a local widow and brought in Irish workers. Two years later it was sold to a retired sea captain, C. L. Sanford, who turned it into an operation capable of producing forty thousand bricks a day. But the most successful enterprise was that of DeWitt Clinton Sage. His Long Island Brick Company employed as many as two hundred workers at its height and supplied bricks for houses and institutions alike—thirty million alone for the construction of the State Hospital at Central Islip.[22]

Born into the brickmaking business in Connecticut in 1837, Sage apprenticed with his father and, after a restless youth, returned to it. In 1877 he founded a successful brickyard on Fisher's Island (technically part of Southold but geographically closer to Connecticut) and, ten years later, purchased 180 acres of land overlooking Peconic Bay at Pipe's Neck near Greenport. A somewhat awed report in the *Long Island Traveler* of the summer of 1887 announced that the clay on Sage's property was "of excellent quality and abundant in quantity," that a kiln shed for holding eight million bricks was to be built, and that the resulting enterprise would be "fully as large" as the enormous Fisher's Island brickyard.[23] The newspaper also noted that a boardinghouse and "tenement houses" were being built for future workers.

Although the Sage brickyard employed some Irishmen and Poles, the majority of its workers were Italian, some recruited at Ellis Island right off the boat, whether as single men or with their families. They epitomized the pattern of migration networks that prevails in many countries and which continues into the present. Several families—the Mazzaferros, the Caffarellis, the Santacroces, the Martocchias, the Corazzinis—followed one another over the course of two decades—from 1890 to 1910—from the same village in the Abruzzo region of Italy. Popoli, which crouches at the edge of a plain leading from the Apennines to the Adriatic coast, had been the seat of the noble Cantelmo family, but eventually fraternal and ducal conflict ended its regional importance. By the late nineteenth century, the beauty of the chamois and the edelweiss in the mountainous region on the western edge—the Gran Sasso—could not compensate for hardscrabble life in Popoli.

So, beginning in 1890 the families came—often a young husband first, wives and children later. (At least one of those immigrants, Gesidio Martocchia, arrived with a wife and three children. When the wife died, he inquired in Popoli whether there was another young woman in the village who was willing to come to the United States to marry him. It is tempting to speculate about the discussions in the village over this proposal, but all we know is that it was accepted and that the new wife bore him another five children.) It was a fateful move for almost everyone. A 2014 Greenport map of the homes of descendants of the Italian brickyard workers of one hundred years ago would be decorated with a thicket of pins.

The work available in American brickyards was both onerous and dangerous. But the Sage brickyard fostered solidarity, transcending the burdens of hard labor and forming cherished memories of Popoli and bonds with neighbors from home. The brickyard also offered housing that was vastly superior to the cramped and filthy rooms that were typical for new arrivals in New York City. The workers lived in nearby boardinghouses or, if they were married, in the cottages erected for them in the woods adjacent to the brickyard. The managers lived among them—in larger wooden houses and, for the immediate Sage family, a modest structure made of local brick. The children attended a little public school that was almost an extension of the brickyard.

Family stories about life in the brickyard fill out the cold data of the census. By 1910 Antonio Corazzini's new life was taking off. He had learned English since his arrival, at age thirty, in 1897 and had become an American citizen. His wife, Anna, had borne him five children; his oldest son, Thomas, age fifteen, was working with him, part of the second generation of brickmakers at Sage. The family lived just outside the main compound where the workers' cottages were, with a root cellar and enough land to grow vegetables and keep a cow. Life was still hard for all the families in the brickyard; they rarely went into the village because they had no money to spend there. But in the 1920s Antonio purchased an eleven-acre dairy farm nearby, which Thomas ran with his brother-in-law—also a former brick worker. By the time Antonio's youngest son, Paul, born in Greenport in 1904, became an adult, the brickyard was in decline, a victim of the Great Depression and of storms that flooded the clay beds and exposed them to erosion from Peconic Bay. But other opportunities arose. Paul worked for the State Department of Transportation for nineteen years, operating heavy equipment and learning to build roads, a skill not unrelated to brickmaking. In his spare time he put crews together to do asphalt work, and when he decided he couldn't rise within government he quit and went into business with his son, also named Paul. (That business is now Corazzini Asphalt, a paving company whose trucks and loaders rumble through the North Fork, fulfilling residential and municipal contracts, including the paving of the campus of Peconic Landing, Greenport's elegant retirement community.) In due time he would regale his grandson—Paul III, but usually known as P. J.—with tales of life in the brickyard.

By this time the connection to Popoli seemed pretty remote. Unlike approximately half of the Italians who came to America at the turn of the twentieth century, the Corazzinis did not return. Antonio's son Paul grew up learning to swear in Italian but not much more; as his parents embraced their new land, they did not encourage their children to use the language of the old one. But the family did not completely abandon the culture they were born with. Four generations later the Corazzinis still make homemade egg pasta and a special Italian Easter cake.

Employers and landlords often cruelly exploited Italians borne on the wave of late-nineteenth and early-twentieth-century immigration. The *padroni* who found them employment in the cities could be more like slave overseers than honest brokers, controlling their movements and taking a large cut from their meager pay. With too many people seeking too little housing, landlords charged exorbitant rents and stuffed whole families—sometimes more than one—into single rooms. But workers at the Greenport brickyards escaped most of such depredations. To be sure, there was some labor exploitation: workers could be laid off at will, and death or injury on the job was unlikely to be fairly compensated. But compared with the urban sweatshop conditions that many immigrants encountered in the era's rush to industrialization, the working environment of the Long Island Brick Company was relatively benevolent. Perhaps the rural character of the workplace and the proximity of boss and worker in daily life eased the inherent divisions of class and culture. For several years after Charles Sage succeeded his father as proprietor, his wife gave English lessons to Poles and Italians in her kitchen. More than one worker's child was named for a member of the Sage family. And time erases many barriers: the granddaughter of Antonio's middle son is married to a great-grandson of DeWitt Clinton Sage, and that great-grandson and P. J. Corazzini are good friends.

The Corazzinis were hardly the only brickmaking family from Popoli to move up and out of manual labor and into positions of influence in village economic and political life. And the process of assimilation began very early. By 1910 Vincenzo Santacroce had left the brickyard to work in a grocery store; the census taker for that year described him as a "merchant." He turned out to be a smart businessman who, despite being illiterate, kept the books for properties he bought on both sides of Greenport's main thoroughfare. While he was still working in the brickyard, he built a handsome brick building on Fifth Street, near the center of the village, where he ran a grocery store. He lived above the store with his immediate family, and the rest lived in a smaller building behind it. At some point, everyone worked in the store.

One of those workers—a reluctant one, she admits—was Lillian White. Her married name obscures her ancestry, firmly rooted in the brickworking tradition of Greenport. As a descendant of both Martocchias and Santacroces, she remembers that when her grandfathers worked at Sage, the workers were all given numbers because the bosses didn't know how to pronounce their names. Martocchia was Number Five, so for much of her early life Lillian was jokingly known as "Number Five's granddaughter." She notes wryly that once an uncle became first the tax assessor and then the Republican town supervisor of Southold, "They all knew how to pronounce his name." Assimilation had been a two-generation, fifty-year journey.

CHAPTER 3

Boom, Bust, and Back Again

Finding a good name for a product or a company is important. The choice must convey the special qualities of the thing to be named and suggest what they can do for a consumer or investor. Naming a community matters, too. The circuitous process that gave Greenport its name reflected the leaders' shifting priorities and an awareness of its future appeal. In 1831 the commercial interests of the village dictated the adoption of a name that would suggest its place in maritime commerce and its development as a shipbuilding center. The owner of the first whaling ship sailing from the village suggested the name "Greenport," a rebranding that might enhance his business and that of other maritime investors. It was the deep harbor, after all, that justified a local newspaper in calling a cluster of fifteen houses and five stores "a place of considerable and increasing business."[1]

Despite this early instance of self-promotion and the successes of its maritime pursuits, Greenport and the hamlets of Southold town were isolated, even by the standards of the early nineteenth century. Dependent on horse-drawn carriages for passenger transport and mail, they relied on ships to carry produce for export to New York, Boston, or the West Indies. But mostly they were limited to raising food for themselves. They were demographically isolated, too. "The people of these villages were of the old New England stock, with very little admixture of foreign blood," wrote a local historian and minister, looking back a century later.[2]

But then came the railroad.

"And the Iron Horse, the earth-shaker, the fire-breather, which tramples down the hills, which outruns the laggard winds, which leaps over the rivers, which grinds the rocks to powder and breaks down the gates of the mountain, he too shall build an empire."[3] Ralph Waldo Emerson's image was rather florid, and it could be debated whether the railroad built an empire. But it certainly built small towns. By the mid-1830s rail lines threaded the Eastern Seaboard, and the Long Island Rail Road started planning its route from New York City—actually from the western end of Long Island—to Boston via Greenport and from there to Stonington, Connecticut, by ferry. (What may seem like an indirect way to get from here to there was, at the time, the only technological possibility, since the unyielding rock of the Connecticut coastline made an overland route impossible.) On an August Saturday in 1844, the village greeted the first train to come all ninety-four miles from New York City. It shortened the New York–Boston trip, which had formerly taken up to seventy-two hours by coach or boat, to a mere eleven hours. And the two-day trip from Greenport to New York became an afternoon's journey. Residents of the several North Fork hamlets could now visit one another without hitching up the horses. At the turn of the twentieth century, the train made up to eight trips a day to New York City.

The euphoria over the possibilities of rail transport was not universal. A nineteenth-century historian of Southold noted, as novelty gave way to realism, "Many opposed [the train], believing it would burn their woods and kill their cattle. And it did to some extent. Its locomotives were wood-burners and their sparks were sometimes devastation, and it took time and trouble [for farmers] to fence in their cattle, but the railroad delivered them from their isolation."[4] For Greenport, the arrival of the railroad ushered in an economic boom. Although it was a shock when, just a few years later, it became technically feasible to build an overland route between Boston and New York, plunging the Long Island Rail Road into bankruptcy, the company survived and thrived as a local carrier. With Greenport as the end of the line, it built a rail center there, creating plenty of maintenance jobs. The freight trains took farm produce and oysters and other seafood to New York City markets and restaurants. The passenger trains brought visitors of many kinds to build and boost local businesses.

Leisure travel was still the province of the affluent, and "tourism" was a new word. But access to the train began to change that. Inns sprang up in Southold and Greenport, which quickly became weekend and vacation destinations for New Yorkers, both well-heeled and ordinary, seeking respite from the dirt and disease of the city. By the time of the Civil War, Greenport had seven hotels and a number of boardinghouses. The Wyandank, which opened in 1845 with a bar (or "tap room," in the parlance of the day) and stables for horses, later became an inn—"Motoring parties will find here a very restful stopping place," promised an ad in the 1919 Automobile Blue Book—and welcomed visitors for more than a century.

Perhaps Greenport's most famous visitor in the mid-nineteenth century was Walt Whitman. Just two years after the coming of the railroad, he marveled at how one could go back and forth to Brooklyn on it on a single June day—"all just as quietly as a man ties his neckcloth in the morning!"[5] He admired Peconic House, a "jewel of a hotel," and noted, "Neat new houses line the streets and gardens adorn them." In 1855—when the first edition of *Leaves of Grass* was published—he spent part of the summer in the village visiting his sister Mary, who lived there.[6] (Whitman had had an earlier, painful experience in the area, when, as a teacher in Southold in 1840, he was run out of town, accused of sexual "goings-on" with male students.[7])

The railroad also brought immigrants, with Greenport often the second stop in their American odyssey. The Portuguese had arrived by boat, and the Italians were often brought by wagon from New York City with their future employers. The new transportation option encouraged a flood of mostly Catholic working people from Germany and Ireland, with smaller numbers from England. Although active recruitment of foreign workers was the norm in the mid-nineteenth century, antagonism about immigrants and the demands they put on social and educational resources was not so different from what we hear in the early twenty-first century. New York, after all, by virtue of its port of entry, was then a border state, with all that connotes.

Aristide Zolberg has made the point that the "foreign paupers" who came to America in this period "simultaneously fostered the American Republic's spectacular economic growth and challenged its original political culture."[8] Most came to the cities. As workers they fueled the new American engine of industrial capitalism, but they also resisted its brutalities with tactics they had learned at home in German trade unions or Italian mutual aid societies. This duality is evident in different ways even in villages like Greenport. Although it lacked the factories and unions of urban centers, its transformation over the second half of the nineteenth century could not have occurred without both the labor and the cultural expectation of the new arrivals. The railroad and the immigrants that it brought enabled a spurt in commercial activity that supplemented (and sometimes displaced) the principally agricultural economy. That growth, in turn, began to challenge the old hierarchies and diversify political and social leadership.

In 1860 the men of substance in Greenport—that is, those who owned valuable real estate—were still principally farmers, with English names like King and Young and Wiggins and Brown. They may have inherited money as the result of nonfarm activity, like Constant Booth, whose ancestor opened the first tavern in 1720. (George Washington is said to have stopped there in 1757 on his way from New York to Boston.) Or they may have prospered from maritime investment, like David Gelston Floyd, whose majestic house is today an ornament on the outskirts of the village. But they still identified themselves as farmers, acknowledging their roles in an agrarian economy.

Yet Greenport already had urban energy in the early 1840s. With its one hundred dwellings and six hundred inhabitants, Thompson's 1839 *History of Long Island* called it "the largest and most populous village in the town [of Southold], and bids fair to become a place of much commercial importance."[9] Whaling, and the associated preparation of ships and equipment, had become an important source of local income. So the mushrooming of the downtown after the railroad arrived is unsurprising. Perhaps "downtown" is an odd word to use for the cluster of stores in a village as small as nineteenth-century Greenport. But the location of the train terminal adjacent to the concentration of shipbuilding enterprises at the harbor's edge constituted a space that encouraged the separation of businesses and residences that became the defining characteristic of commercial development in American cities and towns. And, as in the great city to its west, growth in little Greenport at this time was intense. Grosvenor S. Adams organized the First National Bank of Greenport, Long Island's first commercial bank, in 1864, with fifty thousand dollars. Smith and Terry's shipyard (later to become the Greenport Basin and Construction Company, which still exists as Greenport Yacht and Shipbuilding) expanded and took on the construction of everything from pleasure yachts to fishing steamers. The hotels that sprang up provided new kinds of employment. The Sag Harbor newspaper relocated to Greenport and began publication in 1856 as the *Suffolk Times*.

◆ ◆ ◆

Portuguese sailors and Italian brickmakers weren't Greenport's only nineteenth-century immigrants. Irish immigration to the United States began early in the country's history. Three of the signers of the Declaration of Independence were born in Ireland. Even before the potato famine (1845–1852), which killed one million people and spurred the diaspora of another million, industrialization and commercialization of farming drove landless peasants to find better lives in North America. When the great flood of Irish arrived on the Eastern Seaboard—more than four million came to the United States between 1820 and 1920—most settled in towns or cities, working in textile mills or on the new railroads.[10] Although movement to rural areas was rare, the Irish were already getting a toehold on the North Fork by the 1850s, working on the railroad or on farms. Young Irish women had come to work as maids for Greenport and Southold families even before that; many stayed to marry local lads and have large families.

Most Irish immigrants worked as laborers on the farms or railroads or in the boatyards. A few, however, began their own businesses. James P. Grady, brought to the United States in 1856 at the age of two, worked initially as a laborer in a brickyard but later became a ship chandler and broker; when he died in 1930 his obituary described him as "one of Greenport's most highly respected citizens."[11] Some of the nurturing, fun-loving Irish embraced what now is called the hospitality sector. Late in the nineteenth century there were at least two boardinghouses for Irish workers, and a local business directory listed two liquor dealers with Irish names. In neighboring Southold, the Conway family, whose patriarch arrived in town in 1852, ran a popular hotel for summer visitors for about thirty-five years until it closed at the turn of the century. A family historian notes that Margaret Kelly Conway gave birth to at least eight children during that time and comments that "there were obviously a number of summers when the hotel had a pregnant proprietress!"

For Irish immigrants, Catholic religious observance was important for both spiritual uplift and economic advancement. They worshipped in each other's houses at first, but by 1856 a Catholic priest was in residence in Greenport and land for a church (still the site of Saint Agnes, Greenport's largest church) had been purchased. Many German immigrants, who had also come in substantial numbers with the arrival of the railroad, were Catholic too. The non-Catholic Germans organized a Lutheran congregation and built a church in 1879. Religious institutions were often incubators of immigrant leadership, and Greenport's churches were no exception. Churchgoing Irishmen soon became farmers and craftsmen, while Germans were more entrepreneurial, perhaps reflecting their generally higher skill level. For a time Sunday school was held in J. Peter Drach's Cigar Store on Front Street.

One of the most important German-owned businesses was Jaeger's department store. A little more than a decade after he immigrated in 1878 at the age of twenty-two, Louis Jaeger—hailed as a civil leader and "oldest Greenport merchant" when he died in 1936—gave the village a full-service emporium that endured for eighty years.[12] Shortly after it opened, a local paper gave it the nod: "their prices are very reasonable and the selections they have made show good taste and judgment. They are young men of business and know what they are about."[13] At first Jaeger's leased space on Main Street; then it bought a larger building around the corner where you could buy costume jewelry, wallets, ladies' undergarments, you name it. When linoleum became all the rage, Jaeger's had a whole wall of samples—and would install it for you, too. Louis Jaeger's granddaughter, who worked there as a salesperson and buyer during the middle years of the twentieth century, remembers that the store provided baseballs, team equipment, and uniforms for the high schools in Greenport and nearby towns. It closed in the 1970s as her parents, the second generation of proprietors, aged and competition from big-box stores loomed. "We saw the handwriting on the wall," she says.

Crucial to downtown development in the early days were Central European Jewish immigrants. Jewish peddlers brought clothing, pots and pans, sewing supplies, and the like to isolated towns and villages all over the country. Later they traded their itinerant lives for more stable roles as merchants and thus shaped local retail economies. This seems to have been the pattern in Greenport. Peddling went into decline with the advent of railroad transport, but tinkers and peddlers continued to come to Greenport from New York City. Immigrant storekeepers from Germany and Russia, together with old Yankee stock, turned the maritime village into a thriving commercial center. In the first half of the twentieth century Jews ran (but rarely owned) many of the stores downtown—Kahn's Corner Store (in addition to purveying candy and cigars, "We Clean and Block Hats to Perfection"), Stern's shoe store, Katz's dress shop. The American children of the proprietors began to be politically, as well as economically, influential. Arthur Levine, whose father and uncle had arrived from Russia in 1890 and founded a department store, was a Greenport mayor; his successor was Oscar Goldin, a real estate investor whose grocer father was brought to the United States from Russia at the age of four.

Some of the businesses of the immigrants involved close relationships with the old guard. Lewis R. Case, a farmer and local official whose forebears were landowners on the North Fork in colonial times, owned Louis Levenson's clothing store. Looking back at her turn-of-the-century upbringing, Case's granddaughter wrote, "At regular intervals Louis would come up to Peconic on the afternoon train, pay the rent or the interest on the mortgage, whichever it was, and have a little visit with Grandpa. He brought us nice presents, too. Then he'd go back to Greenport on the evening train. But first Grandma always asked him to have supper with us."[14]

◆ ◆ ◆

For all the hamlets east of the county seat of Riverhead, Greenport became, in the first half of the twentieth century, the place to shop. Haberdasheries, markets, a soda fountain, and an early lending library made it a tiny commercial center; "You could buy anything in Greenport," says an old-timer. But this commercial appeal was only a part of what made the village a lively spot. Seaports are notoriously naughty places, and tiny Greenport conformed. Sportsmen's Cigar Store on Front Street had "cigars downstairs, gambling upstairs, and dirty magazines in the back," chuckles one longtime businessman. Although whaling was long gone, the maritime life of the village—boatbuilding and bunker fishing—thrived, with all the usual corollary activities. Madam Pamn, with her bright wigs and the little cottages she kept for her girls—transported from New York City by train on Fridays—were objects of local fascination. Complaints about bordellos and a casino did not get much traction. (The local joke was that "the mayor was leaving as the police were coming.") "Activities like rum-running and prostitution helped villages like Greenport and others weather the Depression years, as both industries required extensive manpower and, in the case of rum-running, boats."[15]

Immigration plummeted in the 1920s in response to restrictive legislation. The number of people who obtained permanent resident status in the United States fell by 96 percent in the decade after 1924.[16] By then Greenport's immigrant groups, exemplars of the assimilationist ideal of the time, were mostly well integrated to the economic and social life of the village; many of the second generation no longer spoke their parents' language. (While there were surely more serious tensions, a member of one of the old Greenport families jokes that Catholics and Protestants sometimes didn't get along "partly because Italians drank and WASPs didn't.") There were still a few foreign-born arrivals, to be sure. Greeks, reminded of seaside views at home, came to the area and opened businesses in the 1940s, including a limousine service, a lingerie store, and the Coronet, a modest family restaurant that is still a meeting place for local people. But the pace of ethnic diversity had slowed.

Throughout those middle years Greenport was a proud little place, economically and technologically advanced, featuring municipal electricity even before the streets were paved and a sophisticated sewer system built during the Great Depression of the 1930s. Immigrants were gradually absorbed into Greenport life as the village developed its shipbuilding industry and various fishing ventures. They found work in the shipyards that built hundreds of ships for private customers and—most important for the economic development of the village—for the US government. During World War I the navy commissioned sixty-foot motorboats from the Greenport Basin and Construction Company. By 1943 the company was putting nearly a thousand men to work building much larger minesweepers, submarine chasers, and tugboats for the country's World War II defense. Immigrant labor was also vital to the fishing and processing of menhaden. The oyster beds of Greenport provided employment, too; at one point there were fourteen oyster-processing plants, where a low-skilled worker could labor while he learned enough English to find more rewarding pursuits. And there were jobs on the railroad that brought the "summer people" and in the hotels that cosseted them.

But bust followed boom. When World War II ended, so did much of the enterprise that had propelled the robust village economy. Without government contracts, shipbuilding became boatbuilding, and orders for recreational vessels could not take up the slack. The wooden boats for which Greenport builders were noted became obsolete. Other businesses were also in decline. The oyster farms that had supplied New Yorkers—for a while the bivalves were so plentiful that even poor people could eat them frequently—were already succumbing to pollution and overharvesting; the coup de grace had come even before the war, as the 1938 hurricane devastated oyster beds up and down the Atlantic coast. The menhaden fisheries closed, also victims of excessive harvesting as well as of concern that their smelly processing would deter the tourists. Greenport's appeal as a weekend retreat vanished as motels became fashionable and the old resorts looked passé. Greenport became a working-class enclave without many workers.

As jobs were lost and residents moved away, the village became a depressed place. Downtown retail establishments that had flourished since the mid-nineteenth century closed, a trend hastened by the advent of shopping centers that lured customers to the county seat of Riverhead. Motels outside the village now displaced the old hotels, which had hosted community meetings and parties as well as vacationers. The Hotel Wyandank, built in 1845 right near the railroad station where visitors getting off the train couldn't miss it, was still offering dinners for $1.75 in 1950, but it was struggling. By 1968 it was torn down. Vacant and neglected housing and a heroin epidemic seemed more characteristic of Greenport in that period than the graceful Victorian architecture and beautiful trees that still lined its streets. When Mitchell's Restaurant, a former destination for thousands of visitors from western parts of Long Island, burned to the ground in 1979, it appeared to be the last gasp in the struggle to maintain a functional business district.

Yet, for Greenport, the past has indeed been prologue. Nothing was more unsightly than the blight that spread from the rotting remains of Mitchell's. But it would be hard to find a more appealing small-town transformation than the park that, in the 1990s, replaced (and memorialized) the restaurant. It now welcomes visitors to its wide lawns and nineteenth-century carousel and entertains residents with its summer dances and performances of shortened Shakespeare plays. And each December 12, village residents who came from Mexico and Central America gather at the edge of the park to begin the procession around town that celebrates the story of the Virgin of Guadalupe. Once again, Greenport is a village of immigrants.

CHAPTER 4

Migration from Within

We usually think of immigration as the voluntary crossing of national borders. Yet, from the Dutch colonization of New York to the nineteenth century, the most significant migration of human beings to North America across borders was anything but voluntary. The development of commercially successful enterprises—whether shipbuilding in New England, farming on Long Island, or tobacco plantations in the South—was heavily dependent on the forced immigration of slavery. Internal migration has also shaped American life—notably the river of six million southern blacks heading north and west between about 1915 and the mid-1970s. Pulitzer Prize winner Isabel Wilkerson calls the Great Migration "unrecognized immigration" although it crossed only state lines.[1] Like many other Long Island communities, the village of Greenport reflects these movements.

New York, after all, had more slaves than any other northern state, and New York City (New Amsterdam until the British pushed the Dutch out of town) and Long Island had particularly large concentrations. (Walt Whitman's great-grandfather owned slaves in central Long Island until the early nineteenth century; Whitman told his friend and early biographer, "We all kept slaves on Long Island."[2]) Legalized as a response to the need for cheap labor, slavery enabled the rapid development of New York State's maritime and agricultural economies. Blacks were imported from the West Indies at first, later directly from Africa.

This coerced migration shows up on the eastern end of Long Island. The 1687 census of Southold counted 113 whites and 27 slaves—some Corchaug Indians but probably mostly Africans.[3] By the late seventeenth century more than 20 percent of the population of Suffolk County was black, most of it enslaved. A hundred years later the percentage of African Americans was 13.5, with about half enslaved.[4] (Native Americans as well as blacks were slaves then too and, despite a resolution passed in 1680 by the legislative body of the colony, into the early years of the eighteenth century.) North Fork families with slaves usually had only one or two, living with or near the families that owned them. An exception was Nathaniel Sylvester, a successful sugar merchant and the first European settler on nearby Shelter Island, who brought many African slaves from Barbados in the 1650s and who owned at least twenty slaves at his death.[5] And Barnabas Horton, the baker and local official who was one of the founding fathers of Southold, attached slave quarters to his large house.

Scholarly consensus is that slavery was less harsh in the North than in the South—with less physical abuse of the slaves, better working conditions on the northern farms, more personal freedom. But its oppressive heart could not have beaten very differently. Slavery was an instrument of social control as well as an economic boon. Under a 1712 New York law (passed in reaction to a race riot in New York City) slaves were not allowed to own property, own or use weapons, or gather in groups of more than three. Their masters were given the right to punish them, short of taking life or limb, for unspecified offenses. As in the southern states, slaves ran away, and when the Revolution began some took advantage of the chaos and fled as British troops advanced.[6] One scholar has suggested that some escaped slaves from the South reached western Long Island through Underground Railroad stations maintained by local Quakers.[7]

The American Revolution, with its promises of equality and freedom, spurred change in the nineteenth century. Prominent Americans like Benjamin Franklin spoke out against slavery, and groups opposed to it sprang up in New England and the mid-Atlantic states. New York authorized gradual manumission after 1799 and finally abolished slavery in 1827. Motivation for emancipation was economic as well as moral. Cheap white labor became increasingly available in the late eighteenth century, undermining the material benefits of slavery, which had high investment and maintenance costs.

Slaves who obtained their freedom during the interim period between the authorization of manumission and outright abolition bought freedom for spouses and children. Males took to the sea and became a labor source for American whaling and marine commerce, major nineteenth-century enterprises in Greenport. Augustus Griffin, a resident of nearby Orient whose diaries spanned the period from just after the Revolution to just before the Civil War, gives us a glimpse of evolving attitudes and practices.[8] An opponent of slavery, he notes the orderly and frugal character of local blacks who he says would be community leaders if they were white, and he speaks warmly of a local woman who, after manumission, "by indefatigable continual labour united with strictest economy," accumulated a nest egg of more than a thousand dollars, equivalent to approximately a half-million today.

The manumission and abolition laws brought liberty to some but oppression of a different kind to others. As support for slavery declined during the early nineteenth century, so did the African American population of Suffolk County. The anonymity of New York City, as well as its promise of a greater range of jobs, must have been a draw for manumitted slaves as well as for those who escaped. Some stayed where they were, but, caged by the poverty and isolation of small towns and farms, apprenticed themselves or their children to those who had owned them. They traded dignity for security—and perhaps for a chance at education for their offspring.

◆ ◆ ◆

The 1850 census records for Greenport and Southold reflect the pattern of former slaves continuing to work with their former owners. Black residents— children as well as adults—living with whites often have the same last name as others in the household, suggesting a holdover from the days when a slave's surname identified him as chattel of the person whose name he bore. Those records also give us a whiff of lives opening up as slavery becomes history. Jasper Freeman (a changed last name reflecting his new status) is a fisherman living with his wife and five children in Southold in 1850 in a house he owns. His sister, a carpet weaver, lives with him, as does his mother, a former slave named Dorcas, whose minister praised her skill as a seamstress in a remembrance written shortly after her death in 1871: "Thrifty or elegant households all considered it a blessing to have sheets, pillow-cases, table cloths, and other treasures of the linen press made by Dorcas. . . . Her nimble fingers were busy from near the end of the revolutionary war until about six years after the recent civil strife."[9]

Although many African Americans were still personal servants or worked for others on farms or boats, by 1860 they also participated actively in the commercial and cultural life of Greenport. They became entrepreneurial—as dressmakers, barbers, and shoemakers. The Sells family, whose forebears had been slaves of a prominent Brookhaven and Setauket family and had intermarried with Montauket Indians, owned property in the village. Ira Sells apparently prospered as a fisherman, as he is listed as a captain in an 1868 business directory. The black clergyman noted in the 1860 census presumably provided services for the "African" church that is noted on an 1858 map of Suffolk County. In one sense, slavery was behind black residents by then, but its effects would linger in the form of discrimination and thwarted opportunity of many kinds. It would also cling to them through the lives or memories of the next group who arrived to share their community, emigrants from the post–Civil War South.[10] By the turn of the twentieth century, however, it was possible for at least one bright young black man to make his mark as an intellectual; Wayland Jefferson gave talks on local history in the 1930s, wrote pieces for the *Suffolk Times*, and became the first official Southold town historian.[11]

◆ ◆ ◆

In 1904 Mabel Hopkins became the first black graduate of Greenport High School. She looks out from the cover of the pictorial history of the village, a handsome young woman dressed in elegant Edwardian style, a high-collared white dress—batiste or lawn, perhaps—worn for special occasions. A wide white bow affixed to the back of her head—a fashion shared by her five female classmates—belies her serious expression. Nothing in the picture reveals the route by which she arrived at this improbable achievement. Improbable because she graduated at a time when few young people of any race finished high school, especially in rural areas, and many northern schools remained segregated, in fact if not in law.

Even as they pushed for more education in the early twentieth century, African Americans knew that rewards from schooling would not equal those available to whites. And Mabel Hopkins's future appears to fit the pattern. Removed from her refined and unique status as a Greenport graduate, the 1930 census found her, at age forty-two, living still in the village in a mixed black-and-white neighborhood, working as a family cook. She had married a migrant from Virginia who worked as a caulker in the "navy yard," probably the Greenport Basin and Construction Company, which built submarine chasers for the First World War and minesweepers for the Second.

Virginia—specifically Powhatan County, not far from Richmond—was the provenance of many African Americans who arrived in Greenport in the first half of the twentieth century. Much like the chain migration of European immigrants, the Great Migration of blacks northward in that era was a river with many tributaries, most carrying multiple family members or even whole neighborhoods, either in groups or one by one. The arrival of the original migrant in a northern destination announced to relatives and friends left behind that relocation was possible; that migrant's growing knowledge of the new environment encouraged others to choose the same town or city.

Once they arrived, black migrants often found support in religion. Greenport's AME Zion Church was founded in 1922, and a small mission on Center Street held services for a mostly black congregation. The houses of worship also hosted social events. Sometimes these occasions reflected more than one form of recreation; one older Greenport resident remembers being taken as a child to a fried chicken dinner at the AME Zion Church, where the hostess was the madam of the local bordello.

Although most African Americans who came north to Greenport in the early days of the Great Migration were limited to menial jobs and experienced a good deal of racism, they could also find successful, respected families and opportunities for advancement. The Sells family, then living in a large house on Broad Street (its name suggests its elegance), epitomized the potential for success. Leon Sells was a contractor who excavated the foundation of the present Greenport schoolhouse. He and his wife Irene had six children, most of whom went to college.

For the southern migrants, life was harder. Josephine Watkins Johnson, brought to the North Fork from Virginia at age two in 1922, describes her mother's daunting progression from field worker to chambermaid. The daughter of slaves, her mother had decided that there was no future in Virginia because you could make only fifty cents for a half-day or seventy-five cents for a day. She heard from relatives that you could make fifty dollars a month up north, becoming a link in the migration chain. Jo grew up in Greenport, the only black child in her first-grade class and later Greenport's first African American cosmetologist and caterer.

A talented taleteller, Johnson illuminates both individual lives and the social environment of Greenport in the 1920s and 1930s. Poverty runs through her stories, often laced with wry humor. In a recital of Greenport memories, staged in 2003 and featuring a group that called themselves "Greenport Grandmothers," she reminisced: "My mother use to feed us fried bird sandwiches on cold biscuits. She would scatter stale bread and prop up an old wooden storm door over it, and when a lot of snowbirds got underneath the door, she would pull a string from inside the house, the door would fall on the birds, my brother would jump up and down on the birds, and my mother would cut them up and fry them." She also tells stories about how other Greenporters made do during the Depression: "The Long Island Rail Road had a special freight train that brought coal for its trains to Greenport. These coal deliveries always arrived during the night. The engineer would blow his whistle with a secret signal for the poor to come down to 'liberate' the coal, and you would hear cars, trucks, and wagons rumbling down to the station to collect coal in burlap bags and bushel baskets. . . . The railroad complained to the police about the missing coal, but nobody ever went to jail over it."

As difficult as life was for Johnson's family, it was luxurious in comparison with that of the later migrants from the South who came to work on the farms, often planting, picking, and sorting potatoes. (In the early years of the twentieth century Long Island grew a large share of the potatoes sold in New York City.) Recruited by contractors hired by potato farmers, black workers lived in crowded, filthy labor camps during the growing season. Jo remembers that their roots in the Jim Crow South were so deep that, bused in from the fields and camps to buy their groceries, they would wait in the long grass outside the store for the white people to finish their shopping before they would enter. Their labor kept potato farming profitable for a while, but eventually the rising land prices on Long Island, along with root damage caused by the golden nematode, killed the industry. By then, some workers had tired of migrant labor and stayed in Greenport.

Discrimination was a fact of life for African Americans in Greenport during the first two-thirds of the twentieth century. It mattered not whether they were descendants of slaves and Native Americans with a long history in the area or new arrivals from Virginia or North Carolina. Residential segregation limited blacks' ability to buy property except in a neighborhood near the cemetery. It was a major event when Lillian Townsend, owner of the Townsend Manor Inn and a woman ahead of her time, hired three "colored girls" in the 1930s as waitresses, not just chambermaids. They earned a dollar a day plus tips and considered it a decent wage.

Many public accommodations were off limits to blacks. As late as the 1950s Mitchell's, the largest restaurant on the North Fork and a favorite spot to dance and drink for several decades, was at least ambivalent about serving black families in its elegant dining room. In the "Greenport Grandmothers" performance, one elderly African American woman told the painful story of how a black doctor was treated: "He brought his family into Mitchell's Restaurant, and when they would not serve him, he insisted until they did. A friend of mine was in charge of the china and silverware for the restaurant. She told me that when the doctor and his family left, Mitchell's broke every glass and dish and threw out every piece of silverware they had used." On the other hand, one black resident would go to Mitchell's once a year just to demonstrate that he was there and that he was to be served. And he was.

The greatest stain on race relations in Greenport was the presence of the Ku Klux Klan. It still casts its shadow. As the long process that the historian Eric Foner has called "the adjustment of American society to the end of slavery" began, secret societies arose in the South to express the rage of white ex-Confederates ousted from power by Radical Reconstruction.[12] Determined to keep blacks from exercising the rights they had acquired as free men and women, members of these societies intimidated black officials and threatened black voters. They backed up their support for white supremacy with violence—lynching as well as whipping and maiming. Founded in Pulaski, Tennessee, in 1865, the Klan became the most powerful of these organizations. In promoting itself as both a patriotic movement and a religious crusade, the Klan targeted Catholics and Jews as well as African Americans. Federal statutes that criminalized participation in the Klan snuffed out the movement in the 1870s, but it revived during and after World War I. Black soldiers returning to the southern states from the war were lynched, and cross burnings terrorized thousands, sending the Klan's message that this was "a white man's country." The message arrived in Greenport, too.

"Southold and Greenport Covered with Klan Posters," announced *Klan Kraft*, the Long Island Ku Klux Klan publication, on July 8, 1924. The enterprise of Howard Mather, a rabble-rousing Methodist pastor, the paper announced its commitment to "Protestant Christianity, White Supremacy, Protection of Pure Womanhood, Separation of Church and State, Opposition to Foreign Propaganda and Closer Restriction of Foreign Immigration."[13] Mather had chosen an area where many citizens were sympathetic to the message. At least one older resident remembered his schoolboy association of the KKK with "Koons, Kikes, and Katholics." Open-air meetings were held in one of the stately old houses on First Street in Greenport, and cross burnings were common.

Despite the presence of the Klan (which declined in the late 1920s), the number of African Americans in Greenport grew. The Great Migration continued to bring blacks to the North Fork to join family members already there and to labor in the fields, shuck scallops, or work on the bunker boats that provided the fish factories with the smelly menhaden that made excellent fertilizer. By the Second World War, the most egregious kinds of overt racial intimidation had largely disappeared. Both blacks and whites, however, maintain that support for the Klan lingered into the 1960s—perhaps kept alive by the perceived threats of the civil rights movement. Some local residents suggest that Klan members or sympathizers were responsible for the murder in that decade of Carlos DeJesus, a black man who was popular with white women. Racial tension also flared at the high school in 1967 as fights erupted between black and white groups of boys, but the principal asserted that rumors of weapons in school were "vastly exaggerated."[14]

Greenport's black community has not benefited proportionately from the revitalization of the village. During the later decades of the twentieth century, many promising young African Americans moved away, and more recently some have sold their houses and migrated back to the South. Although black residents work in service industries or for the government—as nurses or orderlies in the hospital or the local nursing home, in staff positions in the schools—only a few are becoming prosperous in private-sector businesses like boatbuilding or real estate. And their absence from local politics is notable; a sole African American member of the village board of trustees during the 1990s was not reelected after a new mayor took office in 2007, and no new candidate of color has come forward. Although it is presumed that most Greenport blacks have been supporters of President Obama, many are not registered voters. Turnout was low at a spring 2012 meeting held at the Clinton AME Zion Church to meet the local congressman, obtain information, and organize the faithful for the presidential election.

The legacies of slavery, discrimination, and poverty may have stifled a spirit of solidarity, or at least the public expression of it. Val Shelby, a civic-minded woman who is related to many of Greenport's African Americans—she has thirteen siblings and her father also came from a large family—offers a partial explanation for the lack of civic engagement: "People are too busy trying to make a living, pay the rent. They are too focused on their own individual problems—as we all are these days." A heritage of disadvantage plays a part, too. In a recent *New York Times* column about the necessity of continuing conversation about racial inequality, Nicholas Kristof writes, "We all stand on the shoulders of our ancestors. We're in a relay race, relying on the financial and human capital of our parents and grandparents. Blacks were shackled for the early part of that relay race, and although many of the fetters have come off, whites have developed a huge lead."[15] Despite their deep roots in the village, many of Greenport's African Americans are struggling to catch up.

CHAPTER 5

Is Demographics Destiny?

On a beautiful Saturday in September 2013, Gloria Lopez, who makes excellent espresso and cappuccino at Aldo's Coffee in downtown Greenport, emerged from behind the hissing espresso machine and the stacks of brightly colored ceramic cups to look at the passing scene. It was midmorning, a time when residents would usually be heading purposefully to the supermarket or laundry, stopping for a quick coffee and a chat with Aldo, perhaps, or dipping in and out of Colonial Drugs across the street. But today was the start of the annual maritime festival, and the street was already clogged with visitors ambling among the curbside stands that sold everything from local seafood to knit caps for protection from next winter's storms. While they looked at what Greenport had to offer—wooden boats spread across the lawn of Mitchell Park, art and artifacts made locally or brought in from nearby hamlets—Gloria looked at them: day-trippers from elsewhere on Long Island, weekend guests from New York City, and denizens of the large and small yachts docked at the marina behind the café.

By and large, they didn't look much like her family and friends in the village. They were larger—Gloria is, like most Guatemalan women, petite—and louder and whiter. They appeared to be spending money freely and enjoying it. They were at leisure, a condition Gloria experienced only rarely, at least between May and October. During those months, the tourist economy of the village kept people like her very busy.

There are many people like her living here—that is, recent Latino immigrants from Mexico and Central America who make a modest living during the warmer seasons working at low-skill jobs in construction, landscaping, restaurants, housecleaning, and retail. Gloria is relatively lucky; Aldo's customers depend on his fine coffees, biscotti, and scones all year long. As the weather cooled, she could count on a rise in the demand for hot chocolate. Dispensed with whipped cream and grated chocolate on top, it would reward children who raced through the back door from ice skating lessons in the rink at the edge of the park. For many of the new arrivals, however, the winter would be a time of joblessness and deprivation as plant nurseries closed, fields lay fallow, second-home residents closed their houses for the winter, and restaurants opened only on the weekend.

Latinos are the latest in a long line of immigrants to discover this village. But that line—from the nineteenth-century migrations of Portuguese and African American whalemen, Italian and Irish brickmakers, and Eastern European peddlers to the new influx of immigrants from the Central America—is not unbroken. Unlike the Europeans who came by boat and looked much like the receiving Americans, the migrants from Latin America arrived by plane and on foot (and sometimes in the back of a truck) and were generally shorter and darker than their hosts. Equally important, they began arriving after a half-century in which immigration had virtually ceased and past generations of immigrants had largely been assimilated or integrated into American culture. The traditional issues of immigration—how much? by whom? with what consequences for the country?—had largely been dormant. They now arose in a new context.

What the new immigrants found when they first arrived in the early 1990s was not the bustling commercial hub of the North Fork that visitors see today. Although by then Greenport's fortunes were on the rise—thanks, in large part, to the entrepreneurial talents of Mayor Dave Kapell—the consequences of several decades of decline were evident. Economic misfortunes that followed World War II had taken a human toll that went beyond the material. The village began to empty out, its population dropping by 25 percent between 1940 and 1960.[1] (It was an exception to the mushroom growth of Suffolk County, where the population more than tripled—from 197,355 to 666,784 during the same years, with an increase to 1.1 million by 1970.) Young people left their families—a rural brain drain—and headed for New York City and other points west. The Ku Klux Klan revived locally. Heroin, no longer just an urban scourge, became a Greenport problem. And the decline continued all the way through the rest of the twentieth century. Joe Townsend, a member of an old family of the WASP elite, remembers well what the village was like. He went off to boarding school and college in the 1960s, and he returned in the early 1970s at what he calls "the nadir of Greenport history." "There was no one here between the ages of sixteen and fifty. It was not a self-sustaining community for someone with a college education, so nobody came back." (He did stay, however, and became a mayor who helped to revive his hometown.) For the first time in fifty years, the 2010 census recorded a population increase, though there was almost certainly a serious undercount in 2000, of which more later.

◆ ◆ ◆

Over the longer term the sagging economy's dark cloud turned out to have a silver lining. The village had always had a lot of buildings and apartments for rent, as the purchase of a house was usually beyond the means of residents who fished or worked in the shipyards. Even before World War II multifamily houses were built there. With the collapse of Greenport's housing sector, both one- and two-family houses were vacant. Many were in disrepair; landlords had neglected the apartments for the transient workers who often occupied them. But in an irony of community development, the housing vacancies set the stage for a chain of events that led directly to the diversity and prosperity that have taken hold in twenty-first-century Greenport.

With an abundance of low-cost rental units there and a swelling population elsewhere on Long Island, it was not long before the Suffolk County Department of Social Services began referring welfare clients to village housing—a form of racial steering, in part. Vacancy rates dropped. During the 1950s the owners of empty single-family houses got into the act too; they converted many Victorian and turn-of-the century structures into small apartment buildings, adding to the housing stock available to low-income people.

Landlords did very well as the demand for rentals grew. Although the tenants were poor, the federal government often subsidized their rents through a program (Section 8 of the Housing Act of 1937) that required them to pay only what they could afford and paid landlords for the difference between that amount and the market rate. This assistance to landlords assured stability of payment and reliable referrals. The beneficiaries were often the earlier immigrants—Italians and Eastern Europeans—or their offspring.

Census data can be yawn-inducing. But the history of Greenport jumps out from the population and housing reports for the second half of the twentieth century. In 1940, at the start of World War II, the US census showed Greenport village with 3,259 residents.[2] It had 978 dwelling units, all but 81 of which were occupied, about half by renters. The percentage of "Negro and other non-white units" was just under 5 percent.[3] That a good deal of the housing was rundown is evident from the census; 36 percent of the dwellings are listed as "needing major repair," while only half that share were similarly derelict in Sag Harbor, a village of similar size on Long Island's South Fork. But Greenport was a vibrant community with a distinguished past and enterprises ready to grow. The vacancy rate dropped over the next decade, reflecting the surge of business during World War II, then increased during the postwar slump. The 1960s brought a major demographic shift of the village, reflected in the 1970 census. The numbers tell a tale of both population decline—of 5 percent in just a decade—and racial integration, with seventy-one black heads of household, the greatest number in any community of comparable size (population under twenty-five hundred) in New York State. The houses that emptied out after the war were empty no longer. Thanks to landlords who had done well by doing good, renting to poor and black people, the vacancy rate in 1970 was only 3.5 percent.[4]

More change was on the way. In 1980, for the first time, the census recorded "Spanish origin" for small towns. Greenport had thirty-six people in this category, which probably represented a small, longstanding Puerto Rican presence.[5] Over the next decade the number of Latinos more than doubled. Then came the influx of the 1990s. Even as the general population continued to drop through the decade, the Latino population rose dramatically. In 2000 the US census found more than four times as many Hispanics in the village as in 1990.[6] It would not have been surprising to find a substantial increase, given robust natural growth nationally over the same period. But such a big change in the demographics of Greenport was truly extraordinary, reflecting the beginning of a trend of immigrants settling in small communities as well as cities.

In fact, the change was even bigger than the official record indicated. Former mayor Kapell says of his 2005 visit to the Spanish mass at Saint Agnes Church, "I realized immediately that the 2000 federal census count could not be correct."[7] Being a man of action, he took his insight to the Hagedorn Foundation, which funded a local census that would be more accurate than the official one. The results, which were issued in 2007 and were based on interviews conducted the year before, confirmed Kapell's hunch. The survey estimated that there were almost twice as many Hispanics in the village as were included in the 2000 federal census count.[8] To be sure, some of those people reported that they had been in Greenport for five years or less, so they couldn't have been counted in 2000. But even subtracting that number from the total found in 2006, the undercount of the official census was still significant.

Also significant is the evidence of continuing Latino migration during the first decade of the twenty-first century. Although immigration rose nationally between 2000 and 2006, it began to slow in late 2007. Late in that decade the prospect of better work for better pay in the United States weakened as word spread of the recession and its effects on jobs. Apprehensions of unauthorized Mexicans and Salvadorans, whether at the border or inside the country, fell.[9] But apparently either the immigrants who ended up in Greenport were not deterred by a perception of reduced employment opportunities or they had other reasons for coming—family ties or troubles at home— because in 2010 the US census found that Latinos constituted a full third of the year-round population.[10] That year was the first time in half a century that Greenport's population had risen, an increase attributable primarily to the Hispanic newcomers. For that census, Spanish-speaking residents were hired to canvass their neighbors, so it is probable that if there was an undercount, it was smaller than in 2000.

◆ ◆ ◆

Where did the new arrivals come from, and why did they land in Greenport? Nationally, Mexicans constitute the largest group of the foreign-born— just under 30 percent in 2010—but their rate of increase during the decade 2000–2010 is lower than that of Salvadorans, Hondurans, or Guatemalans.[11] (Central Americans are now the fastest-growing group of Latino immigrants in the United States as a whole, with more than a million Salvadorans in 2011.[12]) This shift is evident in Greenport. Although older immigrants in town tend to be from Mexico, the private census taken in late 2006 found more Guatemalans than Mexicans, with a smaller number of Salvadorans and Hondurans; that proportion probably prevails today. When asked why they came to the United States, most Greenport immigrants have economic explanations. "We didn't have enough to eat," says one Guatemalan simply. "My mother had died, and my grandparents couldn't support me," says a young Salvadoran man. A few people hint at political influences, like a Salvadoran man who got asylum. And America the superpower still has traction with some. "I wanted to see what made the United States so interesting," says a young woman who braved the dangers of the Mexican border five times before crossing successfully.

As for choosing Greenport, the new settlers cite a variety of reasons. They have often relied on hearsay, some of which they discovered was mythical. They heard there was work there, but what kind and how secure was unclear. They understood that rental housing was available, which turned out to be true; in 2010 renters occupied more than half of the housing units, while in the more affluent hamlet of Southold next door less than a fifth of residences contained renters.[13] (In a variant of the logic that "If you build it, they will come," Kapell attributes the increase in the immigrant population primarily to the availability of rentals, which were cheap when the influx began but have become less so.) Underlying these rationales for almost everyone was the pull of a relative who preceded them. A sister had married an American who lived in Greenport, or an aunt already residing there sent the money for a coyote (who smuggles people across the border), or relatives urged a woman in Brooklyn to leave her abusive husband and find a new life in the countryside. As with past generations, the migration chain—more like a necklace really, with beads of varying shapes and colors—carried the promise of a better future.

The surge of Latino residents was not the only demographic shift that was transforming Greenport. The 2000 US census was misleading in another respect. Because no one would want the census to count a person more than once, the portrayal of communities with many second-home owners has a large lacuna. In the past twenty years Greenport has become a destination for such residents. Part-time inhabitants are unlikely to be as involved in the economic or political or social life of the town or village as those who live there all the time, but they make contributions that are not recorded by the census. The privately conducted local census found that Greenport's part-time residents added a thousand people—all of them Anglos—to the official census count of just over two thousand. This finding is supported by another item in the US census, which reported significant vacancy rates in the village attributable to "seasonal, recreational, or occasional use." These data are not unrelated to Latino immigration. The second-home owners tend to be both affluent and busy. They often don't have time to clean their houses and weed their gardens, and the newly arrived Hispanic population meets the need. So the demographic change reflects labor market change as well.

The pattern of demographic change in Greenport since 1990, as seen in the official census data, suggests that even as the village acquires many attractive amenities, both non-Hispanic white and African American populations are still in decline—that is, if the (mostly white) part-timers are excluded. That conclusion is troubling, since it suggests that a significant number of the descendants of the working people that gave Greenport its economic and cultural vigor a century ago are dying out or have given up on the prospect of a viable future there. By 2010 the village reached its pre–World War II population of approximately 3,200 (including part-timers) and regained an energy that characterized it from the time of its incorporation in 1838; but that energy is no longer based on fishing, farming, and maritime industries.

Although there are managers and craft workers and professionals living and working there, much of the reconstituted Greenport is still fundamentally working class. The full-time non-Hispanic white and African American residents—about 1,450 people—work in the shipyards that remain, building and rebuilding yachts and repairing smaller boats, and a few still fish for a living. They support the retail sector, the shops and restaurants that are thriving. They work in the wine industry and in horticulture. Public employees repair the streets and plant the trees for which the village is known; they implement the wastewater-treatment project and maintain the municipal power plant that kept Greenport's lights on during Hurricane Sandy. As they did a hundred years ago, Greenporters serve the tourists, though now that means working for B&Bs and small restaurants (some of them quite elegant) rather than for the large, full-service resort hotels of that era.

This description leaves out in large part the Latino immigrants of the past twenty years, without whom the new Greenport could not be sustained. As workers—and the employment rate among them is very high—they move in a different world from their non-Hispanic neighbors. Some economists and other social scientists who study the labor market see it as divided into segments with different wage scales, working conditions, job security, and possibilities for advancement.[14] Primary labor market jobs pay relatively well, require and reward skills and reliability, provide employment stability, and hold out at least the possibility of advancement. These jobs can be found in all sectors of the economy and include the professions. Secondary labor market jobs, on the other hand, pay poorly, do not require (and may discourage) skills or skill development, tend to be part-time or temporary, and are unlikely to lead to more rewarding or remunerative work.

For the large majority of Mexicans, Guatemalans, and Salvadorans who have come to Greenport, work falls neatly into economists' definition of the secondary labor market. Housecleaning and dishwashing jobs in restaurants are poorly paid, much (but not all) of construction work is low-skilled, and landscaping is often part-time and always seasonal. The instability of these occupations confirms the scholarly analysis; workers must save during the spring and summer for the winter months of unemployment if their work is outdoors or depends on the tourists. Most of Greenport's undocumented immigrants, who are the vast majority of the foreign-born, receive no benefits to supplement their modest pay.

Greenport has the highest percentage of full-time residents of Hispanic background on the North Fork of Long Island. For Suffolk County as a whole in 2009 the share was about half that large. But the Hispanic tide is coming in; the county government's comprehensive plan reported that the Latino population increased by 65 percent in the first decade of the twenty-first century and predicted future gains. (The non-Hispanic white population declined slightly in that period.) The trend is likely to mimic Greenport's reliance on secondary labor market workers. In a tabulation of the ten top job categories in the county, broken down by ethnicity, in the years between 2006 and 2010, Hispanics made up slightly more than 30 percent of the janitors and building cleaners but only 10 percent of retail clerks and less than 8 percent of registered nurses.[15] That Latinos disproportionately fill occupations like truck driver, landscaper, and janitor in both Greenport and the county indicates how functional the segmented labor market is. The allocation of jobs into segments identified in the past, at least in part, by the race and sex of the workers has given way in places like Greenport to distribution by citizenship status.[16] Not having it defines people as candidates for menial jobs and keeps them there. The dual labor market is as confining for the newly arrived Latinos as their lack of skills and education and access to power—and as useful for employers who need low-wage workers. As the white working class of the past has increasingly moved away from Greenport (usually to the west, sometimes just to neighboring Southold), the Latinos who have taken their place in secondary labor market jobs have taken up the slack.

It would be a mistake to conclude that Greenport immigrants never find avenues of upward mobility. Small businesses started by Latinos in the past decade are tucked into corners of Greenport's business district. What they have in common is that they serve the Hispanic community almost exclusively. And despite these enterprises, many people are poor. In a county where the 2009 median household income was $83,620, putting it in the top 1 percent of US counties, Greenport is at the low end with a median household income of $51,042.[17] For non-Hispanic whites, the number is higher ($63,403) and for blacks, much lower ($19,286). The census reports Hispanic household income for this period as $47,171, but this figure is almost meaningless because so much income—*how* much no one knows—is earned "off the books" by undocumented workers and therefore goes unreported. And the definition of "household" is almost certainly understood differently by many Latino immigrants surveyed for the census. Both families and individuals double up within households, making it difficult to compare the village with most of the rest of Suffolk County. The pay scale ranges from the minimum wage to about twenty dollars per hour for the secondary labor market jobs most hold. For families with employment income for only eight months of the year and no other sources of support—undocumented migrants are ineligible for rent subsidies, health insurance, or food stamps, though the latter are available for immigrants' children who are US citizens—survival depends on the limited private charity of soup kitchens and clothing vouchers to be used at thrift stores.

For most immigrants, the challenges of making a life in Greenport are not a deterrent. Unlike many communities where the new arrivals are primarily single men, Latinos there are family-oriented. They are putting down roots, filling the school with their children, and becoming active in the local Catholic and evangelical churches. A few—most often Mexicans—yearn to return to their countries of origin some day. But most don't plan to go home again unless for a vacation in that fantasized moment when the undocumented ones finally get papers. A kind of regional segregation may have fostered community among them; neighboring hamlets and towns are more expensive than Greenport and have far fewer housing opportunities, so the immigrants cluster in the village. The historical pattern of boom and bust in the latter half of the twentieth century has meant that housing vacancies were and are scattered around town, so the immigrants are dispersed widely rather than ghettoized.

◆ ◆ ◆

Greenport has become the narrow end of a Latino funnel that deposits way-farers from El Salvador, Guatemala, Mexico, Ecuador, Honduras, and even Colombia, on its quiet streets. The contributions of the new settlers to the economy as workers and consumers and, less visibly, to the culture of the village are important components of what is today a lively and colorful community. Whether the demographic balance of Greenport in the second decade of the twenty-first century can be sustained, however, is an open question with many unknown variables. The balance of white, black, and Latino residents may shift as birth rates fluctuate, for instance; they are going down for Hispanic women, as for other populations. If the availability of jobs and housing drops significantly, what scholars call the pull factors of coming to Greenport will be less powerful in influencing the migration choices of Hispanics and others.

Finally, what would the current diversity, if retained, mean for Greenport's future? Without an economy based on manufacturing, fishing, farming, or retail, Greenporters are likely to rely increasingly on tourism and the services needed by second-home owners. To the degree that these sectors rely on low-skilled work, the immigrants of the past two decades can fill the bill. But most are notably poorly educated and still deficient in English. The trend suggests a hollowing-out of the essential middle class, leaving rich and poor in an environment of exploitation on one side and dependence on the other. The risk is not the depopulation that confronts small communities in Appalachia and upstate New York but rather the vacuity of resort towns and gated enclaves. On the other hand, as second-generation immigrants mature and are well served by the schools and other local institutions, they may provide new economic and social vigor. If today's immigrant children stay in the village, they will become Greenport's voters and entrepreneurs. A century ago, immigrants were shaping a village of extraordinary vibrancy. It could happen again.

PART III

Classroom Challenges

CHAPTER 6

Schooling New Citizens

Len Skuggevik, Greenport High School's principal, bursts into the English as a Second Language (ESL) classroom. He's an ebullient man, never more than when his school is flying high. And these days—early May 2013—it is. Advanced Placement (AP) scores are up, and the *U.S. News & World Report*'s 2013 Best High Schools report has just awarded it a silver medal for being among the top 10 percent of US high schools. (More about this later.) College admissions are coming in at a good clip. In June, the student newspaper will trumpet, "GHS is clearly skyrocketing toward greatness."

Allowing for a bit of excess in that youthful evaluation, one can still applaud the achievements of the Greenport schools in the early years of the twenty-first century. Emerging from an insular past, the school district has adapted to a rapidly changing student demographic. An immigrant who comes to Greenport with children or who acquires them after settling here can be assured that the schools will provide them with ample protection and stimulation.

In 2012 the student body was 37 percent Hispanic—up from virtually nothing twenty years earlier—with much higher proportions in the lower grades. Along with the challenges of fully integrating young immigrants and the children of immigrants in a largely blue-collar town, the schools are deal-ing with the new Common Core curriculum, new testing requirements, and budget cuts. Managing this congeries of issues is a tall order. The small size of the district—the two schools combined had only 641 students in the 2013–2014 school year—is both a limitation and a plus. On the minus side, the district can provide only a few of the extras found in the schools of affluent suburban Long Island towns. But Greenport offers every child the small-town advantage of lots of personal attention. Class sizes—usually fewer than twenty pupils in the lower grades—would be the envy of most urban public schools; teachers know every student well.

The district's smallness enables a focus on immigrant children who enter the schools at different ages and with different needs. (Immigrant children are here defined as either students who came with or without family members to the United States or the American-born children of recent immigrants.) Children who enter the elementary school at an early age, even if they do not yet speak English, pose few special problems. They usually adapt to American culture and meet academic expectations, though some are at least temporarily impeded by a language barrier or problems arising from their parents' immigration status. Unaccompanied immigrants who arrive as teenagers to join relatives and enroll in high school present more formidable challenges. While the schools go to great lengths to integrate them academically and socially, the results are mixed. These students have problems that go beyond passing tests and fitting in. Failure to keep them all in school and prepare them for the better lives they seek does not lie, however, at the door of Greenport's educational institutions. It is rooted in American immigration policy and in the economic and political forces that wrenched the subjects of this book from lands and people that they loved.

◆ ◆ ◆

Looking at documents and photos of students and teachers from the early twentieth century illuminates one stage of Greenport's diversity. While the old Anglo-Saxon names were present, they no longer predominated. Children lined up for their class photos now included Schiavonis and Malinauskas. And over in the corner of the 1927 third-grade class was Leon Sells, son of the black contractor—also named Leon—who was to dig the hole for the imposing school building that was to come.

That building was a Depression project. Although in 1931 banks were failing and the unemployment rate was hovering around 16 percent, Greenport was just beginning to feel its bite. The previous tourist season had produced only meager profits. Potato prices had fallen, reflecting the finding of the Department of Agriculture that "with the supply of farm hands 40 percent in excess of demand," farm wages around the country were lower than at any time during the past seven years.[1] But Greenport's board of education was determined to create a school district that would house the existing kindergarten, elementary school, and high school under one roof. The yellow brick schoolhouse it built with a bond issue of $550,000 and a federal grant gave jobs to victims of the Depression and pride to the village. Featuring a frieze with images appropriate for Greenport's maritime history—fish heads, chiseled garlands of rope trailing around anchors and conch shells, a masonry ship sailing above the central facade—the building included facilities for home economics and "industrial arts" as well as classrooms for the usual academic subjects. In 1933 students and teachers moved in. The schoolhouse today remains a civic center at the western boundary of the village.

Although assimilation of Greenport's European immigrants was well under way by the 1930s, the elimination of race bias had not kept pace. In 1936 Rose Sells (sister of Leon) went to Washington, DC, with her senior class from Greenport High School. Sixty years later she said of the trip south, "When we got to the Mason Dixon line my classmates acted as if they did not know me."[2] In a neat twist on racial segregation, Rose found better food and more intellectual stimulation at the YMCA to which Jim Crow laws consigned her than she would have in her classmates' hotel for whites only. She had breakfast every day with Carter G. Woodson, the Harvard-educated historian (the second black to be awarded a Harvard PhD, in 1912—seventeen years after W.E.B. Du Bois was awarded one) who promoted the study of black history and founded Negro History Week, the precursor to Black History Month.

Within the next two decades the cultural climate changed. The incorporation of Poles, Italians, and Jews into every aspect of village life was no longer the issue, having been replaced by the contemporary challenge of racial integration. In 1949, discovering that black students would not be able to stay with their white classmates during the senior trip to Washington, the Greenport Board of Education resolved that "any educational tour made by pupils under the auspices of the Greenport public schools be so arranged that any possibility of racial or religious discrimination be prevented."[3] Perhaps the sensitivities of the board members were alerted by the executive order issued the previous year by President Harry S. Truman decreeing the desegregation of the armed forces. Racial reform was in the air—New York State had also passed an antidiscrimination law in 1948—and Greenport was responding. But had she been consulted, Rosa Sells would have testified that this reform was long overdue.

Greenport was about to endure a very dark time in its history. As the ship-yards shut down at the end of the war and the maritime industries of fish-ing and oystering declined, the vibrant village became a depressed backwa-ter. Greenport schools reflected the economic fortunes of the village. Families moved away—to New York City or to Southold, if they could afford it—and the student population dropped from the planned population of one thousand to eight hundred in the 1970s and then to its current level of a little more than six hundred. The social upheavals of the 1960s and 1970s came to Greenport and to the high school, too. The community and the schools struggled with students' exposure to illegal drugs and with occasional racial conflicts.

Greenport High School remained, however, a protective place for black students—most of the time. Connie Solomon, an African American gradu-ate in 1977, remembers that when she was the only black child in the seventh grade section for high achievers, some classmates said, "You people were nothing but slaves." Yet she also had white friends and was a top student respected by most classmates and teachers. Like many young high school graduates from small towns, she yearned to travel and, in particular, to escape the menial labor and limited possibilities for young African Americans—serving ice cream at the local miniature golf course, which her sister did, or picking vegetables for a farm stand. She did indeed escape—to college and graduate school, to work in Virginia with juvenile delinquents, to serve in the Peace Corps in Honduras, and to help set up libraries in Africa as a repre-sentative of the Carnegie Corporation. But she returned home to Greenport, using her MBA as deputy comptroller for the Town of Southold—a tribute to the pull of the village by an exemplar of its schools' success, even in the most difficult of periods in its history.

By and large, the demographics of Greenport schools in the 1970s, when Connie attended them, reflected the European ancestry that had predomi-nated since the early twentieth century, with a smattering of African Ameri-cans, whose roots in Greenport often extended back to the mid-nineteenth century. Federal "national origins" policy had blocked most immigration from countries that had previously supplied many public school parents—Italy, Poland, Ireland, and Russia—so the schools had no new European immigrant students. Although there was no immigrant quota for countries of the Western Hemisphere, Hispanics—with the exception of a few Puerto Ricans, who began moving away in the 1970s—were notable for their absence in the schools as in the town.

That began to change at the turn of the twenty-first century. The North Fork was increasingly appealing to second-home owners and retirees, and Greenport's downtown had become a tourist attraction. When the Latinos that made up Greenport's new working class began to have families, the children headed for the public schools, first in a trickle, then in a stream. While nearby towns with older residents lost school populations, Greenport enrollments held steady and even increased, attributable, in part, to the new arrivals. The fifty-seven-member high school graduating class of 2013 was almost half again the size of the class twenty years earlier and included ten Hispanics.

Whether the trend will hold in the future is an open question. Although birth rates are higher among foreign-born women than among those who are US-born, immigrant women nationwide were choosing to have fewer children in 2010 than in 1990, and the decline in that period was greater than for women born in the United States.[4] Furthermore, immigration from the countries that have sent women of child-bearing age to the area—Mexico, Guatemala, and El Salvador, primarily—is decreasing. So perhaps the enrollments spurred by the new arrivals will prove to be just a bump in the demographic history of the schools. But for the present, the commitment to public education is one of the contributions to Greenport made by the Hispanic community. Without the recent immigrants and their children, the schools could be facing an existential crisis, as the native-born population on the North Fork—and elsewhere around the country—ages and the birth rate of whites (and, recently, of Latinos) declines.

◆ ◆ ◆

Perhaps many small-town school faculties include teachers and staff who themselves went to the school, but in towns only ninety miles from the cosmopolitan commotion of New York City it seems unlikely. In Greenport it is almost the norm. A math teacher, the music teacher, a fourth-grade teacher— even the elementary school secretary—all graduated from Greenport High. And family relationships abound: the father-in-law of the above-mentioned math teacher retired from the faculty recently, and the librarian took over the job from her mother. A recently appointed ESL teacher—herself a graduate of the high school—is the daughter of a beloved science teacher. "It's a close little community," says Joe Tsaveras, a relative newcomer (he started his fifth year as elementary school principal in 2014).

This kind of closeness can mean either continuity or insularity—or both. In the past, village sages have pronounced the Greenport schools provincial and limited, with too few challenges for bright students and attitudes that accepted limited achievement. (A previous, hard-drinking, football-loving district superintendent is said to have announced that you can't expect too much from Greenport, a working-class town of "fish-cutters.") Such criticisms were largely in abeyance by 2014, as new administrators and energetic young teachers took the reins. Whether the changes under way can dispel a lingering impression on the North Fork that Greenport schools are inferior depends on many factors—the willingness and the resources to innovate, the skills and attitudes of teachers, and the commitment of students to their education. Running through all of these challenges is the leitmotif that will remind Greenport educators that a measure of the schools' performance is how well they can orchestrate the integration of new and future citizens.

The State Education Department maintains an annual report card for all public and charter schools in New York. The report card provides data on, among other things, a school district's demographics, teacher qualifications, student scores on statewide tests mandated by the No Child Left Behind Act, and graduation rates. It is sometimes frustratingly crude, but it also affords a glimpse into the changing composition of the classrooms, the students' performance on state tests, and how well the state thinks the schools are doing in living up to standards it has set. In addition, schools within the same geographic area or with similar socioeconomic environments can be compared with one another.

As goes the village, so go the schools. The number of Greenport's non-Hispanic white and African American residents declined in the early years of the twenty-first century, and so did the number of white and black students. In 2011–2012, for the first time in village history, the ethnic domination of whites in its public schools had disappeared; only 50 percent of the students in the two schools were white and the balance had shifted to include more Hispanics and fewer blacks. The big story was in the elementary school, where Latino children constituted more than half of the students, as opposed to a quarter in the high school—and were even more abundant in the lowest grades.[5] Greenport represents a microcosm of the national landscape as the United States becomes, within the next few decades, a majority-minority country.

It might be assumed that the faculty's challenges of adapting to such rapid demographic change, including the need to address language barriers in a significant proportion of students, would result in low student scores on statewide tests of language and mathematical achievement. As a general matter, however, children in Greenport perform, as measured by state tests and presented on the district report cards that the state maintains, fairly well. Poor, black, or Hispanic children, however, lag behind their white and more affluent schoolmates, a discrepancy that persists into the final years of high school.

Gaps in achievement may not matter a great deal in elementary school. Overall, students in grades three to eight in 2012 made "adequate yearly progress" (New York State's general standard) toward proficiency in both math and English, even though all but one of the eight students who were in ESL classes in the third grade were found to have only "a partial understanding of the English language arts knowledge and skills expected at this grade level."[6] Latino students in the sixth grade had largely moved on from ESL and were testing very close to the state average for all students in what is called "English language arts"—reading, writing, speaking, and listening. The sixth grade math scores for Greenport students—white, black, and Latino combined—comfortably exceeded the state average. In 2010 the Greenport elementary school received the national Blue Ribbon Schools Award for "high performance," meaning that test scores of some students were in the top 15 percent in the state and that the scores of its minority group and disadvantaged students were close to those of all students tested.[7]

As any experienced teacher knows, the work is heavier lifting when the faces that look up at you are a variety of shades and expressions, when student writing displays only a faltering command of the language, and when the distractions that impede learning include deprivation and cultural confusion. But many educators (and some parents) believe that the rewards of teaching and learning in a diverse classroom may outweigh modest deficits that show up on standardized tests. And education in this environment, almost by definition, includes exposure to ideas and experience that cannot be reduced to filling in blanks on a state exam.

Greenport teachers generally subscribe to this view. They appreciate both the academic and the social implications of race, class, and linguistic differences among their students. Liz Burns, a fourth-grade teacher, describes the experience of getting her students ready for an imagined visit to Ellis Island. As they prepare, they talk about where their families came from: "With ease, one child told the story of how her Polish grandmother came through Ellis Island, but for the Spanish-heritage kids, this kind of revelation carries greater weight. How their families got here has always been a secret, something unspoken (at least to the native-born), but slowly they begin to tell their families' stories. 'My mother ran through the desert to get here,' one says." Kathy Wallace speaks of the richness of her students' discovery of the holidays of other cultures. "We have 'Christmas around the world' in second grade. Each kid does a country, but not necessarily the country the family is from. Spanish children may do Hanukkah or a Hindu holiday or Ramadan. Often the parents come if their child is doing the country they are from. Once, a Mexican parent brought Mexican hot chocolate; a Jamaican [parent] brought ginger beer. Each child makes a poster or provides a special dish and tells the other kids about how they celebrated."

As immigrant children move through junior high and high school very few remain of "limited English proficiency" (education jargon for those needing ESL instruction) but their test scores may reflect a continuing, if subtle, language barrier. In eighth grade language arts in 2012–2013, for instance, Greenport students overall tested better than average for the state; 53 percent scored in the top categories as compared with 34 percent statewide. But Hispanic students performed less well than white students, only a quarter scoring in the highest categories. The discrepancy was less stark, but still evident, by the time students were in the twelfth grade. In both language arts and math, the twelfth grade scores overall were just a hair below the statewide average, but white students' scores were well above it. Here, too, Hispanic students (African Americans as well) were significantly less likely than whites to score in the highest categories, though slightly more than half reached what the state considered to be proficiency in both subjects. The Regents exams, taken by most students of all backgrounds, showed similar patterns.

Economic status may matter as much as ethnicity when it comes to discrepancies in testing. In 2012–2013 the state considered 67 percent of elementary students and 38 percent of high school students in Greenport to be "economically disadvantaged." Forty percent in the high school were eligible for free or reduced-price lunch; in the elementary school, where Hispanic children were in the majority, that number was 69 percent. The state considered almost all of the non–economically disadvantaged twelfth-graders to be proficient in language arts but only half of the economically disadvantaged. Although state statistics do not reveal the dimensions of an overlap between poverty and minority status, a contrast with Southold, the hamlet next door, is instructive. Greenporters often describe Southold as a place with "a lot of money." And indeed minority residents are rare there, and the median household income is almost 50 percent higher than in the Greenport school district.[8] Reflecting a relationship that prevails all over the country, Southold seniors in 2012–2013 did better than Greenport seniors in state tests of achievement in language arts and math, exceeding statewide averages. Scores on the Regents exams, however, were comparable overall.

Greenport's teachers are sensibly focusing more on the improvements they observe in the classroom than on the dry data the state uses to rate the accomplishments of their students. But they are frustrated by the perpetual, high-stakes testing that is the educational order of the day. Like teachers and parents all over the country, they resent the time that test preparation takes away from classroom instruction, and they doubt that the tests are effective in assessing student learning. Math teacher John Tramontana notes the unfairness of requiring an ESL student who comes to Greenport in the third grade or later to take the state math test right away. And John Kulesa, who teaches history, makes the point that standardized tests cannot measure improvement. "If I bring a kid with a second-grade reading level up to seventh-grade level in one year, that's an incredible achievement, but the system doesn't recognize that."

Also unrecognized is the students' performance in the most demanding academic challenges this small school can offer. Although only 20 percent of students take Greenport's AP courses, they perform well, and their success in the examinations was important in *U.S. News & World Report*'s ranking of the school. The criteria may be narrowly focused on test scores, but the ranking is not as superficial as it may look. It gives the nod to considerations of equality as well as academic excellence. The aim is to reward schools that serve all their students, not just those who are college-bound, which separates the ranking in one important respect from the increasingly test-driven measures of school success. While the *U.S. News* team of evaluators considered state tests in reading and math, they also factored in a school's percentage of economically disadvantaged students, comparing their scores with similar students statewide.[9] Only then, as the comparison moved to the national level, did a school's ability to prepare students for higher education play a part in the ranking. Schools received a "college readiness index" based on the percentage of their students who took and passed AP courses. While Greenport's index (16.8) could not compete with the selective schools that offered more opportunities for college-level study—Stuyvesant High School in New York City, for instance, received an index of 86.6—the school's standing was respectable. Most of Greenport's students passed their AP tests, and 96 percent were considered proficient in English and math, based on the Regents exams. It is easy to see why students, teachers, and administrators were excited with the U.S. *News* recognition of their accomplishments.

American public policy has endorsed inequality in the financing of public schools ever since the nineteenth-century movement that established them. Built into the compromises that Horace Mann and other reformers made in creating a system of free schools were laws mandating that they be funded with local property taxes. This entrenched custom of basing school funding primarily on real estate taxes has prevailed. Rising property values in Greenport have had a paradoxical effect on the supplementary school revenue that New York State supplies: it is reduced, even as the number of poor families with children going to the public schools in the village has increased. With such a situation, it is not surprising that a recent report that found the state's funding of public schools to be "regressive."[10]

During Greenport's dark postwar years, voters in the school district were sometimes reluctant to adopt its proposed budgets; in 1968 it took four votes to pass relief from the austerity plan adopted the previous year. With today's improved economic climate in the village, however, such painful disputes are a thing of the past. In fact, proposed expenditure per pupil for 2014–2015 was $25,567, 13 percent higher than the state median but 30 percent lower than for Southold.[11] Despite occasional grousing in the letters to the editor of the local paper, Greenport voters pass the school budget each year by substantial margins. They can now see the results of a 2010 bond issue in the new roof and refurbished auditorium of the physical facility. The schools are blessed with outstanding art teachers, so officials cleverly schedule the student art show on the day of the budget vote. The polling place is in the school gym, so it is an easy detour to see—and admire—what your tax dollars are buying.

But this is also an era of austerity. New York State enacted a cap on education aid from 2011 to 2013 and a cap on property taxes at a time when property values were plunging around the state. Like most public school districts, Greenport has been affected. The number of teachers dropped from a high of seventy-three in 2003–2004 to fifty-seven in 2012–2013. Budget cuts have taken their toll on what the schools can offer their students. Music teacher Erika Cabral bemoans the loss of opportunities to expose her students to live performances. "We used to go to [New York] city to see a Broadway show," she says, "but we don't have the money for it now." And although some teachers act as literacy tutors at the elementary level, there is no reading specialist, a pressing need in a community where so many students are beginning to read in other than their native language.

Nonetheless, art and music flourish at the school. Art projects blend skills training and art history. The 2013 school art show featured first-graders drawing cupcakes and learning about Wayne Thiebaud, an American artist whose work includes colorful, hyperrealistic paintings of cakes and pies; fourth-graders not only practiced the art of ornamentation in their display but discovered its ultimate expression in Gustav Klimt's *Tree of Life*. The music program includes, in addition to band, junior high and high school choruses and a high school a capella group. Cabral meets with the youngest children once or twice a week, depending on the semester, and guitar instruction is mandatory for seventh-graders. The elementary school concerts—two each year—are lively affairs in which Cabral conducts the whole second and third grades in songs that often involve physical movement—a way to corral fidgeting, perhaps, while the band teacher favors percussive pieces like Sean O'Loughlin's standard for young performers, "The Lost Tomb," and, at the appropriate time, "Santa Claus Is Coming to Town."

The schools are also keeping up with technological advances that can enable teachers to give children more individual attention. Pupils in grades four through eight all get computers. In grades nine through twelve, students receive an iPad from the school, giving students access to worlds that, when first encountered, defy verbal description in any language. History teacher Kulesa wants more from the new technology, in particular an app that would connect his iPad to everyone else's in the room, to give him control over what the students are using. "PowerPoint is too static," he says. "I would like to be able to walk around the room with the knowledge that the students are following what I am showing them and that I can pull back from what is on the iPad or go back to something we have left." Recognizing that the pace of educational technology has left some faculty members behind, the district has paired with Southold to hire a consultant who works with both teachers and students.

Unaffected by the budget cuts are services for the students whose native language is not English and whose command of the language falls below the grade-level standard set by the state. Beginners in English spend two or three class hours in ESL each day; advanced students in high school attend for one hour. To serve these students, Greenport has two certified teachers, and support for the program is generous and consistent. "I have never been refused any budget requests," says Elzbieta Kulon, whose tenure there had extended into the second generation. Her twenty-two years in the school system and experience with both elementary and high school students gave her the long view on the changing demographics of the student body. When she came as a part-time teacher in 1995, she taught five students at a time in a closet in the gym and had no help; later she moved to a large, well-equipped room and had assistants. She had eighteen students in her first year of teaching, fifty-one in 2013 when she retired.

Fortunately for the school's budget, not all immigrant children need ESL. Those who were born in Greenport (and are therefore American citizens) have often completed two years in the Head Start program in Southold, which forces them to use English right away. Despite the growing percentage of elementary school kids that are Hispanic, Wallace says her 2012–2013 second-grade class had only two students with limited English. She attributes her students' facility partly to the increasing assimilation of their parents and to the natural eagerness of seven-year-olds. "They learn to speak very quickly," she says. And they are very motivated. "In second grade, being part of the group is very important; being accepted is a big thing."

Budget cuts might have been worse if district children were not also getting their education outside the schools. The impresario of external education is Joe Cortale, a former teacher who presides over the children's collection in the public library. Each year he runs a foundation-funded literacy program. Several times a year Read a Recipe for Literacy brings together fifteen to twenty kids in grades three to six one day a week for six weeks to expand, through the study of food, their understanding of their community. Learning how a specific food is produced, what it consists of, and why it is good for you, the children then write about it. One year the program sessions were about the potato. A local chef explained the many types of potato, demonstrated cooking methods, and explained the fine points of cooking French fries. A retired pastor gave a talk that he called "Travels with the Potato," elaborating on how different cultures use the potato. A local farmer talked about the importance of irrigation in growing potatoes and described the most successful methods. Other foods that have been the subject of these talks include corn and berries, with guests including the kindly berry farmer whose raspberries often sell out by noon on hot summer days. Cortale also acquaints the children with a wider world; "it's especially important for kids who never get out of Greenport." For one session, he took eighteen children by bus to Riverpark in New York City, a prize-winning urban farm and restaurant. The children were dazzled to see vegetables and herb thriving on the roof of a high-rise building in seven thousand milk crates that were moved around to accommodate to the weather. After their farm visit they went across the street for lunch at the Riverpark restaurant, where they ate a salad that they had created and heard the chef explain how the farm and restaurant work together.

Other activities take students beyond the classroom. Cortale directs 4EC, the East End Education Enrichment Coalition, founded in 2004 with the motto "Pooling the resources of PTAs, libraries, and other organizations dedicated to children." It supports events and programs for grades from kindergarten through twelfth grade that the schools on the North Fork couldn't afford—such as presentations on aerodynamics, trips to the beach to gather trash and learn about its environmental effects, and performances of traditional Chinese pastimes like plate spinning. And David Berson, who operates *Glory*, an electric launch that takes visitors on a forty-five-minute tour of Greenport Harbor, doubles as a nonprofit entrepreneur for Greenport children, with an eight-week summer science program for fifth-graders on his boat and free art and science classes on Saturday mornings during the school year in the little red building that was once the village kindergarten. He also enlists Greenport teachers to help with the children's exploration of the ecology of Peconic Bay and the essays the children write about it. "I liked the part where we dicected [*sic*] a oyster," wrote Jack about his experience on the *Glory*.

◆ ◆ ◆

"Sheep starts with *S*," says Rosie, brightly. She is one of nine children—five boys and four girls, all Latino, ages five and six—in Kulon's 2012–2013 ESL kindergarten class. A visitor would have a hard time seeing the language deficit that qualifies this child, or most of the others, for the services of the program. The teacher starts the class by asking the children to come up and put the day and date up on an easel. They do this without difficulty and when asked about the weather, most shout, correctly, that it is "sunny." They sing a song, "Spring Is Here," and seem to understand the answers to the song's question, "How do you know?"—"I just saw a bluebird/bee/ladybug/butterfly." In fact, they appear to understand everything Kulon says; they answer her without hesitation, even initiating discussion or arguing with her. Any differences in the way they speak are differences of intellectual ability or interest or personality, rather than fluency in English; they all appear to be fluent.

This fluency is deceiving, however. Immigrant children of long ago often entered school without any English at all. But today's Hispanic children—even those whose parents who don't speak English—usually come to Greenport's kindergarten knowing some English. (Only a few of the youngest children are immigrants themselves, brought to the United States as babes in arms.) But when Kulon assessed the language abilities of new kindergarteners, she found that they often did not know the names of many objects familiar to five-year-olds who grew up in an English-speaking home. She would show them a picture of a leg, for instance, and they would identify it correctly but would not know the word for "knee." In 2012, out of thirty kindergarteners, eight needed ESL. They would likely remain in the program for three years, until they received a grade of "proficient" on the New York State English as a Second Language Achievement Test, which schools administer each year to English learners.

The ESL kindergarten class includes exposure to the same concepts and skills that the children's peers who are more proficient in English are getting. This morning Kulon's primary task is introducing her students to subtraction. Using the time-honored vocabulary of "take away," she gives them goldfish crackers in two colors and takes them through an exercise in which they remove some and count how many are left. (Not surprisingly, a few end up in little mouths.) Some children struggle, others guess randomly, but Luis shouts triumphantly, "Nine fish take away three is six!" When a certain level of understanding has penetrated, Kulon slides into using the word "minus," and no one seems confused.

Beyond kindergarten, some of the more stubborn problems of bringing English learners up to the level of their classmates become evident. First-grader Abu, who arrived a year ago from Bangladesh (where English is a familiar second language), has no trouble with the reading about the habits of bees and, when asked for examples of change in their lives, he says confidently, "The babies go find a new hive." But another child does not find it so easy. A shy, slender twelve-year-old, nominally in the sixth grade, Hilda, from Guatemala, can speak fairly well, if slowly, but her reading is labored and she resists the phonics suggestions Kulon supplies. Another child, a fourth-grader named Emilia, spends most of her day getting special, individualized attention—from Kulon, from a special math teacher, from the counseling department. Embarrassed by her inability to read up to her grade level, she is sometimes unrealistically ambitious, choosing books to read that are well beyond what she can handle. She is improving rapidly, however, and would be unlikely to say, as Hilda does, that she likes gym class best—an understandable refuge from the humiliations of being far behind her age group.

The situations of Hilda and Emilia are not typical but not unique either. Greenport teachers worry about the immigrant children who have very limited—if any—education in their countries of origin. Sometimes, in addition to this deficit, they have been moved not only across borders but from state to state or town to town—once again without consistent schooling—before arriving in the village. And some come from families where the parents are illiterate and cannot, therefore, read to their children, even in their native language. Victims of adult decisions over which they have no control, the children stumble in their efforts to relate to their peers socially even as they try to catch up linguistically and academically. Will Hilda and Emilia be able to graduate from high school, let alone be prepared for higher education? That's not a certainty.

At least these girls have many years before the state's obligation to educate them ends. Had they come to the United States as adolescents, they would not be so lucky. With the exception of the students from Colombia, where the educational system is more demanding than in Mexico or most of Central America, the teenagers who arrive with little or no English are at a serious educational disadvantage. It is a race against the clock to complete high school before they turn twenty-one, when public school is no longer an option. Realistically, a seventeen-year-old who is a beginner in English is unlikely to get through the requirements of a New York high school (which include passing the Comprehensive English Language Arts Regents examination, along with four Regents exams in other subjects) before "aging out" unless he or she starts in the ninth grade and keeps up with that cohort through the remaining years. Although Greenport teachers go to great lengths to help them, most of these students get discouraged and drop out. (Although dropouts are not necessarily immigrants, it is striking that in 2011–2012, according to the state report card for the district, nine students dropped out of Greenport High School, but only one in Southold, where immigrants are rare.) "They are here for a year or two," says Kulon with a sigh. "Then they are gone."

Many newly arrived adolescents also face a familial obstacle. They know that they must learn English and otherwise apply themselves. But in their new Greenport homes, they may or may not find support for formal education. Relatives may need them to contribute to rent and household expenses. They may be expected to pay the cost of the coyote who brought them here, which usually amounts to many thousands of dollars. School is a distant second to paid employment. At one level, this perspective—from parents, after all, who have had to beg and borrow to get their almost-adult children to America—is reasonable. Family circumstances may have made education so unreachable in their country of origin that it is not anticipated for their children here. So, for some adolescent students, the strain of conflicting expectations at home and at school is devastating. They have come unaccompanied to join parents whom they may not have seen for years. They may have walked north through much of Mexico (it is more than sixteen hundred miles from south to north) on their way from Central American countries. Or perhaps they clung to the top of the notorious freight train—called "La Bestia" by all who know of it—and were brutalized or robbed by gang members or other migrants. Some took crowded buses, staying in safe houses along the way. Arriving in Greenport in a traumatized state, these young people may find that their dreams of advancement nurtured, perhaps for many years, back home are squelched.

For those teenagers who do go to high school after arriving in Greenport, life is complicated and stressful. Even though they are getting ESL instruction each day, they also have to take content courses—biology, algebra, global history—with vocabulary words that are far beyond them. (Because the school is so small and there are not many ESL students at that level, the state does not require that the courses be taught bilingually.) They usually have part-time jobs—the girls clean houses, the boys mow lawns or install sheetrock—so participation in school sports or other extracurricular events is very limited or impossible. Some extracurricular activities are out of reach financially, such as school trips or sports programs outside the school.

Blanca Lopez, who came from El Salvador at the age of thirteen knowing no English, is one of the success stories. She graduated from Greenport

High School in 2012 and went on to be a liberal arts student (with an additional year of ESL) at Suffolk County Community College. But it was a struggle. "Ms. Kulon was a good teacher—patient," she says. "She gave us extra help, but often I couldn't get it from her because I had to work." A year after graduation Blanca still felt the deficits. "In writing, I know a lot because of Ms. Kulon. The other subjects were really hard, and the only class where I spoke was with her. In math I was OK, but in the other classes, oh my God. I thought my classmates were speaking about me, because you know when you don't understand you think they are talking bad." She appreciated the efforts other teachers made to speak Spanish with her—for example, Tramontana, the math teacher who taught with Google Translate at the ready, and the English teacher who had a Dominican wife and "was really helpful." Blanca's younger sister Rosa illustrates the advantage of earlier exposure to a new language and culture. Having arrived in Greenport at the age of eight, she speaks English more fluently and, as of 2014, had made the high school honor role. She was still, however, two grades behind her native-born age-mates.

The immigration status of some adolescent students presents special problems. Those who have acquired permanent legal residency through their families (or Temporary Protected Status [TPS], a category available to Blanca and Rosa as Salvadorans displaced by earthquakes and violence at home) are generally secure, though even a minor criminal infraction can theoretically expose them to detention and deportation. The implementation of the Obama administration's Deferred Action for Childhood Arrivals (DACA) program has given some students who were previously without papers work permits and Social Security numbers for at least two years; those benefits in turn make them eligible to apply for driver's licenses. Students who arrived without authorization in the United States after June 15, 2007, however, or whose DACA application is rejected by US Citizenship and Immigration Services, are in the metaphorical shadows with adults. An awareness of the restrictions on their educational prospects weighs on them. It is frustrating to know that you cannot apply to the colleges that interest you, that even if you are admitted to your dream school you may be charged out-of-state tuition, and that you will almost certainly be ineligible for most forms of financial aid. (New York State, it should be noted, permits undocumented students to pay in-state tuition at its public institutions.)

Contributing importantly to Greenport immigrant children's adjustment are the sensitivities of both teachers and students. Twenty years ago, when only the edge of the wave of Latino immigration was apparent, some school personnel were indifferent or oblivious to the struggles of the recent arrivals. Native-born students sometimes derided the immigrants' English or made fun of their pronunciation. Attitudes and practices have changed in the new century. With few exceptions, Greenport's teachers and administrators are meeting the rapidly changing school demographics with the resources available to them. Cultural assemblies now embrace a variety of national backgrounds. Letters sent home to parents are now in Spanish, and the outgoing message on the schools' phone line is in Spanish as well as English. Some high school teachers provide handouts in Spanish to supplement English texts. All content courses that include ESL students have an inclusion teacher, that is, a teacher who is certified for special education instruction and who works in collaboration with the primary teacher to help individual students.

It is still true, however, that more could be done to welcome the English learners and their parents. Few teachers speak more than minimal Spanish and there is no Spanish course to help them learn. (The district superintendent has made the Rosetta Stone program in Spanish available at a reduced price and a number of teachers, as well as the elementary school principal, are taking advantage of it.) Parent-teacher conferences—well attended by parents, teachers say—may require the translation assistance of Spanish-speaking aides in the elementary school. The handbooks for elementary and high school are in English only, and the sixty-seven-page document about preparing for college is in English. If you looked only at the website to learn about the Greenport schools, you would have no idea that there were large numbers of Latino children in attendance. Perhaps the website administrator assumes that few immigrant parents and students get their information about the school online.

In the elementary school, it is easier for the teachers to adapt to English learners because most children start with basic knowledge and are using what the British Council calls their "innate language-learning strategies."[12] Or, as Joe Tsaveras, the elementary school principal, puts it, "They are learning their first and second language at the same time." Sometimes the language differences are irrelevant. "The fact that some don't know much English is not a problem," says Cabral. "Music is a universal language; they don't have to decipher it. They all know how to sing; they are repeating the words over and over in a song, first slower and then faster. Singing is great practice for learning the language. And they're in groups; I'm not asking them to speak on their own." Tramontana notes that there are "lots of cognates in math language" and that "math is a show-and-tell game—you're working on the board, doing the problems in front of them." When the language barrier looms, there are resources beyond the ESL classes. Tramontana often gets help from his bilingual students, and he points out that, along with workbooks in Spanish, there are bilingual glossaries in some English textbooks.

In the high school, teachers in the content classes—history, sciences, regular English—expect their students to speak and write in English, but they also know they must adapt to the limited language proficiency of some students. It helps that the school is so small. "We do things so informally here. It's simple and flexible," says Kulesa. Tramontana relaxes the old prohibition against talking with your neighbor in class because "the students help each other." Using visual images is important—maps and photographs for global history (ninth and tenth grade), for instance. Kulesa repeats key ideas three different ways, and if there is a real language barrier he uses gestures and enunciation. He sees his approach as "total immersion," involving kids at many levels, reaching other senses than the purely intellectual. Tramontana says that, with the immigrant students in mind, he is more likely to explain elements of the ideas he is trying to get across; he not only breaks down a problem step by step—something he does for native-speakers, too—but also adds "a discussion about the ideas behind the algorithm."

The teachers must be sensitive not only to the academic needs and deficiencies of their students but to pressures of other kinds—social cues within the school and the ambient noise of immigrant life beyond its walls. Burns notes of her fourth-graders: "When someone in the Hispanic community is deported, the children are tense, even when it isn't someone they know." In the higher grades, the anxiety about family security is less inchoate but also less likely to be expressed to school personnel. The arrest of a relative locally is a source of worry, as it may lead to detention and deportation. The problems of poverty, both in the United States and in the country of origin, are everpresent for some teenagers. What sociologists call "familism"—structural, behavioral, and attitudinal commitments to the family that supersede individual interests—may be on the wane as Hispanics absorb American culture in the twenty-first century.[13] But in Greenport, on occasions where young people are reminded of what were family obligations in the ancestral home, the stresses of adaptation are evident. Often the student who arrives as an adolescent had lived with grandparents before coming to join parents, and the illness or death of a beloved *abuelita* is a source of pain, exacerbated by the knowledge that for those whose entry was unauthorized, going home to bury or console is now impossible.

Greenport's teachers must tread a narrow path between being attuned to their students' interests and cultures and not singling them out as different from their classmates, with whom they need to fit in. For Cabral, this is easy in the early grades: "I use their knowledge of Latin beats, and sometimes when I teach them Spanish songs, I have them speak the words to the rest of the class. They are all into it at that age. Even if their English is minimal, I'm making them teachers in the class, and they enjoy that. They always smile when we are doing that." The students' cultural identity sometimes comes spilling out in moments of excitement. At a recent elementary school assembly, when the performers asked, "What's your favorite fruit?" a chorus of young voices shouted, "Mango," with "Banana" from a smaller chorus. (No one said "apple" or "pear.") High school students are more sensitive, concerned about others' perceptions. Kulesa makes sure that his students know that his global history class will not be oriented toward "America First," but otherwise he waits for topics to come up that engage his students' cultures—soccer or food, for instance.

For the most part, school relationships between the immigrants and the native-born, or the Hispanic children and the whites, are cordial. Elementary school classrooms are comfortably mixed, the teachers say, though they also note that the Latino children often cluster in the cafeteria. In the soccer and basketball program that Cortale organizes, his goal is to engage white and minority children in joint activity. "It's my ulterior motive," he says. "I want the kids to have fun and learn, but even more I want to bring people together." Including the children from the neighboring school district of Oysterponds—a very white area—results in a change of perspective, "breaking down what divides people." "When a kid says, 'He's on my team,' he is seeing the other child as a guard, not a Latino," he says.

The high school is not without teen cliques, of course, and sometimes they take on a racial or ethnic cast. Conflicts may arise between immigrants from different countries; Guatemalan and Salvadoran boys are sometimes suspicious of one another, especially when a few of the latter are wannabes of a Salvadoran gang. And the social hierarchy, for girls at least, makes distinctions according to whether you were born in the United States, rather than in Mexico or Central America. Celia and Augusta Martinez, Mexican

American sisters in the eighth and ninth grades, have both white and Hispanic friends but they are aware of tensions caused by the presence of girls
who are immigrants. "Some kids talk mean about them," they say. For them
language can be a useful defensive tool. Of occasional conflict with white students, Augusta says, "If I have to mock them I speak Spanish." They are very
comfortable with their ethnic identities—both Mexican and American—and
with speaking Spanish at home and English at school. While the girls enjoy
hanging out with their cousins, they don't like it that one brags about being
an American, "especially because she was born in Mexico."

Anti-immigrant and racist currents in high school are complicated
because they are fed by sources outside the school. When white students
reflect the attitudes of their families or neighbors, Kulesa just tells them to
keep it to themselves, but he also tries to foster positive interaction by putting Latino students with others in group exercises, forcing them to work
together. Tramontana says antagonism, either overt or covert, is very rare,
but when it occurs he tackles it head-on, telling the offenders they are ignorant and are making claims they don't understand. Of an occasion in his consumer finance class when students made derisive remarks about people who
shouldn't be in the country, he said, "I used an analogy, asking if they supported the fact that laws dealing with special education gave students rights,
and they did. ESL kids are as entitled as special-ed kids to rights."

An added dimension of ESL at the secondary level is its relationship to
the content courses. Former ESL teacher Christine Aviles-Nott was the go-
between for the content teachers and students, who brought to her problems
they were having in understanding both the language and the cultures of
their students. She was in demand on all sides, sometimes a trying situation. The students might turn to her for technical vocabulary needed for the
biology class, background for comprehending the twists and turns of American history, and skills training for writing essays. But Aviles-Nott had other
priorities, especially with the less advanced students: "If I have to teach the
physics vocabulary, it will take away from my unit on clothing, and the students need to know how to describe clothes." So it became essential to foster collaboration with the content teachers. When Aviles-Nott moved from
teaching in the elementary school to the high school, she was startled to see
that some of the students were eighteen or older and had problems that went
beyond language. "You have to learn English and content materials simultaneously," she notes. So she became a liaison to the other courses. "I knew the

high school teachers from coaching soccer, so I began to visit classes and ask them about what I could do to help my students have greater success in the content courses. The content teachers don't really know what the students can handle. I tell them that you can never assume that a student knows the vocabulary or retains it."

It is difficult to know what the long-term English language deficit means for Greenport's immigrant children. All ten of the 2013 graduates who were Hispanic were ESL students at some point in their time in the Greenport schools. Given this fact, one might expect at least a temporary disadvantage in their academic achievements and prospects compared to their classmates whose native language is English. That appears to be the case. The Hispanic and African American seniors were less likely than their white classmates to graduate with academic distinction. Only three of the Hispanics—all of them male—graduated with distinction as measured by performance on the state Regents exams. They were also less likely than white students to be headed for a four-year college. Hispanic graduates were 17 percent of the class overall but almost a quarter of those going to community college and more than a third of those going to work after graduation.

What happens to the recent teenage immigrants who don't get through high school? The ESL teachers, who have usually been more involved in the students' lives than other faculty members, are surprisingly sanguine. They point to the students who manage to get GED degrees years later at Suffolk County Community College or those who go to work with relatives in large immigrant families that live in Greenport or nearby towns—the ethnic enclave solution. They look at the students' goals with a realism that comes from close observation of difficult lives. They understand boys like Javier, who traveled alone from Guatemala at sixteen and was a volatile and disruptive force in class because he could not control his frustrations at being unable to learn English fast enough.

◆ ◆ ◆

Most immigrant children like going to school in Greenport, and it is easy to see why. Teachers are kind and helpful, and there is enough multiculturalism in assemblies and courses to reassure them that their cultures are respected. But much remains to be done to bring Greenport schools to the greatness anticipated by the young journalists who announced the *U.S. News* award in the June 2013 *Quill*. Limits on what the schools can provide for immigrant students are inevitable in such a small district. Students who already speak the language are bored in the beginning Spanish class that they must take, but a Spanish class for Spanish speakers seems out of reach. Putting together teams for the sport that Hispanic students are most interested in—soccer—is often difficult. As in most American high schools, the emphasis on sports sometimes crowds out dedication to academic rigor. For the most successful and ambitious students, the school's counseling staff is not equipped to develop the best college opportunities for foreign-born or bilingual applicants.

Teachers know they must do more. Their wish lists are predictable. Some would like to take a Spanish course to improve their communications with their students. Restoration of budget lines would enrich their programs. Scholarship money would help low-income students move on to college, especially if their undocumented status renders them ineligible for state and federal aid. (The district has raised money for a modest fund that has helped a number of immigrant students.) Perhaps most of all, the staff wishes that testing could be more limited in scope and less consequential for evaluating both students and themselves. On the one hand, they would like greater rigor in the academic preparation of their students—they don't necessarily oppose the Common Core, which seeks to improve critical thinking—but, on the other hand, they don't want to be passive recipients of standards set by distant bureaucrats.

Beyond specific wants, secondary school teachers feel a general need for more information about their immigrant students that would give them guidance in addressing needs. Tramontana articulates this wish particularly well; he envisions a "game plan for every student":

> I think we could keep track of the students' progress as they enter the district and then move towards fluency with the language. For instance, we could give them entrance tests to see the levels of math proficiency, science proficiency, etc. We could then place them into classes accordingly and have a concerted effort to get them up to their age-appropriate levels. Information could be shared with the subject teachers as to what to expect from each student. Right now, I get no information at all about where a student is when they enter my room. As we discussed, some of the incoming students have major gaps in their school timeline. A student who is dropped into the seventh grade may also need remediation on skills that

were never seen by him or her before. This process of individualizing the game plan would or could be initiated by guidance or the ESL department or some newly created staffing position. I think that our small size can actually be used as an asset, in that we could handle laying out a plan for each student as they enter the district. This might better help us understand if a student is struggling due to the language or missed years of school or due to learning disabilities.

Part of the challenge of teaching immigrant children is that they come to school with different pedagogical issues and different needs. The little ones who were born in the United States to immigrant parents need only to be eased into their peers' competency level in English. But older children and adolescents who have just come to the United States pose more complex problems. Greenport High School is committed to giving these students intensive English instruction and exposure to other course content that will be more relevant when they have conquered their language deficiencies. But academic assistance, of necessity, stops there.

Perhaps the most important step the Greenport schools can take for both immigrant children and the native-born is to continue and improve the preparation of all students for both employment and college. Retired district superintendent Michael Comanda supports a return to vocational diplomas for high school students who are "having trouble with the Regents diploma." Before 2000 there was a general diploma for which one did not have to take a college prep program (though you could take specific college-prep courses). Now all students must be enrolled in a Regents program unless they are in special ed, in which case they receive the individualized educational program diploma, which trumpets their deficiencies. The lack of a general or vocational diploma may contribute to dropping out among immigrants and others as students are frustrated with their efforts to succeed in Regents courses.

Greenport High School has much work to do to improve the prospects of success for college preparatory students. Expanding AP courses, providing more exposure to the world beyond the North Fork, meeting Common Core standards that will soon intensify competition for college admission—these are daunting tasks for any small school. In addition, Greenport must help immigrant students who have surmounted linguistic and cultural barriers but still face hurdles beyond their control. Barriers to higher education may include family indifference or outright opposition. Poverty or unauthorized immigration status may force some students to choose employment over college. Early motherhood remains a popular postsecondary outcome for many Hispanic girls. If Greenport's teachers and counselors, working in both academic and personal realms, can ensure that immigrant students achieve equal adult success with their peers, they will have built a model school for a multicultural America.

Edgar and the Blue Mosque

Hunched over the iPad that Greenport High School has provided, Edgar is studying the Golden Age of Islam, his assignment for world history class. He traces the trade routes depicted in his text with a long finger and peers in astonishment at the graphic representation of the spread of Islam in the eighth century. "I would like to see the Middle East," he says, but then sighs at the unreality of that wish. His English is good enough to understand most of the section assigned, but he is mystified by the phrase "the pillars of Islam." Once he understands that "pillars" in this sense refers to principles, not what holds up a monument, there is another problem. Why is one of those pillars "fasting," which he takes to be an exhortation to speed? He pulls out his dictionary and is illuminated.

Edgar is surprisingly poised and confident, given the upheaval that has defined his life over the past two years. Tall and thin, with a thatch of curly black hair, he smiles easily and seeks every opportunity to use his English, asking for corrections of his pronunciation. He has a friend who is helping him with the hurdles of the new language, and he doesn't seem to be fazed by being nineteen in the ninth grade. Actually, it is a sign of his intellectual accomplishments in Corinto, El Salvador, on the Honduras border, that he has made it this far in an American school. He finished the first grade of high school at home—where he says he was a top student—before heading north in November 2011.

His American high school yields both pleasures and problems. Edgar is immediately identified as a soccer star; in the summer of 2012, before he enrolled, he played in a local league, where he boasts of having made seven goals in five matches, the legacy of a trophy-winning athletic career in El Salvador. He is doing well in his ESL class and in history, which he loves. Earth science, however, is problematic and math is a disaster. He groans when he reads that Islamic scholars developed uses for algebra; his schooling at home did not even include fractions.

But he is determined not to let such a deficiency hold him back. Recognizing that his adolescent dream of being a world-class soccer star is just that, a dream, he hopes to be a doctor or an architect and he has considered the possibility of getting his education through military service. He swears he doesn't flinch at the sight of blood, and he loves to draw. His desire for American education was so great that he lied about his age when he enrolled in high school, worried that he wouldn't be accepted if it were known that he would turn nineteen before the end of the school year.

But he is susceptible to distractions from academic pursuits. "I want to work hard," he says, "but you gotta have fun, too." In his first months he discovered that the public library was a quieter place to study than the cramped room where he lived, but a resolve to work there was quickly abandoned. He made male friends easily, bonding over soccer and shared language, and female schoolmates decided he was a catch. Early on, he intended to resist the lure of the cell phone. "People are always calling, texting, it takes too much time; it is a distraction," he said. The vow evaporated, however, when an uncle gave him a smart phone for Christmas.

His interest in the wider world extends beyond the Middle East and the assignments of his history class. Asked where he would like to go, he rattles off a long list—Spain, Brazil, France, Africa, England. A Brazilian friend with whom he worked installing insulation last summer taught him a few words in Portuguese. Edgar is impressed that this young man speaks good Spanish and some English as well as his native language. He knows that travel will do more for him than merely satisfy his curiosity, but he can't quite define the role he wants it to play in his development. "I need to see the history, the culture, the people of other places," he says. "There are so many people different from me and their history—it's important. But I don't have money; I don't have papers." He buries his head in his hands, frustrated with the current limits of his life and unable to see beyond them.

◆ ◆ ◆

Thus far, Edgar's experience of travel outside his country has given him only pain. His migration was a virtual certainty from early in life, propelled by the pattern set by his family and his neighbors for at least a generation. Although El Salvador's civil war, which killed at least seventy-five thousand people, ended shortly before he was born, postwar catastrophes have made emigration inevitable for many young people. Just as the country was rebuilding, a series of natural disasters hit. First came El Niño, the warming of the Pacific that brought torrential rain and ruined crops. Hurricane Mitch followed, later in 1998, killing more than two hundred people and devastating the agricultural sector. Then, in 2001, earthquakes in January and February left more than a thousand people dead and a million people homeless. As production of the traditional exports of coffee, sugar, and corn fell, so did wages and job opportunities. What was always a poor population became poorer.

International forces as well as local ones drove the coffee crisis of 2001. New supplies from Vietnam and Brazil, increasingly aggressive middlemen to roast the beans, and urbanization that gobbled up coffee-growing areas and shrank El Salvador's share of the world market all had their effect. Prices dropped and revenue fell. Then the Central American Free Trade Agreement (CAFTA), implemented in 2006, removed trade barriers for the United States and flooded the market with farm products that were no longer profitable for Salvadorans to grow. Deprived of rural occupations, people moved to the city, where CAFTA made some new jobs available in textile manufacturing and machine assembly. But those jobs tend to be low paying and temporary; at least in El Salvador, the promise of greater employment opportunity has not been realized. Many people live in abject poverty, whether in San Salvador or in the countryside. Although the country today is not as poor as Guatemala, its per capita income, estimated at $7,700 in 2012, was just half that of Mexico. And net migration figures suggest that proportionately more people are leaving the country than are now leaving Mexico.

So emigrating was—and still is—the normal thing to do for a young man. "Life in my country was very difficult," says Edgar. "I saw people who studied, and at the end they didn't have enough to eat. With them, the only option was for the husband or the men of the family to come here." But it wasn't just the necessity of finding an opportunity for a better life. It was also the obligation to support the family at home. The Central Intelligence

Agency (CIA) estimates that remittances sent from loved ones abroad—at least 20 percent of the population has emigrated—make up 16 percent of Salvadoran GDP and that one-third of households are dependent on them for food, housing, and school fees.[1] Remittances have been such an important source of revenue that in the mid-nineties, the Salvadoran government maintained offices—including one on Long Island—to help its citizens apply for asylum in the United States.

Edgar's family was among those who looked to relatives in the United States for at least occasional assistance. His father had left the family when he was very small—immigrating to California—and showed no interest in maintaining relationships with Edgar or his older brother and sister. So Edgar lived with his mother, four siblings, and his grandparents in a village about an hour from San Salvador. It was an old and interesting town with colonial houses "like museums," he says, unoccupied now but protected by the state. His mother worked as a cook in a restaurant, where sometimes in the mornings he and his brother would visit her and she would make something special for them. His grandfather made enormous cheeses that went to the market in the city. Until his mother died of cancer when he was ten, he looked to her and to his grandfather for succor at home and to three uncles—in Florida, New York, and Virginia—for help from abroad.

The idea of America was all around him in the neighborhood, too. "I was thinking about it always," he says. "When I was little I knew that my father came here. I always knew that one day I would have to come." By the time he reached adolescence, his older siblings had left home—his brother to study medicine in San Salvador and his sister to follow her boyfriend to the United States and thence to Long Island's North Fork. The way forward was clear, even if its details were not: he would pursue his destiny in a place that would at least be hospitable to his dreams of a future beyond milking his grandfather's cows and waiting for his sister's money to arrive.

It was that sister, Jemena, older than he by only four years, who made his pursuit of a future possible. From Greenport she arranged for coyotes—and paid six thousand dollars—to take Edgar from his village to San Salvador, then to Guatemala City, then into Mexico and across the US border into Texas. By this time Edgar's ties to home were loosening; he had no parents and his grandparents were finding it increasingly difficult to support him and his younger brother and sister. Around him he saw other kinds of migration—Guatemalans even poorer than he who were street-corner sellers of ice cream. And, in America, Jemena and those uncles who had helped in the past represented a bulwark against the frightening unknown. His resolution to leave El Salvador was more like the moment when a young lion leaves its mother to fend for itself in the wild than like a considered, individual choice.

Edgar describes the trip as a nightmare, with surreal images and memory juxtaposed. "I went to the capital, then to Guatemala, then to Mexico. The first person who came to my house to get me knew the way and told me where to go to find another person to take me. In Mexico another person picked me up. It's like a chain." It took him twenty-four days—now a blur of rides in cramped vehicles and lonely nights sleeping on his knapsack—to get to the US border. With the Texas desert in view, he swam across the Rio Grande from Reynosa, in the state of Tamaulipas, with his clothes in a plastic bag on his back. As he speaks about the experience, he looks away. "The river was terrible for other people who couldn't swim. They tried to cross holding onto handles," he says. "It was very ugly." He can't explain that. Has he seen people drown? He won't say.

Although Edgar says he "kissed the air" when he was finally on American soil, the ordeal was not over. "It was awful when we walked in the desert, too—very dangerous—the snakes, the cactus." He grimaces. Their guide was experienced and knew the way, he says, but there was no food. "It was three days with nothing to eat—just water." He was living with the risks that have accompanied the increase in border security. As the most common points of entry have toughened, migrants cross farther into the deserts of Arizona and Texas, resulting in more deaths. While immigration officials do not release hard data for particular checkpoints, residents and border workers report that migrant deaths in Brooks County, Texas, directly north of Edgar's river crossing, were almost twice as numerous in 2012 as in the preceding year—127 bodies were found in the area south of the town of Falfurrias, where many properties are too vast to patrol. One rancher found the remains of sixteen people on his 43,000-acre spread.[2] A possible explanation for the concentration of migrants in this area may be that US Route 281 offers a straight shot from just north of the Mexican border to San Antonio; the Customs and Border Protection agency calls the area of the Falfurrias checkpoint "the heaviest area of alien and narcotic trafficking" in the patrol sector.[3]

Edgar survived, however, with little damage other than weight loss and memories that he tries to dispel. As his little group emerged from the Texas brush, a car was waiting to ferry him to a safe house where he ate and spent the night. The next day his odyssey continued with a two-day, nonstop ride in a van to New Jersey, where an uncle met him and took him south to his home in Miami. Weakened by the long trip and lack of food, Edgar spent several weeks recovering at his uncle's house and then went to work in construction to earn money to pay back Jemena for what she spent on the coyotes. School had to wait.

◆ ◆ ◆

"At home, they say, 'Oh my God, the US is a big dream,'" Edgar says, shaking his head in wonderment that he has arrived. And while the big dream is what Edgar was pursuing in his arduous journey, he is also now seeking something even bigger: a new family. Fragments of his El Salvador family waited for him here, to be sure, but it took more than a year to anchor him.

Welcomed by the uncle who took him to Miami, he nonetheless responded when Jemena importuned him from Greenport to come to her. "My sister said, 'Come here, it's best for you, you are my brother. Some day you can go see your uncle.'" The uncle understood. "It's your choice," he said. So Edgar arrived in Greenport in April 2012. Although he liked the village right away, he was surprised to find that springtime in the Northeast was still colder than any winter in El Salvador or Miami. "I had never seen snow; I am always shivering," he says, rolling his eyes and exaggerating the shivers with hunched shoulders.

The weather was the least of his problems. Living with his sister was not easy. He owed her a lot of money, and she expected him to go right to work to earn it. Once again, school could wait; she was too busy to take the time to enroll him anyway, she said when he arrived. For the first few months he accepted what seemed to be his fate and was, as he put it, "working for the coyote." He managed to have some fun by playing in the soccer league of a nearby town. By the end of the summer his construction job had enabled him to repay Jemena half of the six thousand dollars he owed her. But watching the return of others to school in the fall reminded him of the need to activate that future he had dreamed of.

Enter Sister Margaret, who firmly believes that every young person should get an education. She contacted Edgar's grandparents in El Salvador, who gave her permission to sponsor Edgar at school. As his American guardian, she enrolled him in the high school and helped him pay for his room.

That obligation complicated his relations with Jemena. She had acquiesced in their grandfather's request that she permit Edgar to go to school, and she was willing to wait for the remaining three thousand dollars Edgar owed her. But she and her boyfriend needed help with the rent. Like many other immigrant families in town, they could manage the cost of their small house across the street from the supermarket only by taking in boarders. Jemena had other financial concerns also; although she had only a low-paid part-time job, she was sending money home regularly to her grandparents and even to her older brother, the medical student. So every month, whether Edgar was in school or not, he had to come up with three hundred dollars for his room, and he sometimes wondered whether his sister's need for a tenant was greater than her affection for a brother.

Tensions rose. Sister Margaret could not support him indefinitely, but work was unavailable during the winter months when he was in school all week. When he fell behind on the rent, Jemena's boyfriend threatened to replace him with another tenant who could pay on time. Neither his culture nor his situation had prepared Edgar for a heart-to-heart with Jemena about his predicament. "She is always working or being with her boyfriend," he said. Perhaps he and his sister didn't really know each other well, he acknowledged. He worried when her boyfriend yelled at her, and a pall settled over the household. Eventually the boyfriend went for a visit to El Salvador, and the family network there reported that his vacation included cavorting with other women. The breakup of Jemena's romance strengthened sibling bonds, and she and Edgar moved together to an undisclosed location, escaping the threats of the spurned boyfriend. While Edgar was relieved at the outcome, the family conflict had been an unwelcome distraction from his commitments to work and school.

Some relief came with Sunday visits to the family of the uncle who lived in Brentwood, a town toward the western end of Suffolk County. Originally founded as a private colony by anarchists—one of whom, Josiah Warren, is considered the first American anarchist; he coined the phrase "the sovereignty of the individual"—it has become a large Salvadoran enclave, with more than two-thirds of its population of Hispanic descent. Although

Brentwood is a poor community, with high foreclosures and a gang problem, Edgar's uncle's family is financially stable and their home is a peaceful place where Edgar was a welcome novelty, the handsome cousin they
were getting to know. For Edgar, the best part of the visits was the family
soccer games. "Even my uncle plays," he says in wonderment, perhaps
thinking of the fatherly attention he hasn't had. Praise and generosity
from his uncle is precious, a reminder that family ties can cross borders
even if he can't.

With the arrival of spring in his first year back at school, he sacrificed
some of the Brentwood visits to do paid work on the weekends. And during the summer he was fully occupied, installing insulation in houses with
the employer he worked for when he first arrived. He planned his budget
for the next year. With his summer pay he would reimburse Jemena for
the remainder of her expense for the coyotes and, in addition, put away
enough to pay his room rent during the winter months. "I need to save
$2,100 in the summer for seven months when I go back to high school,"
he said matter-of-factly. Grateful for the seasonal work, which paid almost
twice the minimum wage, he also liked the fact that his boss had jobs
all over the East End. His curiosity about the world extended even to the
small American towns he saw on Long Island. And once again he had a
relationship with an older man, not quite a father figure but someone he
admired. "He's a respectful person," he says of that boss, who teased
instead of scolding when Edgar was late for work.

◆ ◆ ◆

Edgar has now been in Greenport for more than two years. He has been
soaking up American norms and values and even critiquing them. He reads
the *New York Times* when he can; he has opinions about current events,
national and international. Through memories of life in his Salvadoran
town, he probes some of the strangeness of American ways. Why are
eggs different in the United States? The supermarket eggs have pale
yolks, while he is used to the darker yolks and richer taste of the eggs
of Salvadoran chickens that ran around his grandfather's yard. Why don't
more Americans play soccer? It's so much more civilized than football and
it's played by all kinds of people all over the world. He chuckles at the
recollection of the two little dogs his family kept. There were lots of dogs

where he lived, which people called either Indian dogs (small) or Gringo dogs (large and aggressive). Despite his guffaw indicating that he knows and appreciates the associations of these images, he is ready to join the gringos, if not to embrace their occasionally bellicose style.

But joining the gringos, whether in Greenport or elsewhere in the United States, has become increasingly problematic, and Edgar must now face that reality. Handicapped by a lack of material (and sometimes emotional) support, he is up against myriad obstacles, some of his own making and others imposed by family pressures and his immigration status. New York State's obligation to educate him in the public system expired when he turned twenty-one in April 2014, two months before his last opportunity to graduate from high school. Even though his English had improved by leaps and bounds, he could not master the language sufficiently to pass the Regents tests the state requires, let alone overcome his deficiencies in math. A promising alternative was to sit for the new high school equivalency Test Assessing Secondary Completion (TASC) exam, which, if he passed it, would at least give him the chance to attend the local community college. Initially, he vowed to study for the test but soon found excuses to reject the preparation help that teachers and friends offered. Finally, as the exam date approached, he buckled down and worked on practice tests into the night after his construction job ended. "I need to have a future," he reminded himself.

Immigration policy loomed large over that prospect. With comprehensive reform stalled in Congress, Edgar is consigned to be "out of status" for the foreseeable future, maybe forever. He is ineligible for the DACA program initiated by President Obama in the summer of 2012 because he arrived after his sixteenth birthday and was not in the United States on June 15, 2007. In the unlikely event that the immigration reform bill passed by the Senate in 2013 to legalize most of the estimated eleven million undocumented immigrants in the country became law, he would probably not be one of that number because he would have trouble proving that he had been in the United States long enough. And he is not eligible for any form of family reunification. His sister is unlikely to become a citizen, and even if that happened—probably through marriage to an American citizen—the family unification category for siblings has very low priority; this route is effectively blocked for now. His young cousins who live in Brentwood were born in the United States and are therefore citizens, but even when they mature and are supporting themselves they will be limited to legalizing only parents, spouses, and minor children. As of late 2014 his only realistic option for setting out on the so-called path to American citizenship would be to marry into it.

What were the alternatives? If he returned to El Salvador, got a university education in an area of high labor demand in the United States—perhaps a STEM field (science, technology, engineering, and mathematics)—and applied for admission to the country with professional status, he might have a future here. As a boy from a town where everyone is poor, however, that is an unlikely scenario—and besides, his talents don't lie in that direction. ("There is no royal road to geometry," said Euclid—and Edgar agrees.)

At least he is unlikely to be deported. In 2012 the Obama administration vowed to prosecute only undocumented immigrants who have committed serious crimes or are a risk to national security. So far, this policy has not provided relief in much of the country; only a little more than 10 percent of prosecutions filed in immigration courts nationally in early fiscal 2015 were for criminal activity.[4] (Most prosecutions were for "entry without inspection" or other immigration offenses.) But negative public response on the North Fork to police cooperation with immigration agents in recent years and the White House vow to concentrate on deporting only felons has made local raids unlikely. Edgar is probably immune to the lure of crime of the kind that would alert immigration officials to his unlawful presence. He does not drive drunk or sell drugs. Although he knows other Salvadorans who tell him of gang activity on the North Fork, he stays away from it. The closest he has come to felonious conduct was in his head—the urge to defend his sister from her aggressive boyfriend.

◆ ◆ ◆

By the time of the high school equivalency test, during the summer of 2014, Edgar felt prepared. He had signed up to take it in Spanish. Buoyed by his strong performance in high school history and good reading comprehension skills, he was confident about all the sections except math. His new boss had given him time off to take the test, telling him he was too smart to spend his life drilling holes in the ground. He had enlisted friends to drive him to and from the test site.

But it was hard—not harder than he expected but harder, he feared, than he could handle. As he waited for the results, he became increasingly desperate. It didn't help that he wondered if Jemena, always hostile to his academic progress, had earlier thrown away test instructions sent in the mail. He now wondered if she had also discarded the precious document that would give him at least a toehold on his future. He felt abandoned and alone and began to see Greenport as a cold, uncaring place, full of "people who just kill me and play with my heart." From Virginia, another uncle assured him of steady blue-collar work if he wished to migrate once again.

Edgar was depressed. He doubted that he had passed the test, and he couldn't summon the strength to consider retaking it anytime soon. Virginia felt like an escape, another chance to start over. But how would that benefit him—without legal status, with only menial jobs, without an education to propel him into the middle class? He was incapable of making a plan or of holding onto his dreams. As he prepared to move to Virginia, he announced, "I don't have any opportunity in this world." He did not wait to get the test results. Resigned to a future very different from what he wanted when he kissed American air, he knew he was unlikely to see the Blue Mosque or climb the Eiffel Tower.

PART IV

Settling In

CHAPTER 7

Housing or Houses?

On a late afternoon in August 2013, James Olinkiewicz—a developer, builder, antique dealer, and speculator from the neighboring town of Shelter Island— appeared before Greenport's zoning board of appeals to request variances so he could subdivide a lot he owned on Fifth Avenue. A large, handsome two-family rental house currently graced the property. The site plan for the subdivision, if approved in a separate action by the village planning board, would enable him to build an additional two-family house that he would also use for rentals.

It was not an easy sell. A gaggle of Fifth Avenue neighbors had come to the public hearing to oppose his plan. Several testified that there were already too many renters on the block, that traffic on the street had increased since Olinkiewicz had purchased the existing building the year before, and that the quiet neighborhood had become, in the words of one, "saturated with people, more people than were meant to live on this street."[1] One witness said that he had counted "a minimum of sixteen people at times" living in the three-bedroom upstairs apartment of Olinkiewicz's building and that "there's anywhere between six to ten [vehicles] at any time during the week. They're coming in all hours of the night, speeding down the road." Letters from other homeowners were read aloud and agitated interruptions from the audience peppered the board debate.

Discussion veered away from the consideration of Olinkiewicz's application to complaints about problems elsewhere on the block—beer cans thrown in the street, loud music late at night, poorly maintained properties. At one point, the village municipal services came under fire—unplowed snow, ineffective stickers on illegally parked cars. One resident invoked a stabbing that occurred down the block on Christmas night eight years earlier.

When it was time for Olinkiewicz to respond, he tried to pacify his antagonists. "I understand the neighbors have passion for the neighborhood," he said, stressing that he welcomed inspections of his property to determine whether his apartments were in compliance with the village code. Defending both his right to build another two-family house and his record as a landlord of good character, he touched on another rationale for his project: "I built two brand-new beautiful houses for people to rent to help with the overpopulation of rental people."

But the audience was having none of it. They saw Olinkiewicz as an outsider seeking a quick profit from change that would disrupt the peaceful enjoyment of their street. As a letter from one neighbor put it, "Adding density to a family-oriented block simply for the financial benefit of someone who does not even live in Greenport is not in the best interest of the village and those who love it." In a small town, everyone may be privy to your business: it was widely known that Olinkiewicz had purchased the property with a large mortgage at a high interest rate and that without the rental income from a house on the newly subdivided lot he would be unable to recover his investment.

Parking, traffic, and nighttime noise are classic and legitimate objections to the disruption of neighborhood peace and quiet. But what is expressed as a threat to the residential character of a neighborhood may also mask darker impulses. "I tried to sell my house when I first built it, and I couldn't sell it," said one of the more volatile neighbors, "because there's eight Mexicans sitting on the wall out front drinking in the middle of the day." "With the new people coming in, we don't know where they're from," said another. Whatever discomfort some of the neighbors felt with these remarks, an ugly subtext traveled around the room.

◆ ◆ ◆

Olinkiewicz could not have known that his zoning variance application (and the concurrent request for a subdivision from the planning board) would have such far-reaching implications. Churning up from below the surface of a relatively simple land-use issue were all the housing problems of a small town undergoing profound economic and social change, and lurking beneath the housing issues were wrenching questions of village identity. Until recently,

Greenport had been a housing mecca for new arrivals. The village was not spacially segregated, and relatively reasonable rents were available. So housing was both an incentive and a reward for immigrating to the village. By 2014, however, it was threatened as a resource that can sustain the working-class population, whether native-born or immigrant. Greenport's success in reinventing itself as an attractive and economically viable small town has come at a cost. Rental housing is in short supply—and, therefore, increasingly expensive—as new, more affluent residents convert multiple dwellings to single-family homes. With little room in the village for new construction and sharply curtailed federal and state subsidies for renters or first-home buyers, gentrification looms as a disruption of the demographic balance of classes, races, and ethnicities that has prevailed in the last twenty years.

A case could certainly be made that the neighbors of Olinkiewicz's rental house were justifiably concerned with traffic and parking problems on their street. And in an area where nuclear families were the predominant residents, a cluster of beer-drinking males might reasonably be a cause for uneasiness. But lurking behind these superficially neutral complaints is a regressive tendency—a departure from Greenport's history of absorbing immigrants—for some native-born Greenporters to express, however indirectly, discomfort at sharing their quiet streets with Hispanic newcomers. Although the neighbors' ostensible target was Olinkiewicz the person, he focused their ire as the avatar of invasion, the sponsor of people who would lower property values and bring disorder to their community. Academics have labeled this kind of neighborhood protection NIMBY-ism (derived from NIMBY, which stands for "not in my back yard").

NIMBY-ism can be seen as a form of informal policing, erecting boundaries to preserve residents' control over physical spaces. At its core is the pressure that dominant groups put on the government to deny access to marginalized people, whether immigrants or others, to spaces or services. That pressure inverts the inequality between the groups, casting the protesting citizens as victims of abuse by disadvantaged people who are portrayed as intruders.[2] The Olinkiewicz proposal brought out this perspective. In an escalation of the Fifth Avenue residents' protest, a few brought their complaints to a meeting of the village board of trustees two months later. One resident railed against "low-income people" and "people being subsidized by the government" on her street, predicting danger to children and the general deterioration of her neighborhood.

NIMBY-ism sometimes results in threats to the people to be excluded. Although the Olinkiewicz proposal generated a political reaction, there was no evidence that the neighbors intimidated his tenants. While a few Greenporters argue that the village is unfairly housing immigrants who work elsewhere (would they say the same about affluent, white Westchester County, where the bulk of residents commute to work in New York City?), landlords are only too glad to rent to the newcomers, and no one bars Latinos from the enjoyment of Greenport's beautiful bayside park. Efforts to deport a vulnerable immigrant are rare and related only to the commission of a serious or repeated crime. Nonetheless, the outcome of exclusionary tactics in Greenport neighborhoods will be to reduce the amount of living space available to minorities, poor people, and longtime residents' young-adult children who would like to remain in their own community. Furthermore, the NIMBY-esque rumbles in the village are occurring at a time when other forces—a modest amount of gentrification, in particular—are pushing up rents, creating a severe scarcity of affordable housing.

◆ ◆ ◆

For more than one hundred years Greenport has needed to find housing for its immigrants. Providing it has often been good business. In 1850 David Graham, age twenty-five, and four other young Irishmen were brickmakers in the Hashamomuck neighborhood at the edge of town. They lived in a boardinghouse then, but ten years later Graham, now with a wife and seven children, was running his own establishment, taking in German as well as American and Irish boarders.[3] By 1870 his boardinghouse was a sort of annex to the brickyard where he, three of his sons (he now had nine children), and his ten boarders worked. In all, twenty-one people lived in Graham's household, and the tenants were presumably a good source of income. By 1885 his oldest son, William, had risen from the working class on the strength of his knowledge of brickmaking; he leased land with deep clay pits on the other side of the bay and started a new brickyard in Sag Harbor.

Boardinghouses and rooming houses were usually urban phenomena, expressions of the mushroom growth of cities in the nineteenth century. Factory workers who couldn't afford private dwellings, immigrants looking for a toehold in American life, sailors between voyages, young people escaping the confines of small towns—strangers were plunged, willy-nilly, into a form of communal living in Boston, Chicago, and New York. Boarders were common in some smaller communities, too, especially if, like Greenport and nearby Sag Harbor, they were ports. A number of prominent writers—Herman Melville and Nathaniel Hawthorne, for example—lived from time to time as boarders, either renting a single room from a family or sharing the common table in a boardinghouse.[4] Walt Whitman "boarded out" in New York City and on Long Island on and off for thirty years, though probably not in Greenport, where he could stay with his sister.

In Greenport's downtown, boardinghouses shared space with elegant homes owned by prominent local families. They housed seamen and men who worked in the boatbuilding trade. Bars and flophouses contributed to the reputation of the village as a freewheeling spot where you could earn a buck and have a good time. But by the turn of the twentieth century, the five remaining boardinghouses increasingly housed tourists who couldn't afford the several resort hotels and also housed the young women who worked in them.[5] Many of the single-family houses were being turned into stores and renovated beyond recognition; the last to display the grace of old woodwork and a cherry banister—built before 1837, town records show—now houses the Blue Duck bakery.

The demise of the boardinghouse—and of the practice of renting single rooms to boarders—had many causes. As transportation options improved, people could live farther from their workplaces. In the cities, rising affluence fed the desire for the privacy and autonomy afforded by an apartment. In small towns and suburbs, single-family houses became more affordable, with building booms in the Roaring Twenties and after World War II. On the North Fork, assimilation of the Italian, Polish, and Irish immigrants during the late nineteenth century heralded new construction, and many of the new houses belonged to descendants of those immigrants. And for many decades there were few new immigrants to house.

◆ ◆ ◆

Alarms about the shortage of rental housing in Nassau and Suffolk Counties are common. "Long Island's 4.3 percent rental vacancy rate means that there are fewer available rental homes than in any other suburban area in the New York region," announced a report by the Regional Plan Association in 2013.[6] If young people and low-wage earners cannot find affordable rental housing, the report warned, businesses would not stay in the area and the economy would stagnate. But if you looked only superficially at Greenport, you would be hard-pressed to believe that Long Island was in the throes of a rental housing crisis. In its analysis, the Regional Plan Association noted Greenport as an outlier; more than half of its homes were rentals, compared with only one in five for Long Island as a whole. The village today has at least four hundred rental units, located on a thousand parcels of land, private and public (including parks and cemeteries.) It's an idiosyncratic feature for a town of only twenty-two hundred full-time residents, but it has been, until now, a major contributor to economic health and renewal.

Greenport has always had a lot of renters relative to owners. Even in a time when fewer people owned their own houses, it was unusual (on Long Island, at least) to have more rentals than owner-occupied dwellings, as Greenport did in 1940.[7] In nearby Sag Harbor, for instance, a village of similar population size, property-owning households exceeded rental households by one-third; and in Southold town (excluding Greenport), by 30 percent. Probably the dominance of rentals was even greater in the preceding century. Most of the workers in Greenport's industries—fishing and shipbuilding—did not earn enough to afford single-family housing, although one charming remnant of Greenport's architectural heritage is a cottage that once belonged to a ship's carpenter.

Those workers began to leave after World War II. Now that there were no more minesweepers or tank lighters—flat-bottomed boats with a ramp that could carry tanks—to build for the government, the bottom fell out of the labor market. Fishing, too, was in decline. Oystering, a boon to local prosperity for fifty years, had been, since the 1930s, a victim of pollution and overfishing and, finally, of the 1938 hurricane, which destroyed the oyster beds. Pollution and an algal bloom called brown tide destroyed the harvesting of menhaden (also called bunker), the smelly fish that had been a mainstay of the local economy since the Indians showed the settlers how to use it.

The effect of depopulation by working people after the war is apparent in the housing census of 1960. While renters occupied more than half of households in 1940, they constituted only one-third of households twenty years later. (The number of people affected was probably much greater than that statistic suggests because some of those dwellings held more than one family.) About 12.5 percent of dwellings were vacant (and not in the manner of today's vacancies, which mostly signal second homes for city people); in

many cases they were abandoned. The census found many structures needing repair; it recorded 14 percent of all housing units and 24 percent of rental
units "deteriorating" or "dilapidated." Although the census-taker considered
95 percent of structures in nearby Sag Harbor to be "sound," only 86 percent
in Greenport were.[8]

Nature abhors a vacuum, and so do landlords and social planners. In
the nineteenth century, as American cities expanded outward, the elegant
townhouses of downtown became tenements and boardinghouses, serving
as rental resources for young and restless migrants from small towns. So,
too, a hundred years later, Greenport adapted to demographic change: as
single-family houses emptied out after the war, their owners turned them
into multiple-unit dwellings of various kinds. Sometime after the 1971 zoning map was drawn up (it's still in effect), the village liberalized the code
to permit the conversion of single dwellings into two-family houses, and by
1980 they dotted the village. They provided relatively small living spaces—
though not less than "1,000 square feet of livable floor area," mandated by the
village code—and relatively reasonable rents.[9] Rooming houses—different
from boardinghouses in that they provided rooms but no meals—also met
a need. Manaton House, with up to twenty tenants in a rebuilt carpenter's
house from the 1850s, was the last rooming house; it burned down in 1991.

With a postwar housing crunch all over the country, including Long
Island, Greenport's rental housing was a boon not only to landlords and
tenants but also to local and federal governments. Employees of the Suffolk
County Department of Social Services were delighted to be able to send welfare clients to a place where low-cost housing was available. While some landlords exploited the poor and black families who had replaced the departing
shipbuilders and fishermen as Greenport renters, others offered help. One
civic-minded landlord with a heart was Oscar Goldin. The son of Russian
immigrants, he was born in Greenport in 1905 and spent his whole life there,
where he owned the furniture store and, for a time, a market, and worked as
an auctioneer and appraiser. ("Buys and sells everything for cash," said the
ad he ran for many years in the local paper.) A local school board member
and village trustee for many years, he served as mayor from 1953 to 1955. He
also invested in real estate, buying up cheap houses and then renting to the
poor. He did well by doing good, benefiting from the state subsidies but also
lending his tenants money and giving them food—some said in exchange for
their votes when he ran for office. According to local sources, he was popular

with his tenants but not so much with some other residents, who resented the influx of black families in many of the houses. But even in a town where some residents harbored support for the Ku Klux Klan up until the 1960s, segregated housing was the exception.

It helped that the federal government stepped in with the Housing Choice Voucher Program, better known as Section 8. Currently providing housing subsidies for more than five million Americans, the program pays landlords up to 70 percent of the rent for eligible tenants. Section 8 supports many rental households in Greenport; although the reporting requirements are rigid and the monitoring tedious, most landlords find it a reliable source of income. To qualify for Section 8 housing, residents must have incomes that fall below a regional standard—$31,750 for a family of four in Suffolk County in 2013. They must be citizens or legal permanent residents (green card holders), or visa holders of some other kind.

That undocumented immigrants are barred from this subsidy has not deterred them from moving to Greenport. In the early days of the current immigrant wave—the mid-1990s—market rate rents were low and inventory high. And members of a family from Mexico or Central America who discovered the village sent out the word to others, who, over the years, joined them, thus setting up networks of extended families for mutual support (and sometimes conflict). According to both the mayor and the housing inspector, Latino immigrants now occupy most rental properties except for those with Section 8 vouchers—and new ones are still arriving. But will they find places to live? Or will they have to move to Riverhead, the county seat, where urban decay still keeps the rents low?

◆ ◆ ◆

Greenport has managed to avoid the social and physical problems that many cities have had with low-cost housing. No faceless, badly built high-rises or barracks announce that this is where poor people live. No neighborhood could reasonably be considered a slum, though there are a couple of places where houses are run-down and Saturday-night excess sometimes spills into the street. Discrimination against black and brown renters may exist, but it is rare and far below the radar. Unlike most of Long Island, Greenport immediately assimilates Latino immigrants residentially into working- and middle-class neighborhoods. Since most of the village is zoned for one- and two-family houses, they usually move right into a peaceful residential area within walking distance of stores and transportation.

The most common accommodation is a two-family house where each unit holds at least one traditional family, sometimes with an additional boarder or two. What is considered a traditional family, of course, varies by country and culture, with large extended families assumed to be the norm among Greenport's Latinos. These households are often beacons for an even more distant relative or the close friend of a cousin in Guatemala who needs a room (or perhaps just a mattress in the corner of the living room) while figuring out how to survive independently. They are nodes of family and community networks. They connect recent arrivals with those who, by now, know the ropes locally and reunite family segments that are well established here with those that remain at home. Newcomers can often expect to be housed and fed for at least a few months, though they may also be expected to contribute financially as soon as possible. In general, household demographics are country-specific, though a Guatemalan family may take in a Salvadoran or vice versa. Sometimes this heterogeneity breeds conflict.

True apartment houses are rare in Greenport, unless you count three condo developments whose residents are often second-home owners who enjoy views of the bay and ample parking. One development with eight apartments is a Section 8 project that houses few immigrants, but most must rely on the private market because they are undocumented. A few multiple dwellings include small rental apartments available to immigrants: former mayor Kapell has seven above his antiques store, which also serves as his real estate office. Downtown, the people who live above the stores are not the merchants, with a notable exception; only in the case of Di Angela Leather—"home of fine leather goods and accessories"—does the upstairs resident have a financial interest in the enterprise downstairs.

Immigrants live in single-family houses too, an indication of either upward mobility or the kind of group living that some native-born residents object to. A few of Greenport's immigrants have managed to join the fraternity of homeowners and thereby facilitate rapid entry into this totem of American life. A few more are renting a house from a landlord who charges them less than usual, with the understanding that they will fix up the property by making repairs and painting. More frequently, single males rent rooms in a house and share a kitchen and bathroom. These are the sons and fathers who are doing hard labor during the day, having a few beers in the evening, sending as much of their pay as they can to families in Mexico and Central America, and waiting for the day when they can return to their homeland and start a business or enjoy the house their remittances have built. The housing inspector, Eileen Wingate, is most often called to group houses. "When boys are living together, it's usually a mess," she says. "When women move in, it gets much better; there are usually two couples. And then babies arrive and there's overcrowding."

Her job is often thankless. Subject to casual disdain and death threats alike, Wingate persists in her tasks of observation and correction. A former landscape architect, whose quick smile belies her toughness, she has tremendous responsibility but little power beyond the ability to respond to the complaints of police, firefighters, or neighbors concerned about perceived code violations. She is more critical of landlords than of tenants. Some landlords don't care how bad the conditions of their rental units are, she says, and especially when the tenants are unauthorized immigrants, "the people who live there are too scared to say boo." When she finds problems, she issues a notice of violation, then an order to remedy, and finally, if there is no correction of the problem, an appearance ticket, which she refers to the village attorney, who may or may not take the offender to court.

Perhaps because bad news travels very fast and can be damaging in such a small community, the village is pretty casual—some say lax—about prosecuting housing code violations. In late 2013, a woman who owned and lived in a house on Kaplan Avenue finally appeared in court to respond to ten counts accumulated over a five-year period. Some violations were deemed fire hazards by the fire department and Wingate. Part of the outside of her house had no siding, merely a plywood shell that absorbs water. She had replaced the roof a couple of years earlier without getting a permit. The backyard was full of discarded toys and equipment—a bruised kitchen sink on its side, a stroller with only one wheel. But the response of the homeowner to the charge against her was fierce: her partner stormed the village hall, threatening physical harm to Wingate. It's because of this kind of thing that her office door is locked at all times.

Although it often pains her, Wingate can be just as tough on tenants as on landlords. If your electricity has shut down because you have overloaded the circuits, she won't turn it back on without an inspection. "The worst part of my job is when, in the middle of the winter, I have to close a building and put people out," she says. Having seen all sorts of strategies to disguise overcrowding—piling up mattresses, hiding a tenant in a broom closet—she is full of stories. Investigating a complaint about day care being provided in an apartment, she found ten toddlers sitting in front of the TV and only one adult present. "I asked the kids to count, and when we got to the end, one kid said, 'Jose is sleeping,' and I pulled back a curtain to find three more children asleep." The day care service had no permit and no smoke detector.

The quest for a safe and stable rental can be daunting. For a Latino immigrant in Greenport, moving frequently is the norm—sometimes by choice, as when a family relationship becomes conflictual; sometimes of necessity, because a basement has flooded or an overloaded circuit has caused a fire. Life changes propel housing changes, and moving has become more and more difficult for immigrants, especially those without legal status. Landlords increasingly require Social Security numbers, pay stubs, or other evidence of steady jobs. What seems like plenty of room for a Latino family accustomed to close living conditions may run afoul of code provisions or state laws that mandate square footage per person.

Greenport's landlords represent a plethora of perspectives and behaviors. There's the developer of rental housing who refused to spray for bedbugs, the immigrant landlord who rented to his countrymen but didn't put in adequate electrical circuits to keep them safe, and the woman who rented out her illegal basement apartment that continually flooded. But there is also the landlord who lowered rents during the Great Recession (officially December 2007 to June 2009 in the United States), and Carolyn Tamin, whose eyes fill with tears when she contemplates having to evict a tenant if, yet again, the rent is late. Overall, conditions in rental units are passable if not ideal, and Wingate says they are improving. Asked whether there are properties where repeated complaints require repeated inspections, she says, "There used to be more. Now I do only one or two a year; they [landlords] seem to be learning."

◆ ◆ ◆

With so much rental housing spread out over the village and in so many forms, it was perhaps inevitable that controversy over how it should be regulated would arise. It began in 2011 when members of the village board of trustees first met to consider a proposal requiring rental permits and expanding authority for inspection. Initiated by David Murray, a local builder, in consultation with Mayor David Nyce, it reflected similar legislation enacted in other Suffolk County communities attempting to preserve neighborhood character through zoning and housing code policies. The legislative intent of the law was to "prevent unsafe conditions arising from the rental of dwelling units that are substandard or in violation of the New York State Code or Rules and Regulations or the Greenport Village Code."[10] Noting dangerous and crowded conditions he had seen in some buildings, Murray explained at the first of several hearings on the matter that his concern was with the safety of the tenants. "If you have been in some of these dwellings . . . they're run down. The electrical sockets have more things plugged into them than you can throw a stick at."[11]

So the stated intention of the law was to prevent and correct such conditions in rental properties and to protect other residents from "blight, excessive vehicle traffic and parking problems." Landlords renting out apartments and buildings that they did not occupy would have to register their property with the village, submit to inspection of the rental units as a condition of receiving a permit, and comply with local and state rental regulations. Permits would be reviewed by a licensing review board and issued by the village building inspector, who would then be authorized to make inspections "to determine the condition of rental properties," obtain a search warrant to enter properties if the landlord or tenant refused to permit an inspection, and revoke the permit where the rent regulations had been violated. Penalties for law violations initially included jail terms on top of fines, but they were deemed too harsh, and later drafts eliminated them; fines were to be assessed against both owner and tenant.

As stated by its proponents, the target of the law was the landlord who either hides the fact that the premises are rented or maintains them with indifference to unsafe or unsanitary conditions. But of equal concern were also multifamily occupancy and overcrowding. The proposed law provided that "[a] rental property shall only be leased, occupied or used by one person or a family," with family defined as "two or more persons that are related by blood, adoption, civil union or marriage, or up to five persons that are not related by blood, adoption, civil union or marriage" who live together. The bill detailed "presumptive evidence of multi-family occupancy" that is prohibited—for example, more than one electric meter, more than one satellite dish, or separately locked bedrooms within the household. Evidence of over-occupancy included more than two mattresses in a bedroom and the presence of more vehicles than would normally be warranted for a single family.

In the United States, both law and culture have endorsed residents' interest in creating and preserving quiet, homogeneous neighborhoods. The use of zoning law to improve housing conditions is widespread and widely endorsed. (As Supreme Court Justice William Douglas wrote in 1954, "The misery of housing may despoil a community as an open sewer may ruin a river."[12]) Limiting density in a residential neighborhood is also constitutionally permissible, the Supreme Court has said, as long as restricting the number of unrelated people who may live together is based on rational and constitutionally permissible goals like reducing noise and traffic.[13] But regulating crowded housing must not be aimed at particular groups or deny fundamental rights of those it displaces. And courts at both state and federal levels have shown considerable discomfort with definitions of family that, for the purpose of excluding some tenants, bear little relationship to the legitimate goal of preserving a neighborhood's quality of life. The highest court in New York, in fact, has suggested that the state constitution bars a definition of family for zoning purposes that treats related and unrelated persons differently by restricting the number of only unrelated people in a household.[14]

Greenport's proposed law, on its face, was not aimed at immigrants. It was certainly possible that native-born families might live with some of the prohibited conditions; one witness at a hearing, an American, challenged the two-mattress provision by noting that her mother put four children in bunk beds in one room. But, by and large, it was immigrant residents who were widely known to crowd into spaces that were unsuitable or illegal for more than one family, however defined. While landlords would have to put up with the inconvenience and intrusion of closer scrutiny, many of those most likely to suffer the greater harm of losing their homes as a consequence of inspection would be immigrant families. Newly arrived residents were often hard put to pay for housing, and a popular solution was to share space and expenses with friends or extended family members.

So the battle was joined. Supporters of the law presumed that substandard rental housing was proliferating and that exploitative landlords—some of whom were not Greenport residents—should be held accountable. Wingate, who felt the existing code did not allow her to initiate inspections (as opposed to responding to complaints from police, firefighters, or neighbors), welcomed the added authority the law would give her. "It will give me the tools I need to get into apartments and check the safety, size, light fixtures, windows that provide outside access, CO_2 detectors, smoke detectors," she said. But at the first hearing before the board of trustees in July 2012, not a single speaker supported the law. Landlords predictably resented what they saw as an intrusion on their property rights and defended their stewardship of clean and safe dwellings. Other residents expressed concern that the law would be administratively unwieldy and costly and that it provided penalties that the village was not authorized to impose.

A word never used in the hearings that stretched over more than a year was "discrimination." Yet that was the subtext of the much of the opposition to the bill. The requirement that a dwelling can only be used by one family suggested to some that an objective of the legislation was the eviction of immigrant households. The specific exclusion of required inspections for seasonal rentals—the summer leases that, in other communities, provoke concern about hordes of hard-partying young people jammed into small cottages, heedless of safety and security—aroused suspicion that the bill's real targets were poor and Hispanic year-round residents. And who but single male Hispanics would be affected by the law's prohibition of boarders?

Particularly fiery attacks on the bill at two separate hearings came from Kapell, Greenport's previous mayor and the man generally considered the impresario of Greenport's revival. He derided the assumption that substandard conditions were proliferating, noting that housing conditions were vastly better than they had been a generation ago. He advocated more aggressive use of code provisions against a few noncompliant landlords instead of intruding on the rights of others. Calling the bill an "abomination," he predicted that it would impose "severe hardship" on the immigrant community, which he described as "coming to Greenport to make a future" and providing "the service in the community that we need."[15] At the first hearing, he made the distinction between intent and effect. "I take it for granted that this [bill] comes from a good place," he said, "that this is not intended to be bad or evil. But the effect of this is . . . to create a screen, essentially, for who gets to live in Greenport." A year later his assumption regarding the proponents' best intentions had vanished. "It reads like a fascist manifesto to attack immigrants and low-income families that distinguish this village," he bellowed to the board of trustees at a hearing in June 2013. "It's a cruel and unnecessary law" that will "gut the economy" by driving away many of its workers, he said. Similar testimony came from Ed Reale, a board member of the North Fork Housing Alliance, which helps low- and moderate-income families find housing throughout Southold Town (in all its hamlets as well as in the village of Greenport) and builds low-cost housing. He called the bill "vindictive, not what I thought was the spirit of this village" and noted that courts had found similar rental regulation schemes—in particular the search warrant provision—unconstitutional.

Despite these objections, the proponents prevailed. Ignoring last-minute legal concerns raised by the director of Long Island Housing Services, the board of trustees voted three to two to enact the rent regulation law. It was a foregone conclusion that Murray, who had initially proposed the law, would endorse it, and the mayor's affirmative vote was expected, since he had also supported it from the beginning. The other "yes" came from Julia Robins, a new board member who was a real estate agent; as a tenant herself, she welcomed the chance for the village to make landlords provide safe spaces for residents. Opposed was Mary Bess Phillips, a long-time resident and landlady, who found the bill intrusive and cited the difficulties of enforcing it with only one building department employee. And Deputy Mayor George Hubbard voted no, out of concern, he said, that "we can't handle the code that we have now." Since the law's requirement that each of the more than 400 rental properties in town be inspected seemed an impracticable goal, a common view in the village was that enforcement would be either selective or nonexistent.

◆ ◆ ◆

It would be very short-sighted for decision makers, backed by discomfited citizens, to head down the path of restricting—intentionally or unwittingly—immigrant housing. While Greenport's working class is not entirely Latino and black, immigrants make up the bulk of the housecleaners, landscapers, dishwashers, and construction workers who drive the revival of the village. As they learn English, they are an increasingly visible presence in stores and restaurants, as clerks and waiters and small business owners. Many are consumers with large families who shop in the supermarket and pharmacy, and the modest commercial network that they have created—convenience stores, a barbershop, a *pupusería*—relies entirely on their trade. Greenport would have no school district without the children of its immigrants.

The usual analysis of the effect of immigrants on a local economy is to see the influx as boosting employment—filling jobs that native-born residents don't want and providing labor in emerging industries. But the economy also benefits from immigrants as tenants and ultimately as homeowners. The dynamic is especially evident where housing has been abandoned, eroding the tax base and contributing to crime, which further depresses the housing market. Immigrants can help to break that vicious cycle, in small towns as well as in cities. One recent report suggests that their contribution is particularly significant where they are low-income people hunting for low-cost housing.[16] As soon as they move in and pay rent, the value of the house rises, adding to tax revenue; as soon as they go to the local Home Depot or hire a local contractor, at least a few local incomes rise.

Greenport fits the pattern of housing decline and immigrant-led revival. Vacant and decrepit housing after World War II contributed to high crime and general desolation in the village, more like the decay of New York City in the 1970s than like the rural depression of upstate New York. Kapell, who was the community development director before he became mayor, notes that a 1979 report by the Suffolk County Health Department described Greenport as having some of the worst slums in the county. The village remained a depressed backwater even into the 1990s. House values were low enough so that in 1997, according the Long Island Index, 87 percent of home sales in the village (twenty out of twenty-three sales) were at "affordable" prices—that is, less than 2.5 times the Long Island family income.[17]

The new century changed that, for good and for ill. On the one hand, the village flourished as Greenport's amenities (often serviced by immigrants) attracted both tourists and new residents—second-home owners, retirees, and families looking to escape suburban sprawl or urban anonymity. Mostly gone were the slum conditions Kapell had noted, partly as the result of his efforts. Immigrants had contributed by renting some of the older houses that had been repaired. "Everybody has been lifted by the renaissance of Greenport," says Robins, the village trustee, whose thirty-year experience as a carpenter and builder has given her a firsthand look at the changes. By 2010 house prices had shot up everywhere on the North Fork, including Greenport. That year only seven sales, out of twenty, were at the "affordable" level ($268,105 or less), none in the village center where Greenport's attractions are.

But the new century has also brought rising inequality, the Great Recession, and antagonism toward government efforts to strengthen the safety net. What the secretary of housing and urban development calls "the worst rental affordability crisis that this country has known" is one of the consequences.[18] It is more profitable to respond to demand from the rich than from the poor, so landlords and developers focus on housing them, while families whose homes have been foreclosed compete with lower-income workers and young people for rental units, which have remained flat or declined in number. And federal and state governments are either too strapped or too indifferent to respond with new rental opportunities for native-born or immigrant residents. So for all but the affluent, supply is down and demand is up.

Tiny Greenport has not been immune to these forces. As the village lured new residents who could afford to buy and renovate the old houses—and, importantly, convert them back into single-family homes—the number of rental properties shrank. With scarcity comes inflation, and rents rose, affecting everyone who couldn't buy. Opportunities for subsidized housing were also shrinking. Although the state had awarded Greenport's housing authority eighty-seven Section 8 vouchers in 2013, only seventy-eight were in use because of the sequester enacted by Congress. The problem had shifted from an excess of vacancies to a scarcity of affordable housing. And now the new rental regulation law was likely to worsen the crunch by displacing people in crowded households. As one outsider observed, "It appears that the ordinance is allowing development at one end of the market to thrive while strangling the other, lower end." In this respect, Greenport was joining the rest of Long Island—and much of the rest of the country.

◆ ◆ ◆

From Titus Maccius Plautus, a Roman philosopher of the second century BC, to Evan Carmichael, a twenty-first-century webmaster for entrepreneurs, business advisors have counseled that you must spend money to make money. It's not just good guidance for budding corporate moguls; it's also pertinent for governments and small businesses. The current housing squeeze affects the availability of housing that low-wage workers of all kinds—young people starting out as well as immigrants—can afford. Commitment to greater density and to smaller homes will be expensive, both economically and politically. But without safe, comfortable places for ordinary families to live— whether renters or buyers, immigrants or native-born—the delicate balance of diverse demography and rural charm will be upset. Greenport will become merely a getaway for the affluent, with services imported from hardscrabble ghettos that working people can afford.

It's not just Greenport's problem. Most of the hamlets and villages that border the bays of Suffolk County are frozen in no-growth paralysis because they are not providing housing for the people who will generate economic activity. As Kapell put it in a 2004 article in Long Island's principal newspaper, "Population growth, skyrocketing property values, exclusionary zoning and aggressive environmental protection have eliminated opportunity for small lot, cluster, and rental housing development needed to meet the needs of the average family."[19] In December 2011 the North Fork Housing Alliance had a waiting list of 426 households. It probably hasn't improved since then.

Over the years entrepreneurs and politicians have brought up several proposals for consideration by the village and town. None of them have come to fruition. One developer's plan for erecting a small condominium development on a vacant corner in the middle of town would have provided subsidized units for middle-income buyers—nurses, teachers, and other local people who cannot afford the rapidly rising house prices but would be eligible for the required, modest mortgages. The building's location would have given residents easy access to stores, restaurants, and transportation (trains as well as private and public buses); they would connect to municipal utilities. While that project would not have benefited the immigrants or native-born low-income residents, it would have moved a few people into home ownership and eased the rental market slightly. Ostensibly blocked by a (potentially solvable) zoning problem, the plan got a chilly reception from local politicians, who seemed to be worrying that the units would house undesirables and suggested that the corner was unsuitable for children. (A number of children living within a stone's throw of the corner seem to be thriving.) After the project had languished before village committees for several years, the developer gave up and sold the lot in 2007. Seven years later it was still vacant, an urban bruise on the small-town landscape.

Kapell's plan, proposed in 2004 when he was mayor, was more ambitious. He sought to stretch the village boundaries to take advantage of Greenport's zoning. Unlike the large-lot, single-family standards of Southold, Greenport's pattern of one- and two-family homes on small lots would prevail, enabling the construction of affordable houses, up to five per acre. ("Affordable" in planners' parlance means within the reach of families who earn no more than median income.) An income limit for buyers would keep prices down, and two-family houses would give owner-occupants an opportunity to derive rental income from the half of the structure they didn't live in. The expanded village would extend the housing density that has given the village a walk-able downtown and a concentration of the goods and services that answer most daily needs. A modest amount of infrastructural development would be needed, but the village would get new tax revenue and the underpopulated schools would get additional students.

Although a group of residents cried foul—"What are we talking about, a socialist government?" complained one—the village board of trustees voted unanimously to endorse the mayor's request to the county and state to fund a feasibility study of the idea.[20] But the town of Southold, which includes the village of Greenport, balked. Annexation would be a complex legal pro-cess, a public referendum would be contentious, and the increased demand on the schools would drive up property taxes. Instead, the town instituted inclusionary zoning, which, while not altering the prevailing large-lot pol-icy, required developers of five or more housing units to provide 20 percent of that housing as affordable. Loopholes abound, however: there is no such requirement for smaller developments, and a reluctant developer can take advantage of a buyout provision in the legislation, paying a substantial sum to the Town Housing Fund. (As of 2014, a buyer would have to pay the town $210,200 for each unit *not* built.) So far, the only developer to fall under the new requirement is so reluctant that he has filed suit against the town, alleg-ing that the buyout amount is too high.

Southold's town board may finally be summoning up the political will to encourage affordable housing. It has put developers on notice that it will help navigate bureaucratic twists and turns to get projects approved. A new compre-hensive plan for the town stresses the importance of making more moderate-income housing available for buyers and renters alike. And Greenport's trustee Robins plans to pressure Southold decision makers to make good on their paper commitments. But sentiment in the town has always favored the status quo—leaving ordinary workers to fend for themselves in Greenport.

◆ ◆ ◆

In the end, James Olinkiewicz decided to withdraw his initial request for zon-ing variances that would have enabled him to build an additional two-family house. Instead he planned to submit a new request. This time he would seek a variance that would allow him to subdivide his existing property so that he could build a single-family house next to his first house, which would also revert to single-family use. This outcome would reduce low-cost housing by two units (the apartments in the first house around which the dispute raged) and increase traditional one-family housing by two units—the reconverted house and the new house. The neighbors had won. And Olinkiewicz's effort to ease the housing crunch in Greenport turned out to be futile: the two single-family houses he proposed to rent (or, perhaps, sell) would not be affordable for the potential tenants whose need is greatest.

Perhaps he was disingenuous when he cited the need for housing as a primary motivation for his construction and conversion of two-family rental housing. But he identified and accurately described the local problem: "You sell a house in the village that was a two-family, it gets converted back to a one-family, now you've displaced all of the people, and so you have over-crowding." He might have added, "And soon those who are displaced will move away."

If they did, Greenport would be in big trouble. For small communities that depend on manual labor, whether performed by foreign- or native-born, struggles over land use and housing are existential. They are also more than the crisis of the moment and of the North Fork. The warring messages of rejection and support for the immigrants, as evidenced by the village disputes over the construction of two-family houses and the rental regulation law, are symptoms of a much broader dilemma. Political and financial commitment to housing production or rent supplements for low- and moderate-income people has been a sometime thing for almost a century, usually spurred by an upheaval like the Great Depression of the 1930s or a moral imperative like the needs of veterans after World War II. Without such an incentive for either developers or the government—or, most likely, both—to get into the game, houses for those who are comfortable are always more popular investments than housing or subsidies for those who need it most. It's not new. More than forty years ago Ada Louise Huxtable, the architecture critic of the *New York Times*, wrote, "The hard truth is that there is absolutely no way, with current tools, procedures, and appropriations, of solving America's basic shelter problems."[21] The same could be said today of Greenport.

PROFILE

Sofia's Quest

It is 9 AM on Thanksgiving Day, and Sofia Martinez is getting ready to take her children to a holiday dinner at the Catholic church in Riverhead, the county seat. Celia and Augusta, ages fourteen and fifteen, are still asleep, but Jorge and Luis, ages eight and six, are in high gear, excited about the day ahead. One of their tasks before leaving is parrot care. Their two birds are small, as parrots go, but lively and noisy, avian mirrors of their boy masters. Their names are Mango and Kiwi, with plumage to match. Jorge confides that Kiwi, purchased only a couple of weeks ago, was expensive—"so much that more than one person had to help to buy him"—and that he is still getting used to his surroundings and stays in the cage most of the time. Mango, however, often flies about the apartment, alighting comfortably on the refrigerator or a bed or a human extremity. Sofia, age forty-six—small, bright-eyed, doyenne of pixie charm—coaxes Mango onto her finger and then to Jorge's shoulder while her children watch admiringly. She turns to them with a smile of such joy that it is hard to believe that her life is full of turmoil and worry.

Jorge isn't actually her child. He is the son of her son Robert, age twenty-six, whose many medical problems have necessitated that she assume Jorge's care. He is a jittery boy who can't stop talking even when the parrots aren't exciting him. But he is also a companion for Luis, two years younger, which helps keep the littlest boy out of his teenage sisters' hair. Celia and Augusta are fully engaged with sports and music—guitar, flute, and trumpet—and they would rather not have too much to do with the boys. They are gracious about occasional babysitting duty, however, and they enter into the controlled chaos of trips to Riverhead in Sofia's elderly Volkswagen to eat at the *taquería* or shop at the big-box stores.

Like most single mothers, Sofia lives a life that is a perpetual juggle of work and family. After-school activities necessitate different schedules for her four school-age children. She has multiple appointments with teachers and counselors who arrange special education classes for two of them and medical attention for Jorge, whose jitters signal severe attention deficit hyperactivity disorder (ADHD). As a housecleaner with multiple clients, she commutes across the harbor to Shelter Island as well as serving households in Greenport. And she must make frequent trips to Riverhead and to New York City to deal with Robert's problems; he lives with his father or uncle when he is not in a treatment center.

In the past Sofia considered returning to Mexico, to Izucar de Matamoros, about an hour south of the city of Puebla, where her mother still lives. Her beloved grandmother recently died, and she was bereft at being unable to comfort her in her final days. Her mother has osteoporosis and needs the care that a daughter could bring. Luis's father once gave her that opportunity; he had become disillusioned with life in the United States and decided to go back to Mexico and try to get an education. And her dear friend Gabriel, after many years of installing windows on the North Fork, had saved up enough money to go home and invest in the small store he had always wanted. Sofia watched him leave with mixed feelings. The burdens of life here pressed hard on her. But she had made a commitment to her American children and she would keep it.

◆ ◆ ◆

The Mexican state of Puebla, source of the holiday of Cinco de Mayo (Fifth of May) has a rich political, artistic, and culinary history. Its military importance stretched from the repeated invasions of pre-Hispanic times to 1867, when the future dictator Porfirio Diaz routed the French in one of the final battles of the Franco-Mexican War (also called the French intervention). Its colorful Talavera pottery and the melding of chiles, spices, nuts, and chocolate that is mole poblano are appreciated around the world.

Although the modern city of Puebla is the fourth largest in the country (almost two million people in 2010), the state as a whole is rural. With a population that strongly supported the Mexican Revolution (1910–1917), it embraced the reform that broke up the haciendas and gave peasants communal lands known as *ejidos*. But in the decades that followed, many forces combined to hobble the state's noble goal. By the 1930s the benefits of agrarian reform were almost nonexistent, and even during the era of relative prosperity between the mid-1940s and the late 1960s, peasants in Puebla suffered. Spurred by a national president who prioritized domestic manufacturing (what economists call import substitution industrialization), the successes of the Mexican Miracle could be seen in the skyscrapers rising in Mexico City and in the highways and railroads that connected the corners of the country. But investment in agriculture benefited landowners, not peasants, and government improvements in infrastructure favored large farms in the northern states, not Puebla.

It was a time of fevered urbanization. In 1970 more than five times as many people lived in Mexican communities with more than 15,000 residents as in 1940.[1] Perhaps because it was near Mexico City, Puebla became an industrial hub. Manufacturing increased and agriculture declined, a pattern that remains to this day. Volkswagen had opened a plant in the city in 1967, the first of what is now the largest auto manufacturing center in North America. Thermostats, stainless steel machine parts, candy, and Coca-Cola—they are all made in Puebla.

The industrial growth of the mid-twentieth century brought some economic benefits to subsistence farmers and other workers by driving them out of dying farming communities. It also forced social and cultural sacrifice. The cities offered jobs that paid more than growing corn and beans, but families were splintered and traditions abandoned. The country's financial collapse in 1982—the result of political unrest, profligate government spending on fantasies of industrial power, and the collapse of the peso—wiped out the advantages of urbanization for many people, leaving them in poverty.

For Poblanos (the people of Puebla, as well as the name of a mild chili pepper), migrating to the city was not the only opportunity for betterment. Campesinos and urban workers alike were joining the trek to the "other side," emigrating to the northern colossus, where even rising unemployment during an American recession was a lesser evil than starvation at home. Most of them did not go to the western states, where Mexicans had put down roots for many generations. They initiated a new pattern of Mexican migration. Before the 1990s just a trickle of migrants had come to the Northeast, but in that decade the trickle became a river with many tributaries as Mexicans moved in significant numbers to several states. In New Jersey, they made up 2.5 percent of the population by 2010, and the census that year counted 457,288 New York residents of Mexican descent, 319,263 in New York City.[2] Most came from the state of Puebla.

◆ ◆ ◆

Sofia and some members of her family followed the double migratory path common to Poblanos in the late twentieth century—first seeking work in the city of Puebla and then, finding little opportunity in Mexico, emigrating. When Sofia was small her father left home to be with another woman whom he later married. Her mother was left to support Sofia and her five siblings, which became increasingly difficult after Sofia's grandfather's small store burned down with all his corn inside. Sofia had helped him in the fields, and the fire was a loss to her as well as to her grandfather. "I knew him as a man still trying to grow his corn, but he was ruined," she says sadly. It put the final stamp on the dissolution of her nuclear family. With her mother and older sister leaving to work in Puebla, Sofia's brothers went to live with their father and she was sent to aunts and uncles. She would have liked to continue at school after the sixth grade, but it was impossible. "I thought my mother would help me, but she was too poor; she needed me to help her." So Sofia followed her mother to the city.

Although Mexico's informal economy is not as large a percentage of the country's GDP as that of Central American countries, it is enormous. In 2008 an International Monetary Fund analyst estimated it to be 28 percent of economic output early in the new century, while other estimates suggest a higher number.[3] (Because it is, by its very nature, "informal"—that is, unrecorded in any official repository—this part of the national economy cannot be measured with any assurance of accuracy.) The most widely accepted number of informal sector workers—defined as workers who don't have a fixed place of employment and don't register with taxing authorities—was over fourteen million in 2012.[4] How large this number was in 1982 when Sofia—smart and strong but still only fifteen—went to Puebla to help her mother is unknown. But it is clear that the *ambulantes*, vendors without a fixed address selling goods in urban streets, were already a common sight in every big city. (In 2006, it was estimated that more than two hundred thousand ambulantes were working in Mexico City alone.[5])

Sofia and her mother joined them, peddling smuggled goods from the United States—T-shirts, watches, knockoffs of designer handbags—and liquor. For several years, they lived in a single room with her older sister and two younger half-sisters. Although all her sisters tried to help their mother, they also found ways to move on: one left school in the ninth grade to get married at fifteen, another simply disappeared—"a rebel," says Sofia.

Sofia's escape was bolder. Life was better elsewhere, she knew, and the opportunity to explore it was close at hand. Her father's second wife had brothers who had found jobs in New York with better pay and better working conditions than they could have found in Mexico. If Sofia's father could leave his job as a maintenance man in the local movie theater, those relatives would help pay for him and his daughter, now eighteen, to come to the United States. So in December 1986 they set out. Getting from Izucar de Matamoros to Tamaulipas, a northern manufacturing state, was easy—just a long day's drive. The hard part of the journey was hiding in an empty boxcar overnight to cross the border. "We were alone with two other migrants and a coyote," Sofia remembers. "I was afraid and very cold." But they arrived at a Corpus Christi hotel without further trauma and flew to New York City a couple of days later.

That trip was only one in a lifetime of tests of her strength. To survive her past and continuing travails, Sofia has developed a sturdy philosophy of life. She accepts her twenty-eight years spent in the shadow of illegality in the United States but will also embrace the moment when one or more of her children are mature and settled enough to petition for her legalization. Her evaluation of the hardships of her trip north is typically measured. "It was very difficult, but it was not bad like the trip of many other people who have to run in the desert or cross the river," she says. "It was OK. I cannot complain when I hear the stories of people who were raped or killed or beaten."

Her odyssey was not complete, however. Where material deprivation had been the defining problem of her life in Mexico, hostility and violence followed her for the early years in New York. Her stepmother, with whom she lived when she first arrived, turned on her when her father went back to Mexico. The debt Sofia had incurred as the price of migration became justification for holding her hostage, even after she paid it off; "I wanted to leave and go back to Mexico, but she had all my papers—passport, birth certificate, everything." So she moved in with a friend but soon moved again—from Brooklyn to Queens—to get away from an abusive boss. At nineteen, living in a room in Queens with no job and no money, she met Robert's father and soon became pregnant. "Guillermo was a good person because he respected me and took care of me," she says. But he was also young and inclined to drink and smoke and miss work. "He was living the life of youth in the streets, not taking his responsibilities." He was also very macho (her word) and would not let her work. "What he said was right; I had to do what was proper for his wife. I was very submissive until it was necessary to go to work." Fleeing from his jealousy and occasional brutality, she finally arrived in Greenport in 1995. Its leafy calm has sustained her ever since.

◆ ◆ ◆

Even within Greenport's tiny perimeter, Sofia has lived a peripatetic life. When she first came to Greenport with seven-year-old Robert, she stayed with a cousin in an apartment on a side street. She rented the cousin's living room for two years until she met and married a fellow Mexican and moved with him into a small, comfortable house in a modest development at the edge of town. It was a house with a yard, a good place to raise Celia and Augusta when they were born a few years later. But conditions there deteriorated, and her landlady sold the house. The new owners removed Sofia and her family, saying they wished to renovate and pointing out that she had paid a very low rent for eight years. Next came a brief stay in a two-bedroom apartment on Main Street, where the landlord decided that her family—now augmented by two when her teenage son brought his pregnant girlfriend into the household—was too large for the space. "It seemed like a big apartment to us," Sofia says ruefully. "But for them it was too many people—and they robbed me of my security deposit!" Her marriage did not survive the next apartment, and for a while she lived in a single room with her son and the girls. When she finally found a place, the landlord objected to her son's friends coming around, so they had to move again, though by this time Robert had found his own place. She liked the new apartment, but the landlord had not told her she would be responsible for water and electricity, and she found she was also paying for power for the store underneath her. Finally, in 2010, she got lucky. She and her daughters and a new baby and the son's baby (abandoned by his mother) found a comfortable apartment above another store. This time the landlord was responsible—"He is a good person," Sofia says with relief in her voice. The rent was reasonable, and she didn't have to pay a real estate agent's commission, as had become the custom. Her odyssey had at last led her to an oasis.

Sofia's work helps her deal with other problems. "I like to work, a lot," she says. Her dedication to clients and her general competence have paid off in steady employment and a flexible schedule. By middle-class standards, it would be a stretch to find in her present arrangement real occupational advancement over the years she spent laboring in factories, kitchens, and hotels. But by now the people she works for know her well and cherish her abilities and spirit. While psychic income is hardly a substitute for permanent employment with benefits, it enriches her in ways that supplement her pay. She generally earns two or three times the minimum wage, and every month since arriving in the United States, she has sent something home to her mother.

Her income is not totally dependent on housecleaning jobs. Sofia also sells salsas made from several kinds of chili peppers that she cultivates in a nearby community garden. "I like to grow things," she says. "My family says I inherited that from my grandfather." Celia and Augusta's father pays child support, and despite her undocumented status, the Suffolk County Social Services Department subsidized her expenses as a foster mother for Jorge. In 2013 she went to court to adopt him, undaunted by the attention she will need to give to his learning disabilities. The ironies of immigration policy come into play in this situation: New York State does not permit Sofia to drive, and the federal government prohibits employers from hiring her; but the county is willing to put her permanently in charge of raising her needy grandson.

Sofia's immigrant status impinges on her life in many ways. Some of the concessions she must make to it carry real risks. She often has on her person a wad of hundred-dollar bills as a substitute for what legal immigrants and citizens would have in credit cards. Like most undocumented adults, she drives—"very cautiously," she says—without a license; living in a rural area, she would have no reliable way to reach her clients without a car. She "owns" her car by having it registered in the name of a licensed driver to whom she pays the insurance premium; she takes care of all maintenance and repair costs.

Even if Sofia is convicted of a traffic or other minor offense, she is unlikely to be detained or deported. She is the primary support for four American children, one of whom is considered disabled by ADHD, and she has a long history of steady employment and law-abiding behavior. In recent years she has been paying income taxes. She may be eligible, as the parent of citizens, for a temporary reprieve from deportation through the new Deferred Action for Parent Accountability (DAPA) policy, part of the Obama administration's effort to enact modest reforms with executive action. But fragile stability does not amount to reliable security. The slight but ever-present threat of apprehension haunts her. She would like to participate in early childhood research being undertaken at Luis's school but is afraid to have him traced to an undocumented mother. She has recently been advised to have mammograms, but she is reluctant to identify herself at the hospital. Blatant local references to her illegal presence remind her that her situation affects even her children. She hurries them past the barbershop around the corner where the barber has taunted them—"Aliens!"

◆ ◆ ◆

Although Sofia's disposition is generally sunny, sadness is a frequent companion. She still misses her country—the friends who remain there and others who shared her New York life for a time but have returned to Puebla. Her teenage daughters would like to see Mexico and meet their maternal grandmother, but Sofia cannot take them to her and she wonders if her mother, whose obesity has caused medical problems, will live long enough to know the girls. Sometimes the challenges she faces seem overwhelming. All of her children have struggled academically, and no one knows whether Jorge will grow out of the hyperactivity that requires medication and a great deal of patience.

Yet Sofia is also aware that problems she grapples with in her Greenport life are more likely to be solved in New York than they would be in Mexico. Although Mexican law guarantees that children who need them will receive special education services, usually integrated into regular classrooms as in the United States, few teachers are trained to deal with children with ADHD, especially a child with conditions as pronounced as

Jorge's. Special education is most likely to be found in cities. In 2010 the US State Department reported that fewer than half of Mexican municipalities provided special education at all, while an earlier report estimated that only 8 percent of schools were providing it through middle school: "the reach of the special education services is not far and not deep."[6] In contrast, Greenport gives Jorge daily attention, both medical and academic, and her older children continue to get help with homework, even in high school.

Sofia's greatest sadness is the helplessness she feels about Robert's illness. She wonders whether his problems began when, at seven, he started acting up at school and telling her he couldn't stop thinking about his father hitting her—something that Sofia says did not happen often. Perhaps his worries were a precursor of what was to come. Even in more peaceful surroundings in Greenport, Robert had trouble in school and dropped out in the ninth grade. He fell in love at sixteen and impregnated his girlfriend, the mother of Jorge. A sweet-faced young man who was, however, still functionally illiterate in his early twenties, he spent several years getting and losing menial jobs. Although his affect and attitudes hardly suggested the stereotypes of depressives or the criminally inclined, he nonetheless was convicted with an accomplice of holding up a clerk in a convenience store at knifepoint—an offense he couldn't explain. Spending six months in the country jail was not a solution. A few months later, in early 2011, it became clear that his experiment with deviance was also an expression of illness. Sofia had allowed a young cousin who was just getting out of prison to come live with them briefly while he found work and housing. But he went back to dealing cocaine, and Robert joined him as a consumer. One night they both had too much, and the cousin collapsed on Front Street. Too stoned to act, Robert did nothing. By the time someone called the ambulance, the cousin was dead. Robert was so traumatized that he was hospitalized for two weeks with depression.

But it wasn't only depression. As he recovered, he took on weekend work as a busboy, something he enjoyed and was good at. But he often had terrible headaches and couldn't get up in the morning. After he was late at the restaurant several times, he was fired. It is hard to know whether that brought on the downward spiral or whether the spiral was already upon him, a tornado taking everything with it—family relationships, employment, hopes for the future. Sofia found him increasingly aggressive at home, and he admitted to violent fantasies, frightening his sisters. One day he disappeared into New York City. After two frightening days of looking for him, Sofia finally found that the police had sent him to the psychiatric emergency room of a Queens hospital, dazed and incoherent, hearing voices. He pleaded with her to give him his "pistols," convinced that he was supposed to be going into the army.

Now, at least, there was an explanation: he was schizophrenic. As devastating as such a diagnosis would be to someone who was at least minimally knowledgeable about mental illness, Robert saw it as worse than six months in jail. At first he rejected the professional determination that he had an incurable disease and refused to accept the probability that he would need to take antipsychotic medicine for the rest of his life. He insisted that his natural desires to be a productive adult, independent of his mother but protective of her, would prevail over what seemed to him merely a series of bad choices. But two years after his diagnosis he enrolled in a program in Riverhead that would monitor his medications and subsidize housing for him until he could return to school or part-time employment. Perhaps his hopes for the future were, as many around him thought, illusory; Sofia tried not to dwell on that possibility.

She had another worry, more pressing if less painful. Her children had fallen in love with a dog, now just a playful puppy but soon to be a large, intrusive presence in her modest apartment. Her landlord gave her several months to move but held firmly to his view that one adult, four children, two birds, and a dog amounted to a definition of overcrowding. Conceding that this was a reasonable position, Sofia knew that, once again, she would have to move. Initially she turned for help to her daughters, who had become adept at surfing the Internet. But when that approach lured her into a Craigslist fraud, she realized that the search for housing would now be even more difficult than in the past. Where could she find a safe, comfortable rental for her brood for $1,500 or less? Hers is an extreme case of the quest for affordable housing in gentrifying Greenport.

◆ ◆ ◆

Sofia will probably never return to live in Mexico. Except for her bond with her mother, her family ties are now stronger here, where many relatives have also made the trip north, than in Mexico. "We talk occasionally, but very little," she says wistfully. "It is hard to keep in touch when it has been so long." Her situation exemplifies an irony noted by many students of immigration policy: the restrictions actually ensure that the population of undocumented people in the United States remains large because, if they go home, they will have to stay there, unable to return to the United States to see friends and family. As long as she remains subject to deportation, Sofia cannot benefit from the transnationalism that defined the lives of several generations of Mexicans. If she qualifies for DAPA, she will be protected from deportation for at least three years and will be issued a work permit, but without more, she is no closer to legal permanent residence or citizenship than before President Obama announced the initiative.

Sofia accepts her transplantation. Thinking of her most vulnerable child, now both son and grandson, she says without ambivalence, "I can't go back to Mexico and leave Jorge; he has to be here, and if I am going to help him I have to stay here." His problems and Robert's have also given her opportunities to deepen her roots on the North Fork. Her contacts with social workers and psychologists have opened up avenues of knowledge that astonish and excite her. "I'm learning so much," she says. As a requirement for being Jorge's foster mother, she opened a bank account, which she has learned to manage. Her English is improving rapidly, partly because she wants to know more of what her teenage daughters are talking about and partly because she has begun to text her clients on her cell phone. She anticipates the moment when, as adults, the girls can help legalize her American presence, but, as always, she is patient. "I have now spent more than half of my life here, so what does another few years matter?"

PART V

Toward Community Health

CHAPTER 8

Cobbled Care

One Saturday in May 2012 Edgar was cutting a bluestone paving tile for his job with a contractor. He wasn't very experienced at this kind of work, and his hand slipped. As the knife sliced into his finger, he let go of the stone, which slammed down on his wrist, crushing it. Bleeding and in pain, he rushed to the emergency room of Eastern Long Island Hospital, where the doctor on duty stitched the finger, bandaged the wrist, gave him something for the pain, and referred him to Stony Brook University Hospital for surgery. But Stony Brook did not find him eligible for emergency Medicaid, and his insurance—funded by the state children's insurance program (Child Health Plus, which covers the undocumented as well as legal residents and the native-born)—had expired when he turned nineteen the previous month. As an undocumented adult he could not get coverage elsewhere, and in any case he could not have afforded it. Eventually the local community health center helped him get treated at the Surgery Center of Southampton Hospital. The cost—much reduced from the market rate—was shared by Edgar's sister, an older worker who knew his family, and the owner of the home where he was working when the accident happened. He went for physical therapy at a low-cost center in Greenport, and six months after the surgery, his wrist had regained most of its range of motion.

This is a fairly typical story of the way the American health system works—and doesn't work—for immigrants in Greenport. The local hospital responded as best it could, honoring the federal mandate to assist anyone who requires emergency care, regardless of ability to pay or immigration status, until the condition has stabilized—which means, as the Emergency Department director put it, "until the risk is past."[1] And Hudson River Health Care (HRH-Care), which sponsors the community health center that provides primary care to most of the Hispanics in Greenport—as well as to non-Hispanic whites, including the mayor—carried out its mission by coordinating the continuing help Edgar needed. But the distinguished teaching hospital of the university turned him away because it was constrained by rules about whom it can serve and at what price. Hospitals can get federal reimbursement from Medicaid for delivering babies of undocumented women, but that's about all. (As for emergency care, more than half is uncompensated, the American College of Emergency Physicians estimates.[2]) Edgar was very lucky to be in a community where private and public resources could be cobbled together to take care of him. But that outcome does not alter the reality that a nineteen-year-old was on his own with limited access to the safety net, forcing him to rely instead on relatives and friends to bear most of the expense, out-of-pocket, of repairing his wrist. Had he been a citizen or a legal resident who had been in the United States for more than five years, he would have been eligible for insurance—probably Medicaid—to cover most costs.

◆ ◆ ◆

Even in the best of times the American health care system has left out the poor, whether they are American or foreign-born. Either they cannot find the medical attention that every human being needs or they cannot obtain comprehensive insurance for one reason or another. In the early years of the twenty-first century the inequity intensified, with one study finding that during 2011 almost three out of five adults in poor households were uninsured at some point.[3] While there is no comparable survey of immigrants, they were surely even worse off. Whether poor or affluent, they have faced additional barriers—ineligibility for affordable insurance because of their status or the lack of information about where to find treatment. Almost by definition, if they are uninsured *and* undocumented, their range of choices is very narrow—and for some, it's getting even narrower with the Affordable Care Act—of which more later.

Not all obstacles are externally imposed. Some are psychological, products of fear and misunderstanding that see the effort to get help as a step into the unknown. Because the very act of showing up in the office of medical professionals requires creating a written record of one's name and identifying characteristics, many immigrants (though few in Greenport) fear being exposed to the possibility of deportation. People who are undocumented feel the greatest anxiety, of course, but being legally present in the country does not guarantee security. Any noncitizen immigrant who has a condition that needs attention knows that he or she may be vulnerable to policies that could send him or her (or a family member) back to the home country. An old record showing that asylum status was denied or that the fine for a traffic offense was unpaid could trip you up. Federal legislation passed in 1996 provides for the deportation of any migrant—not just those without papers—convicted of an "aggravated felony," defined so broadly as to include shoplifting and minor drug offenses.[4] For the undocumented especially, the prospect, however unlikely (and illegal), that health records would find their way to the Department of Homeland Security is enough to deter some people from turning to doctors even when their health problems are acute.

Oversensitivity to immigration enforcement practices and policies is not the only reason that immigrants sometimes avoid health care that is available and superior to what they would have had in their countries of origin. Sometimes cultural sensitivity makes them loath to entrust themselves to a foreign, English-speaking doctor or nurse. At least some of the Latinos in Greenport believe that taking medicine or asking for treatment is to be avoided at almost all costs, even if getting help earlier may save your life. Many perceive the unpleasant truth that Americans—political decision-makers as well as ordinary citizens—are often deeply ambivalent about assisting newcomers by sharing resources. They may feel guilty and defensive about using public services and wonder if seeking diagnosis and treatment will hurt their chances of becoming "real Americans."

The question of what rights are owed to the foreign-born has been with us since the early days of the republic. Thomas Jefferson and Alexander Hamilton were at odds over it after Jefferson recommended, in his first State of the Union address in December 1801, that immigrants receive citizenship immediately. Hamilton's scorn was withering: "To admit foreigners indiscriminately to the rights of citizens, the moment they put foot in the country, as recommended in the message, would be nothing less than to admit the Grecian horse into the citadel of our liberty and sovereignty." The concern behind Hamilton's position—a view that Jefferson shared in an earlier document—was that many immigrants will bring with them loyalties to their old regimes and, therefore, be unable to embrace "that temperate love of liberty, so essential to real republicanism."[5]

Less lofty and abstract considerations came into play as more ordinary Americans were torn between wanting the human capital of immigrants and denying their human needs. The threat of diluting the whiteness of Protestant America was much debated. And as America absorbed people regarded as Europe's rejects, concern rose about "convicts" and "defectives" entering the country. Aristide Zolberg summarized the justification that contemporary pundits offered for the "foreign-pauper scare" of the 1830s: "While a thriving industrial society can be entrusted to generate constructive stimuli and thereby overcome the political difficulties arising from the immigration of economically desirable cheap labor, to achieve this it must not allow itself to be burdened by the additional problem of paupers and convicts."[6]

Longstanding prohibitions by states (and colonies before them) against admitting migrants who could become a "public charge"—that is, dependent on the state for financial or medical support—were sweeping, excluding people who were not only poor or had communicable diseases but also those who were mentally ill or just slow. Federalized by 1882 legislation barring "any convict, lunatic, or idiot or any person unable to take care of himself or herself without becoming a public charge," the doctrine remains a barrier to legal admission to the country and to many services that legal residents and citizens enjoy as a matter of right. The Immigration and Nationality Act still provides that someone who "is likely at any time to become a public charge" may not have a green card or become a citizen—and may, in rare instances, be subject to deportation. And the list of conditions that might render someone inadmissible—mumps and measles as well as "mental disorders"—is long and comprehensive.[7] (President Obama lifted the HIV ban in 2010.)

As a practical matter, the public charge doctrine as applied to the use of health services has more impact as symbolism than as substance. Its sweep is much reduced in the twenty-first century. As long as an immigrant is receiving only noncash benefits like treatment for disease or short-term rehabilitation, or special programs like children's health insurance and prenatal care services, she is unlikely to fall under the public charge rubric.[8]

The antagonism, however, that for over a century has sustained both federal law and public attitudes toward immigrants who use public resources continues unabated. Many Americans are ambivalent about providing even emergency services to immigrants and harbor a suspicion that undeserved benefits routinely accrue to people who are not legal residents. Political leaders are not immune to such resentments. When President Obama, in an address to Congress in 2009, commented that undocumented immigrants would not be eligible for subsidies—or, indeed, for any assistance at all— under the Affordable Care Act, a Republican congressman shouted from the audience, "You lie!" The spirit behind that outcry casts its shadow on immigrants' health care decisions every day.

◆ ◆ ◆

Staying healthy requires having the opportunity to find help, getting care that responds to basic and specialized needs, and being able to pay for it. Everyone's health care decisions are inevitably dominated by this triad of considerations—access, quality, and cost. A casual observer might think that all of these matters would constitute obstacles for Greenport's Hispanic immigrants. After all, the quality of health care in rural areas is often lower than in the suburbs or cities for everyone—let alone for immigrants, who are often quite isolated in the countryside. And most of those immigrants are poor, which may make the cost of even primary care prohibitive.

But for residents of Greenport, quality is rarely an issue. Medical services are somewhat bifurcated, to be sure; when people with private insurance need a doctor they go to private practitioners, rather than to the community health center. Nonetheless, the services that immigrants in the village and the nearby hamlets, regardless of status, can find are generally of high quality for both routine complaints and critical health problems. Recent research based on more than 31,000 visits to primary care doctors has found that, for uninsured patients and those that rely on Medicaid or community health centers, the length and content of primary care visits does not differ significantly from what is provided to patients using private insurance.[9] That conclusion would not surprise users of the Greenport Health Center. And North Fork specialists deal competently with most symptoms that patients present. Medical personnel at Eastern Long Island Hospital in Greenport respond quickly and caringly to emergencies brought to them—chest pain, nausea, accidents, sprains, and concussions—and sometimes to non-emergencies when patient demand is overwhelming the health center. For problems the local institutions cannot handle, the hospital is affiliated with Stony Brook University Medical Center, less than fifty miles away. The largest academic medical facility on Long Island, Stony Brook has more than twenty clinical departments and a national reputation.

Paying for care is a greater concern. Specialists may be beyond reach. Many do not accept Medicaid and, in any case, undocumented patients are ineligible for it, although New York State, relatively progressive where medical benefits are concerned, allows coverage, regardless of immigration status, for prenatal services and pediatric care as well as cancer screening, diagnosis, and treatment for people over fifty. The Greenport Health Center has resources to overcome some financial obstacles. It treats people who qualify for the federal Migrant Voucher Program, which offers discount cards to uninsured patients who work in agriculture—broadly defined to include landscapers and greenhouse workers—and their families. Walmart's prescription drug program offers many medications at four dollars for a thirty-day supply. Zwanger-Pesiri, a radiology company with offices in a dozen Long Island communities, provides free screenings and exams to uninsured, low-income people, regardless of immigration status. Immigrants can often rely on networks of family and friends, as Edgar did, together with public and private programs designed to address particular needs. Financial support for services beyond primary care becomes a form of bricolage—the construction of solutions from disparate sources in creative ways.

For Greenport's immigrant children, paying for health care is rarely a problem. If they are undocumented, Child Health Plus, the state program, will cover them up to age nineteen. But most low-income, Hispanic children in the village were born in the United States and are, therefore, eligible for Medicaid, usually obtained through Fidelis Care, the nonprofit New York State Catholic health insurance plan. Sofia has reason to be grateful for this benefit. One day her youngest child Luis was eating chips, stuffing them in his mouth along with a quarter, which he swallowed. It didn't go down very far and got lodged in his throat. The emergency room at Eastern Long Island Hospital did not have the capacity for pediatric endoscopy, so the doctor there sent Luis to Stony Brook, where anesthetics calmed him and an esophagoscope found and extracted the quarter. To Sofia's relief, Fidelis Care paid for everything.

High-quality professionals and manageable costs are a boon only when they are available. Until recently the biggest problem facing Greenport's Latinos when they needed health care was access. Medical attention was a very scarce resource for most of those who arrived in Greenport in the 1990s, when the influx of immigrants began. "There was nothing here for poor or uninsured people," says Maria Rivera, who came to the North Fork in 2002. "People used to phone friends and relatives at home in Mexico and describe their symptoms when they had pain or an accident, and then those people would send them the medicine they thought was right—very dangerous." Some immigrants drove twenty-five miles to Riverhead, the county seat, to find a clinic. That situation has changed, however, since then, Maria says. "Health care here is now a good opportunity for Spanish people." After a period of uncertainty about the safety and reliability of the proffered services, Hispanics living in the village and nearby hamlets have flocked to doctors, nurse practitioners, and midwives in the area who are committed to serving them.

◆ ◆ ◆

Greenport immigrants' health problems often arise from the work they do: heavy lifting in construction causes low back strain, prep work in a restaurant kitchen can bring on repetitive stress injury in the elbows. If you are working in landscaping or viniculture you are exposed to deer ticks. "We see Lyme disease left and right," says Ligia Soto, whose ten years of experience with migrants in the fields and greenhouses make her an expert. Many who are affected suffer in silence, she says, because they have never heard of the disease—it is virtually unknown in Guatemala or El Salvador, though common in Mexico—and can't understand why they feel so lousy.

As Soto travels up and down the North Fork to provide on-the-spot health counseling, she learns of other medical issues. Diabetes, obesity, and alcoholism are common, as they are among the native-born. Blaise Napolitano, the family practice doctor who heads the staff at the Greenport Health Center, thinks that the prevalence of obesity increases as immigrants adapt to the fast-food culture of the United States. Among the children he sees—mostly American-born to immigrant parents—pediatric obesity is troubling. "But the medical issues are less important than psycho-social disorders like depression and neglect," he says. He worries about the effects of poverty on Greenport's immigrant children.

Not all health issues are problems. Because so many of Greenport's immigrants arrive as single people but stay to form families, there are lots of pregnancies. And if there is one area where health care is readily available, well understood by Greenport immigrants, and free, it is prenatal care. Any pregnant woman in New York State, regardless of immigration status, can now get a wide range of services—checkups, lab work, hospital care, information about childbirth and postpartum issues, even nutrition counseling. Paid for by Medicaid, comprehensive care for the new baby continues for two months after birth, and heavily discounted hospital care is available after that through New York's Charity Care program. To be eligible for these services you need only live in New York and have an income at or below the poverty level (as of 2013, $1,963 per month for a family of four, with the expectant mother counting as two people). Most pregnant Latino immigrants in Greenport qualify.

They flock to nurse practitioner Pat Alcus, whose Center for Prenatal Care, a satellite of Southampton Hospital, prepares thirty-six to fifty women for motherhood each year. (Babies are born in the hospital.) In operation since 1995, the center was much in demand from the moment it opened. The demographics have changed since then, however; reflecting the population of Greenport in general, fewer of her patients are white and African American now and the majority are Latina. Most of those are undocumented immigrants, sometimes very poor; the staff winces at the recent memory of a woman seeking prenatal care who was sleeping in her car. But poverty and immigration status become, at least momentarily, irrelevant when the women have accomplished what they came for. The proud but guarded faces of dozens of mothers who have given birth with assistance from Alcus look down from photos on the wall of clean, spare waiting room—a gallery of images of mothers with babies, new citizens all. The women leave the center fortified by improved understanding of human biology, referral to social services to help them cope with added family responsibilities, and an appreciation of what it means to have help at hand when you need it.

◆ ◆ ◆

The War on Poverty initiated by President Lyndon Johnson in the 1960s has taken a lot of heat lately. Conservative media pundits and political figures like to announce that "poverty won" and reject the proposition that poor people need government help to better their lot. "We actually have a pretty solid idea of the keys to getting out of and/or staying out of poverty," says Michael Tanner of Fox News. The alternative to government handouts is simple: "(1) finish school; (2) do not get pregnant outside marriage; and (3) get a job, any job, and stick with it."[10] The Republican vice presidential candidate in

2012, Congressman Paul Ryan (R-WI), campaigned on a budget plan that would slash Medicaid and food stamps, relying on block grants to states to take up the slack. Keeping himself in the political spotlight in early 2014, he softened his message only slightly. He used the commemoration of Johnson's State of the Union address fifty years earlier that called for action—"We shall not rest until that war is won," said Johnson—to attribute poverty to "crime, drugs, and broken families." He called on the Obama administration to "dump decades-old programs" that Ryan thought had "deepened the divide" between the poor and the middle class.[11]

Medicaid and food stamps may be on the block, but one safety net benefit that is not likely to be dumped—originally an experiment within Johnson's Office of Economic Opportunity—is the community health center program. Surviving the shredding of the safety net in the Nixon and Reagan administrations, it has been popular ever since as the federal effort to provide primary and preventive health care in communities with many poor and uninsured people. According to the National Association of Community Health Centers, the centers operate in more than nine thousand locations, providing about twenty-two million people (including 20 percent of low-income children in the United States) with comprehensive primary and preventive health care. The Greenport Health Center exemplifies both the strengths and the limitations of the national movement to provide what its proponents call a "medical home" for people whose medical needs would otherwise be overlooked in the private health care system.

The origins of that movement predated President Johnson's War on Poverty, but the support and the spirit of the war gave it a big boost. Until the repressions of apartheid closed them down, the clinics that served some of South Africa's poorest townships were models of community-based health care. They were a source of inspiration for a young American doctor, H. Jack Geiger, who had spent a summer at the center in Pholela (now in Kwazulu-Natal) and who subsequently saw that he could realize his dream of practicing what he called "social medicine" for patients in the poorest communities at home. With the passage of the Economic Opportunity Act of 1964 ("to eliminate the paradox of poverty in the midst of plenty in this nation," its preamble announces) the American model of nonprofit, low-cost, patient-directed clinics funded by both federal and local sources was born. Geiger and a colleague founded the first two, in rural Mississippi and in a Boston neighborhood.

In 1975 Congress made the centers permanent institutions (now called Federally Qualified Health Centers) and later expanded their reach to cover housing projects and homeless shelters; it also authorized related services like education and transportation to make health care more accessible. Section 330 of the Public Health Service Act now sets forth standards for the program, and the federal Bureau of Primary Health Care funds and administers it. The centers must focus on populations that are medically underserved—which usually means low-income people, whether migrant workers, central city minorities, or undocumented immigrants. In 2013, 73 percent of health center patients had incomes below the federal poverty level and 35 percent were uninsured.[12]

In the early 1970s four women from Peekskill, New York, set in motion the development of HRHCare, the organization that now operates federally qualified health centers in the Hudson Valley and Long Island, including the Greenport Health Center. In a story reminiscent of Rosa Parks as a catalyst for the civil rights movement, Mary Woods waited all day one day in 1971 for an appointment for a child's checkup at the county hospital and then missed the last bus for her two-hour ride home. That did it; her crusade began the next day. Inspired by the example of Martin Luther King and by the antipoverty activism of the time, she enlisted three friends—the four are referred to at HRHCare as the Founding Mothers—to do something to bring access to health care to their poor African American community. Spurred by the belief that health care was a universal right, they employed the tactics of 1960s organizing—door-to-door surveys, petitions, endless community meetings—to convince others. Doctors, clergy, local politicians, and the Westchester County Health Department joined Peekskill residents to propose a community health center that would provide the town with affordable and comprehensive care. With a federal grant of $285,000 for three years, the new organization opened the Peekskill Area Health Center in 1975. Forty years later HRHCare serves eight-five thousand people within its network of twenty-two centers; its 2013 grant from the Bureau of Primary Health Care was for $858,333 to open a new site in Hudson, New York.

HRHCare came to Greenport in 2004 with a grant for providing services to migrant workers. At that time a nurse practitioner was providing adults and children with primary care and prenatal services in the space now occupied by the Greenport Health Center. She did not have the resources that HRH-Care was prepared to put into the health center, and HRH Care eventually bought her business. (In a sign of what is to come in the provision of primary care, the nurse practitioner has taken her shingle to other Long Island towns, establishing retail clinics in Walmart stores.) Although family care and the special programs funded by the state and the federal government are delivered locally, HRHCare retains a managerial role with the centers. The Greenport Health Center doesn't even have a bookkeeper; HRHCare handles all financial transactions of consequence centrally and electronically. The center isn't burdened with fundraising, either; "We survive by having people who apply for grants," says Napolitano gratefully.

For middle-class Greenporters with private health insurance (or Medicare or Medicaid), the Greenport Health Center is nearly invisible. Located in a Front Street building that looks like many other nineteenth-century clapboard houses in the village (expanded to accommodate examination rooms and offices), it announces itself with a single sign. But all of Greenport's Latino immigrants and many of its other low-income residents know that they can find there two primary care physicians (one part-time), a pediatrician, nurses (one a midwife), medical assistants, and a case manager. On Thursday afternoons Leonila Rodriguez comes to advise patients about insurance and sign up those who qualify for Fidelis Care. Two patient representatives dispense equal amounts of information and charm to connect patients to the medical professionals.

Partial support for the center comes from Medicaid. Because of the rural economy of the North Fork, many of those who are ineligible for Medicaid (i.e., unauthorized immigrants) can be covered by the Migrant Voucher program. Support from the federal Children's Health Insurance Program (CHIP) and Child Health Plus enables the center to treat everyone under nineteen at no cost. Patient fees—charged on a sliding scale, from $15 to $50 per visit—cover a negligible share of the center's costs. But there are always people who don't fall into any category that HRHCare can compensate. Finding ways to pay for the care of adults who lack insurance—about half of the patients, Napolitano estimates, most of whom are undocumented—is a constant struggle. He doesn't ask about immigration status or financial resources, however. "We don't turn anybody away."

On a typical day the waiting room—about the size of a single-car garage—is full to overflowing most of the time. Behind the receptionist's desk, a tiny file room (little space is needed now for computerized records) leads to a set of steep stairs where the representative from Fidelis Care coaxes low-income and immigrant families into its plan; in late 2013 and early 2014 she also helped all but the undocumented negotiate the New York State health exchange created by the Affordable Care Act. Downstairs, signs in both English and Spanish announce the availability of flu vaccines and the prohibition of cell phone use in the examination rooms. Brochures advertising training for breastfeeding—"Healthy Babies, Happy Moms"—and summarizing Medicare benefits decorate the receptionist's counter.

Nancy Montoya is at the front desk greeting patients, inspecting their documents, explaining medications, or giving directions to a specialist's office, while juggling telephone calls in Spanish and English. Nancy began working at the center as a fifteen-year-old intern more than a decade ago, when it was still the nurse practitioner's clinic. Now her title is senior patient representative, and she likes her work, but in the future she hopes to become an electronic medical records technician, a growth occupation in the era of Obamacare. In the meantime, there is little about the center that she doesn't know. The daughter of Guatemalan immigrants, she is attuned to facts of life specific to center patients and adjusts to them. She also knows the behavior patterns of this small town. As she fills out the registration form for a new patient, she is careful to get the name and number of an emergency contact. She knows that most patients use prepaid phones and that when their minutes expire they will be unreachable, either because they will have a new number or because they can't afford to buy more minutes. She also knows that a few will be illiterate in any language and that some will not know their addresses.

Nancy's colleague Maria Perez has found a clever way to deal with illiterate patients. When she cannot give written instructions she puts small stickers on their medications to indicate frequency of dosage—one sticker once a day, two stickers twice, and so on. Maria, who arrived from Guatemala at age fourteen, goes to Suffolk County Community College most mornings and works in Greenport later in the day. She is studying to be a practical nurse and will move on to the RN program when she is certified. For now, she checks vital signs, draws blood, makes referrals, and schedules appointments. She sends people to the New York State cancer services program, which provides free mammograms, Pap smears, and colorectal screening. Like Nancy, she sees her job, in part, as education. "I talk to the diabetic patients about the disease while I am taking their blood, and then if we have insulin in the office we give it to the patients and teach them how to use it. We are all teaching all the time," she says.

Maria takes pride in the individual attention that every patient who walks through the center's door will get. "Dr. Napolitano personalizes everything," she says. "The great advantage of the Greenport Health Center is that it is small, and the community feels comfortable because they know the staff." It helps that more than half of the employees, including Napolitano, speak Spanish. Establishing trust in the Latino community took many years, and not just because those who were undocumented were afraid to be identified. In the rural mountain culture from which many of the immigrants come, going to a doctor was unlikely except when the situation was dire. Ligia Soto, working with the Migrant Voucher program, emphasizes the importance of convincing patients not to wait until they are ill to use the center. "Promotion is key," she says. She uses the nonmedical services she provides—translation, referrals to social welfare programs, transportation from the fields or vineyards to the center or to appointments with specialists—to convey the message. "The tendency of many is not to go to a medical professional unless they are sick. They don't use the service unless they understand maintenance. We tell them, 'Your body is like a car; it needs maintenance.'"

Professionals at the Greenport Health Center would never utter the bromide that an ounce of prevention is worth a pound of cure, but they live by it. Counseling in nutrition and diabetes prevention are priorities. For every patient, a member of the staff checks to see that immunizations are up-to-date, reviews medications, and computes the body mass index that signals a warning when steps should be taken to stave off obesity and its consequences. (These measures are required for reimbursement by the center's various monitoring bodies, but even if that were not the case, they would be done.) The flow of a patient visit starts with intake by Nancy, moves to readying the patient for a doctor or nurse practitioner, and returns after the consultation to Maria for explanation of medications and referral to other providers, if needed.

Although the center's philosophy supports close attention to an orderly and comprehensive process, an additional nudge comes from the new electronic medical records system mandated by Obamacare for health care providers who take Medicaid and Medicare. (As necessary as it is, the extra recordkeeping can cause frustration, "Doing these things is important," says Napolitano, "but documenting them is cumbersome.") Reinforcing the emphasis on prevention and coordination is the designation of the center as a "medical home," the result of a quality assessment by a nonprofit organization, the National Committee for Quality Assurance. To get the NCQA seal of approval, a practice must adhere to a set of criteria intended to "transform primary care into what patients want it to be." The list is too long and detailed to reproduce here; suffice it to say that the must-pass elements for managing care include the kind of continuity, communication with patients, and follow-up on which the Greenport center prides itself.[13]

Coordination of primary care with specialized services and hospitals is not perfect, however. Louis Schiff, director of the emergency department at Eastern Long Island Hospital, acknowledges that there are gaps. "Follow-up is sometimes tricky," he says. "The admitting doctor should arrange follow-up with Dr. Napolitano, but it is not done well enough. We leave it up to the patient to bring records to the doctor. We need a dedicated coordinator so that the doctor has already got the information from the hospital." Nonetheless, both he and Napolitano are optimistic about the progress to be made with the capacity to share medical records electronically, with the push of a button. Soon they will have integrated records from the primary care doctor, specialists, and hospital, with a portal so that patients can see their own health information. "We can send everything electronically now," Schiff notes. And for the present Napolitano uses the telephone to follow up with the hospital when he sends a patient there.

Blaise Napolitano is the embodiment of the primary care physician who loves his job. A graduate of Cornell and the Ponce Medical School in Puerto Rico, he took his residency in family medicine at Stony Brook University on Long Island and was chosen for his job in 2006 by the chief medical officer of HRHCare. "I was never going to get something better than this," he says. "The gratitude of patients, the chance to help someone who really needs it." He is keenly aware of the consequences of leaving festering conditions unattended in his uninsured and undocumented patients.

> Suppose a patient has a kidney stone. It's not an emergency that could send him to the ER; the urologist won't take him because he can't pay; and then he gets an infection. Now he is admitted to the ER but can't be released immediately because he isn't stabilized. If he can't pay, the hospital sends a social worker who assists him in applying for emergency Medicaid. It would have been cheaper if he had been treated as an outpatient before the infection—also less suffering for the patient and less likely to result in lost work days. Or take the diabetic with chest pain. We say he has stable angina. A cardiologist is willing to see him for $350 for a consultation,

which he can't pay. One day he has a heart attack. He is sent in an ambulance to Stony Brook, where's he's in the ICU. It costs us a lot more and the patient suffers; it's always easier to treat a patient electively than emergently.

He sighs. "Public health is the last stop on the train; otherwise patients would be hospitalized."

As the achievements and problems of the Affordable Care Act play themselves out, it becomes increasingly clear that immigrants who are unauthorized—and some who are legally present as well—are losing in the health care lottery. The Affordable Care Act not only excludes undocumented immigrants but also requires that insurers market their products solely through the health insurance exchanges. The result is that even an undocumented immigrant with sufficient resources to buy insurance on the private market cannot do so. And recently arrived immigrants (except for asylees) with work visas or green cards are not eligible for Medicaid until they have been in the United States for five years. It's a perverse and punitive twist on the declared objective of Obamacare to make health insurance available to all.

As of 2010 more than eight million children in the country were uninsured, about a million of them noncitizens and many more of them the citizen children of low-income parents.[14] Insuring children might be thought to be the most compelling (and least controversial) case for health care reform. And, indeed, one of President Obama's first initiatives in 2009 was signing federal legislation that greatly expanded public free or low-cost insurance for children. Because most children in Greenport's immigrant families were born in the United States and are therefore citizens, they are eligible for the benefits of the Affordable Care Act. But Napolitano worries that the parents of some of those children will be unable to afford to insure them, regardless of their immigration status. "I'm hearing that it's still too expensive, even with subsidy." He's right. Many immigrant families are employed in seasonal work and have very little income in the winter. While insuring a single child may be manageable, insuring several can be prohibitive, even with the subsidies. Furthermore, many immigrants work for small businesses that may not be required to pay health insurance for their workers, while some employers will cut their workers' hours to avoid the obligation to insure them. If parents are not covered, children will suffer, according to recent research.[15] And the Greenport Health Center will have to support more uninsured patients, rather than fewer.

◆ ◆ ◆

The national debate about the desirability and legitimacy of the Affordable Care Act can be viewed through many prisms. There's the question of whether the country can afford to have everyone covered with comprehensive, affordable health insurance. Lurking beneath this ostensibly neutral bookkeeper's dilemma is the far more politically charged question of whether we really want universal coverage. After all, that goal would mean that government—much maligned for even the modest safety net it now provides—would have to increase its assistance to low-income (and many middle-income) families. Then there's the issue of what insurance companies get out of the law: is the individual mandate to buy insurance a windfall to boost profits or simply a necessity to make the new system financially feasible? Finally, is the legislation, as it is implemented, heading the country in a direction that goes beyond ensuring health care coverage for individuals to a fundamental shift in how we commit one-sixth of the American economy to the health of the population?

Most of what nonprofessionals know about the Affordable Care Act addresses who is covered for what and how much it costs. But more important for the improvement of Americans' health care overall is what Obamacare contributes to the revolution just barely under way in how health care is delivered. The promise is nothing less than the transformation of fragmented, unequal, expensive, often arbitrary health care into an efficient, fair, patient-centered, comprehensive system. Commentators outdo each other with metaphors for the vector of the changes: Will it be an asteroid, flattening hidebound institutions? A tsunami, washing away obsolete practices? Whatever the image, the hyperbole blithely overlooks the entrenched interests that must be thwarted and the complex bureaucracies that must be reformed to realize the revolution's goals.

The Affordable Care Act focuses on multiple areas of reform: a priority for preventive health measures; a reduction in expensive, superfluous procedures; decentralized delivery of primary care; the use of electronic wizardry to make comprehensive medical records available to both professionals and patients; and improved coordination among the institutions that serve patients. ("Holistic," "access," and "information technology" are the buzzwords.) This is a tall order for large cities, little rural communities, and everything in between. Among the institutions that Obamacare contemplates to further its ambitions are accountable care organizations—the bill calls them ACOs. These are networks of hospitals or other sizable care centers that commit themselves to coordinating all levels of care for a specified group of patients. New York State has recently received $8 billion to assist hospitals that serve poor patients with the development of these networks. The ACOs will be paid for the outcomes they achieve for their patients, not for the appointments they keep or the procedures they order. Bill Keller of the *New York Times* calls them "the Silicon Valley of preventive care, laboratories of invention driven by the entrepreneurial energy of start-ups."[16]

Whether the laudable aim of the ACOs succeeds or not is an open question: will it spawn unwieldy, centralized mastodons or lean, efficient partnerships? One worry is that ACOs will prove to be oligopolies that worsen the fragmentation of health care. And Atul Gawande, the award-winning surgeon and medical journalist, warns that "under conditions of true complexity— where the knowledge required exceeds that of any individual and unpredictability reigns—efforts to dictate every step from the center will fail. People need room to act and adapt."[17] This perspective has relevance for small towns like Greenport where the demographics are shifting and a large number of patients will continue to be uninsured or underinsured.

How it plays out will become evident in short order as ACOs affect the provision of health care in the village. HRHCare, as an ACO, will soon manage services for Medicare patients in its health centers, including the one in Greenport. And the Stony Brook School of Medicine aims to develop an ACO that "establishes and implements best practices across our inpatient, faculty outpatient and captive physician networks."[18]

In its small way, Greenport has been ahead of the transformative curve, at least for its immigrants and low-income residents. It has lived by another of Gawande's pithy observations: "We have trained, hired, and rewarded people to be cowboys. It's the pit crews that we need."[19] Greenport's pit crews still base health care payment on the old fee-for-service model, but the principles that support payment reform are much in evidence. Cost is still a worry for both patients and providers. People who remain without health insurance— all of Greenport's undocumented immigrants except children and pregnant women—must still rely on the kindness of Greenport's loose network of health care providers. But for most immigrants—meeting their basic medical needs and anticipating what might be needed in the future—this small-town network is making it all come together.

An Accidental Nurse

Rigoberta is returning from a doctor's appointment. Fog and intermittent rain are doubling what should be a fifteen-minute trip. Abruptly the rain ends, and a watery sun casts steamy brilliance on the road ahead. "This weather reminds me of winter in Guatemala," she says. Her thin face, charmingly surrounded with tendrils of curly hair, is alight with a smile of remembered pleasure. She used to walk from her town to the village six kilometers away where she was a primary school teacher. There was a bridge on the way, and as she walked over the bridge the weather would be transformed—on her side it would be cloudy or foggy and when she crossed over the sun would be out and the air much warmer. "Sometimes a car would pass—only two or three for the whole walk," she said, "and I would refuse the offer of a ride, though once I accepted a ride on a tractor. And once a relative suggested that he take me on his horse, but there was a steep hill going down and I was afraid I would pitch over the horse's head." She liked watching the seasons change as she walked. There are only two seasons in Guatemala, she says—winter and summer.

For Rigoberta this nostalgia is a rare moment of distraction from a life of anxiety. She is the mother of three little girls, the oldest profoundly disabled and requiring twenty-four-hour care. Amelia, six years old at this time, suffers from dwarfism and related problems—respiratory failure, pulmonary artery hypertension, congenital heart disease, and latent tuberculosis, along with an assortment of other, less threatening ailments. She is about two feet tall and will never be taller.

Amelia's condition determines every hour of Rigoberta's day—and many hours of the night, as she or her husband Carlos must get up several times to suction the tracheostomy tube inserted in Amelia's windpipe through which she breathes. When Amelia is awake and active, Rigoberta constantly monitors her oxygen levels and the condition of the ventilator and nebulizer that keep her alive. Every couple of weeks there is a medical crisis—fluid in the lungs, a blood pressure spike, an infection—that sends her, with Rigoberta, to the local emergency room or to Stony Brook University Hospital, fifty miles away. Although there is a flock of medical personnel attending to Amelia, her mother is the live-in, full-time nurse.

Rigoberta's journey from Guatemala to the North Fork was harrowing, and her future in her new country is uncertain. Unlike many undocumented people, she is a highly visible resident of Greenport. Although local people are unlikely to report her to immigration authorities, her daughter's disability is known to dozens. But, given Amelia's condition, Rigoberta would rather be here than in her home country.

In Greenport (and the broader community that includes doctors, clinics, and hospitals in Suffolk County) she has found succor of many kinds—medical expertise that would not be available in Guatemala, child care and therapy for her middle daughter Ashley, caring village employees who will not disconnect her electricity when the bill has not been paid, and the maternal concern of Sister Margaret, who steps into the breach with rent assistance on occasion. She has made friendships that transcend national and linguistic boundaries. The trigger for much of this help has been her daughters' status as American citizens, born to Rigoberta and Carlos when they met and married here. But she has benefited, too. Services to Amelia, Ashley, and baby Clara are often extended to her, as when the visiting nurses inquire about her health issues as well as the girls', and she enjoys indirectly some safety net protections available to poor families that include US citizens—heating subsidies and food stamps, for instance.

For Rigoberta and Carlos, the indignities of being undocumented are real but secondary problems. They suffer most from poverty and from a child's illness that keeps them mired in it. They cannot pay for copying hundreds of pages of medical records to support the court claim that Carlos should not be deported because he supports a disabled child, or for an MRI for Rigoberta, who has crippling migraines. From time to time, they cannot afford to buy the phone minutes that are Amelia's lifeline in a medical emergency. Although legal residence would open doors, it would not usher them into a comfortable American life.

◆ ◆ ◆

For most Latino immigrants, leaving their country is not a choice in the sense of a considered and informed weighing of options—where can I best develop my talents/find a good job/speak freely?—and then acting on the results. It is, rather, a propulsion driven by hunger or violence at home and rumors of opportunity and security abroad, whether based on good information or poor. Rigoberta's is an extreme case of having no choice. She literally fled for her life, escaping death threats rooted in a culture of superstition and intimidation.

Guatemala is one of the most violent countries in the world. The 1996 peace accords that ended its thirty-year civil war curtailed the death squads that targeted students, labor leaders, and anyone who might be thought to sympathize with the guerillas. But they didn't usher in a peaceful, democratic society. Political violence continued, with the killing of a Catholic bishop who exposed human rights violations during the war, murders of dozens of political candidates and their family members before the 2008 presidential election, and assaults on civilians by decommissioned members of paramilitary groups. Gang assault, kidnapping, and murder have succeeded political violence, permeating urban and rural areas alike. And the failures of police and courts to stem violence in the lives of ordinary citizens have fed vigilantism, reinforcing customs and beliefs that encourage ordinary citizens to prey upon each other. (The government acknowledges corruption in the national police force that cannot be controlled. Rogue officers are said to be more effective at providing protection to organized crime than to ordinary citizens.[1]) In 2004, the year before Rigoberta escaped to the United States, the murder rate in Guatemala City was 78 per 100,000, much higher than that of Detroit (42), considered the most murderous American city; by 2006 it was 108, according to the US State Department. Although murders began to decline in 2011, the drop could not be attributed to effective law enforcement, and the rate of violent crime still warranted the department's rating of the situation as "critical."[2]

Guatemala's powerful patriarchal traditions have led its Human Rights Commission to declare it "the most dangerous place for women in all of Latin America." Attributed to organized crime, gangs, and domestic violence, femicide rates are astronomical; in the year Rigoberta left, 665 women were murdered in this country with a population of less than that of the New York metropolitan area. The commission assigned blame for post-conflict violence on brutality from male partners, official indifference to the safety of women, and the transformation of government-backed death squads into "clandestine operations that have become entrenched in every facet of Guatemalan society."[3] Rigoberta's experience reveals one of these facets, dominated by female predators and based on class envy and belief in witchcraft.

She grew up in a stable and loving family—middle class and relatively educated—with a brother and two sisters, all of whom remain in Guatemala. When she was small, her family lived in Guatemala City, but when the nearby volcanoes threatened, they moved to Palencia, a town of about fifty thousand people twenty-seven miles north of the capital. For a decade after she finished her education—twelve years, with some university studies—she taught seven-year olds in Palencia. Recognizing her intelligence and commitment to elementary education, the head of the school asked her to assist him in preparing other area schools for annual audits. Deeply religious, she also began to work with a local priest, holding prayer sessions in the villages—"sharing the word of God," she says, with people who had left the church.

She also knew young people involved in the gangs—primarily the vast network of proudly violent groups known as MS-13 that spread, in the last decades of the twentieth century, from Los Angeles throughout the urban United States and Central America and even into Canada. "There was a program to bring them back to the church, but they had to make a commitment to follow Christ," Rigoberta says. "Some changed and became evangelists, others died; some who wanted to be reunited with their families separated from the gangs. Some promised they would go back to church but it wasn't real, and then it was tragic for them. It was a big risk to separate from the gang." (After Rigoberta left for the United States the priest she had worked with was murdered—shot in the head by unknown assailants as he was giving the Eucharist to the ill in the neighborhood, perhaps because he was steering people away from the gangs.)

For Rigoberta, moving in this world was also a big risk, though she didn't think so at the time. "I depended too much on God," she says. "I thought He would send the angels to protect me." When the gangs came to her house to collect their "fee," she and her mother refused to pay. "My mother talked to them, said no, we go to church, we haven't done anything to the gangs, we don't criticize their way of life. So we didn't have to pay; they weren't going to bother us." They thought they were safe.

But she had become both visible and notorious, the subject of poisonous rumor—she was a prostitute, a drunk, an informer, a witch. Threats against her escalated until an anonymous letter arrived saying that if she continued her work her throat would be slit. A local evangelical minister warned her that her life was in danger and urged her to leave Guatemala. Within three days she was gone.

Rigoberta's trip through Mexico and across the US border, while brutal, was actually less horrific than that of many others. Although her coyote deserted her, he didn't do so until she was at the border city of Matamoros. Although for part of the way she traveled in a stifling, fetid cage with one hundred other people in the back of a tractor-trailer, she did not suffocate. Although she was kidnapped and held hostage at the border, she was not sexually assaulted. (Some women going north are so sure of being raped that they take contraception injections before they leave, according to social workers in Mexico and Central America.[4]) The corruption of the Mexican police (and perhaps of our border guards) actually worked in her favor, as they paved the way for her to cross into Texas. The woman she knew in Los Angeles who had agreed to help her did not come through with ransom money, but an unknown friend of a friend—who later became her husband—provided it. Perhaps religious faith protected her—or the fear of God that remained in the minds of her captors. "When they threatened me and snatched the rosary off my neck," she says, "I told them God would save me. I prayed a lot, and finally they let me go and sent me across the border. He did save me."

◆ ◆ ◆

Amelia is standing on the scale in the pediatrician's office. Her tubes trail behind her, her diaper sags, and her deeply brown eyes are full of fear. She does not wail or cry, however—perhaps because she is a brave little girl who has suffered so many medical indignities in her years of half-living, perhaps because the ventilator on which she depends does not permit her to utter more than squeaks. Five years old at the time of this visit, she weighs twenty pounds.

The doctor examining her suspects that she has pulmonary aspiration—food or liquid lodged in the respiratory tract, which can cause pneumonia or death. The nurse pokes a tiny suction catheter through the hole in her throat—the tracheostomy—to test for the passage of fluid or worse into the lungs. Sure enough, traces of phlegm and food are found entering Amelia's lungs. This triggers the call for an ambulance, and soon Amelia is on her way to the hospital for yet another ordeal of X-rays, evaluations, and treatments to forestall the inevitable. As she is being belted onto the stretcher, she squeaks, "Mano!" a request for the tonic of her mother's fingers.

In addition to the pulmonologist, pediatrician, and cardiologist who will attend to Amelia at Stony Brook University Hospital, a battery of caregivers has been attending to her since she was a baby. It's not just the nurses who come to the house and are paid by Medicaid for sixteen hours a day and sometimes stay overnight, unpaid, just because they want to help. It's also the inspector of Amelia's machines who has counseled Rigoberta on how to fight for her rights to the best medical care for Amelia and has given her his personal cell phone number to call if she needs advice or immediate service. It's the technician who comes to the house after Amelia has had surgery to test her blood levels; a large fellow, he leans over Amelia and says, rather glumly, "She knows I gotta stick her." But she is a better patient than many he has to stick. On his way out the door, he says to Rigoberta kindly, "Take care of my girlfriend."

In this village, interdependence complements diversity. Sympathy for Rigoberta's family extends beyond medical providers. Lee Beninati is the understanding boss who knows when Carlos cannot come to work because he has to stay with Ashley when Amelia and Rigoberta are at the hospital. Carolyn Tamin is the concerned landlady—she has a daughter with kidney disease and she understands the tensions of caring for a sick or disabled child—who sometimes has to wait for delayed rent payments. Family friends clean and cook in times of stress and are ready to play with Amelia and Ashley in a propitious moment, knowing that Rigoberta would do the same if she could.

Since Amelia can't go to school, the school comes to her. Sandra Rosanti is the home-schooling teacher, a cheery blonde presence who, in 2012–2013, guides Amelia through most of the first-grade curriculum. (She also manages to find time for Ashley, the wild child whose needs must take a back seat to those of her sister.) One day the children who attend the regular first grade pay a call on Amelia. Standing in the yard, they hold up their names for her to see, as they stare at her tiny figure waving to them from the porch. For them, it's a field trip to another world. Back in the schoolroom, they ask many questions: Will she grow? Why is that machine attached to her? What is the tube in her throat for? Can she speak? Amelia has passed the tests in reading and math to move into the second grade. Today she is all smiles.

Of course there are moments when the scaffold of care shudders or collapses, often because of small but significant flaws. On one such day, transportation to Amelia's usual pediatrician is unavailable and Rigoberta has gone to a new pediatrician nearby. The doctor announces peremptorily, and without looking at her or requesting translation, that the family must face the possibility that Amelia's condition will not improve and that the parents should consider committing her to an institution. Rigoberta's face crumples, and she shakes her head as though a spider has landed on it.

A couple of months later Hurricane Irene is on the way. Rigoberta is spending the day trying to ensure that her family will have power during the storm because Amelia depends on uninterrupted electricity for life support. Early in the afternoon she discovers that the Greenport school, which she thought would be the place of refuge for people who must evacuate, is locked and the parking lot empty. Perhaps the Southold school is a better bet. It, too, seems unprepared to admit people seeking shelter there. Rain is coming down now, fat drops from a still, sultry sky, only a promise of the wind to come. But it's the wind that will bring down trees and power lines, threatening the life of her child, so she is anxious. Perhaps not coincidentally, as she contemplates her next steps, Rigoberta's first migraine crashes down upon her, a searing, blinding agony. Light and sound have become environmental assaults; she vomits over and over.

But at this moment her support system kicks in. At the hospital emergency room, the doctor and nurses don't care that Rigoberta is undocumented; they hustle her onto a bed, give her an injection, and assure her that her pain will dissipate quickly and effectively. It's a bit like the projected hurricane—a swirling attack but soon over. Rigoberta summons her remaining energy to pack up her family and call the fire department to take them to the school's shelter when it is available, since Amelia's machines are too large to fit in a regular car.

More troubles await. At the shelter, a doctor advises against staying there because of the possibility that Amelia might pick up an infection from others seeking refuge against the storm. Returning to their home—now without power—the parents pray that the batteries for Amelia's machines will hold out. They do. And in the morning firefighters arrive with a generator. Crisis averted; the hurricane is merely a nuisance in the scheme of these complicated lives.

◆ ◆ ◆

An observer of the agonies of poverty and illness in Rigoberta's household might conclude that immigration policy has little effect on the family's rhythms of life. Because her daughters are citizens, they get good medical care through Medicaid. The girls' food stamp allowance puts food on the table for the whole family, and federal Supplemental Social Insurance (SSI) for Amelia supplements Carlos's income, which is seasonal. But Rigoberta is dependent for her own health care on a bare-bones insurance policy, available through a New York State program for low-income people that costs almost nothing and does not deny coverage to undocumented families. The specialists in her managed care program are far away, and many procedures are not covered. If she were documented, she would have a broader range of choices. But in her present situation, the causes of her vertigo and migraines go undiagnosed, and surgery for the hernia caused by lifting small children is unavailable.

Without legal status, Rigoberta and Carlos cannot take advantage of housing opportunities available to other poor families. Finding adequate and affordable housing for a sick child is always difficult, nowhere more than on Long Island, where, in many towns, the rental shortage is acute and subsidized housing is rare. Rigoberta and Carlos lived for a while in nearby Peconic in the upstairs apartment of a house surrounded with roses, which Rigoberta loved. But Amelia's problems made it impossible to stay there. An inspection by the supplier of her machines concluded that the power source in the apartment was inadequate in an emergency, another tenant in the building had dogs that might carry sources of infection, and the upper-story location made it difficult to get Amelia out quickly.

Greenport has more rental housing than most Long Island communities, so the family found Tamin's comfortable, ground-floor apartment just two blocks from the health center and ten blocks from Eastern Long Island Hospital. But the $1,300 monthly rent was often too much for a family with a single breadwinner, so Rigoberta and Carlos began to look for rental assistance. On a gray December morning in 2012 they bundled up their two older daughters—arranging Amelia's ventilator and oxygen tank around her in her wheelchair and putting Ashley in a stroller—and pushed them through Greenport streets to the office of Asha, the housing administrator of the village. They were hoping for help with housing costs through the federal Section 8 program. The little girls were uncharacteristically quiet as the family settled in for their appointment; perhaps they sensed a bureaucratic hurdle before them. And indeed their parents' immigration status proved to be the immovable obstacle that collided with the force of their obvious need.

Section 8 subsidizes private housing for poor families, giving a portion of the rent directly to landlords. Although it does not support undocumented families, "mixed families" can be eligible—that is, families that include, in addition to citizens or legal residents, members *sin papeles.* The benefit of the subsidy is prorated to exclude the undocumented family member. (Presumably the rationale is that the taxpayer won't want to be assisting someone who is in the United States illegally, but this rationale undercuts the core objective of helping vulnerable families, since the undocumented person is likely to be the most vulnerable adult in the household and the least likely to make substantial financial contributions to paying the rent.) So Rigoberta and her family could qualify as a "mixed family."

Asha's gentle voice and warm smile were encouraging. She accepted the application Rigoberta and Carlos had filled out and went over each section carefully. Household Composition—husband and wife with two citizen children. (Baby Clara had not yet been born.) Household Income— low enough to meet the eligibility standards. Assets—none. Current Landlord Information—a compassionate neighbor, herself the granddaughter of an immigrant (the successful Greenport merchant Louis Jaeger). Criminal Background—a couple of old Driving While Intoxicated (DWI) charges (after which Carlos completed an alcohol treatment program) and one for driving without a valid license. Nothing there to disqualify the family. Then she turned to the obligations of a family that has received a Section 8 voucher—to cooperate with inspections, to comply with the lease, to supply information needed by the program—and the rather stern warnings about the consequences of fraud or failure to report such matters as change in income, moving house, or participating in crime. Finally, she requested recent bank statements, income tax returns, and documentation supporting Carlos's immigration status.

Here his work permit and Social Security number failed him. As a Salvadoran, he had been entitled to Temporary Protected Status (TPS), a concession to countries with wars or environmental disasters that prevent their citizens abroad from coming home, either because it is unsafe or because their return would impose too much of a strain on the country's resources. El Salvador was one of those countries. In early 2001 earthquakes killed more than twelve hundred people, injured about nine thousand more, and left hundreds of thousands homeless—numbers that increased as landslides magnified the damage all over the country. Carlos soon applied to the US Citizenship and Immigration Services for TPS and received a Social Security number and work permit pending approval of his request. But he never provided the evidence necessary to support his application, and his work permit expired in 2003. Oblivious or indifferent—it is hard to know which—he continued to make use of his Social Security card, working as a seasonal laborer. Without legal immigration status, however, his family was not eligible for the Section 8 housing benefit. Asha said she would preserve a voucher for them until March, hoping that Carlos could have a valid work permit by then, but everyone knew this was unlikely. It turned out that even if Carlos or Rigoberta had become a legal resident by early 2013 there would have been no voucher, as the sequester passed by Congress had frozen the program.

For Carlos, the failure to get housing assistance was a setback but not a body blow. The real threat to his American life was his criminal record. Although he is a devoted father who never hesitates to care for his other children when Amelia's situation demands Rigoberta's full attention, Carlos is sometimes overwhelmed by the hand he has been dealt. His anguish over erratic work assignments and health crises at home manifests itself in a cluster of troubles—a string of arrests, a persistent dental infection, a tendency to drown his sorrows rather than bear them. Eventually, they landed him in immigration court, where the prospect of deportation loomed. But in an ironic twist of immigration policy, his bad behavior brought him to the path to legality.

"The US won't send parents of a disabled citizen home if they can find a reason not to," says Sister Margaret. Carlos's was such a case. His lawyer was able to convince the judge that he was a responsible father, the sole support of a severely disabled American child, and should receive a "cancellation of removal" and a one-year work permit. Whether this respite could lead to legal permanent residency—that is, a green card—depended on several unknowables, including whether Carlos could stay out of trouble and whether he could make the case, after a year, for renewal of his permit and the opportunity to petition for a green card. He is stubborn and proud, controlling expenditures and decisions about money in the belief that women shouldn't be involved in such matters. ("He is not modern," says Rigoberta. "He talks to his macho friends.") And an albatross hung around his neck—the possibility that Amelia would succumb to her many life-threatening conditions. Carlos and Rigoberta would then lose both their daughter and their quasi-legal justification for remaining in the United States

◆ ◆ ◆

Rigoberta is an optimistic person who appreciates the small pleasures. Even when the burdens of their lives were all-consuming, she and her family found ways to take advantage of some of Greenport's amenities. They would put Amelia in her wheelchair on a summer afternoon and go to the ice cream parlor or walk to the beach to scatter breadcrumbs to grateful seagulls. Amelia celebrated her first communion not only with the usual ceremony at Saint Agnes—much of the Latino community in town attended—but also with a grand party supported by Make-A-Wish America, the foundation that grants the wishes of children with life-threatening conditions. But Rigoberta also has moments of despair; she never forgets the dangers that lurk in limbo. She lives in fear of "giving people too much information," as she puts it, wondering if the many nurses she comes in contact with may inadvertently (or purposefully) reveal to others their knowledge of her undocumented status. She sees herself as hiding behind Carlos, whose evasions worry her. He says he will be getting a green card any day now, but what if he didn't really qualify? What if he breaks under the strain of his obligations and abandons his family? The darkest shadow is her knowledge that Amelia will never grow, that this tiny frame cannot much longer contain the internal organs pressing on it.

So at some level, she was prepared for the reality that intruded when Amelia's cardiology and respiration problems intensified. The expanding brain and aorta gave her headaches, fevers, and high blood pressure. Weeklong stays at Stony Brook University Hospital became more frequent. Her good days, when she laughed and played and greeted the home-schooling teacher with squeaks of welcome, were fewer. Doctors told Rigoberta that it might be possible to remove the tracheostomy tube, easing Amelia's breathing, but first she would have to undergo a test of her cardiac capacity for the procedure. That test offered both promise and peril. It required admission to the Weill Cornell Medical Center of the New York–Presbyterian Hospital, so in September 2014 Amelia and Rigoberta rode an ambulance into Manhattan.

The test was the coup de grace. Amelia went into a coma and never came out. On October 19, 2014, she died. At the funeral home, the crowd who came to say goodbye to her spilled out the door. Rigoberta sat immobile, listening to the tributes to her smart, funny daughter. "No matter what her obstacles were, she just charged right through them," said Sister Margaret. No one who had seen her use her baby hands to paint her fingernails or play computer games would disagree.

◆ ◆ ◆

Rigoberta's faith may console her with an image of Amelia at peace in the arms of God, but she is also suffering terribly. And beyond the personal loss is material insecurity of a very immediate kind. As a disabled American citizen, Amelia received Supplement Security Income (SSI), which was discontinued at her death. The bureaucratic wheels turned very slowly to requalify the children for food stamps—now for two rather than three—and for a time the family depended on the local food bank. During the winter that followed Amelia's death there was little work for Carlos. Rigoberta sought housecleaning jobs to make up for the loss of subsidies for Amelia's care, but she had a lot of competition. She and Carlos could not pay for oil, so they survived the cold weather with space heaters.

As they ran up their overdue electric bill, at least they did not need to worry that their power, supplied by the municipal system, would be cut off. Small-town sympathies set in, no less because this was an undocumented family. For a while the ladies at Village Hall would tolerate arrears. At Greenport's elementary school, plans were under way for the annual talent show to feature a tribute to Amelia; Rigoberta collected photos to be included in a video about her child. Concern extended beyond Greenport: Amelia's long stays at the Stony Brook University Hospital had made her many friends, who gave Rigoberta a plaster cast of her small hand and donated a brick for a hospital walkway.

But what does the future hold for Rigoberta? It is hard to see beyond housecleaning to an opportunity that makes use of her talents. As an educated Guatemalan who has learned some English and is increasingly sophisticated about various medical procedures and equipment, Rigoberta could contribute to her new country in myriad ways. She would like to work with flowers or food; she could return to school and formalize the medical knowledge she has acquired; her skill at stimulating and distracting a small child in pain could be put to good use. But starting over with her career would be difficult here, so she thinks about going back to Guatemala and continuing her studies on child development. The gang problem remains, however; violence is even worse now, her mother tells her. Besides, she is still the mother of two little Americans.

Rigoberta may be able move on from the pain of loss to a celebration of the daughters who remain and a new commitment to life outside the home. That prospect, however, is contingent on distant and fickle events and politics. As the parents of American citizens, she and Carlos may be safe from deportation, though Carlos's criminal record remains a threat. Even with a work permit, Rigoberta must navigate an overwhelming present and seek a professional future that, at present, seems chimerical.

PART VI

Dilemmas of Control

CHAPTER 9

Legal Limbo

In January 2014 the criminal case of Erick Ramirez jolted Greenport's immigrants and locals alike. Ramirez, age twenty, who had arrived from Guatemala a year earlier to join his mother, was arrested for raping a twelve-year-old girl. (While the charge did not allege the use of force, New York law, like that of most other states, makes sex with such a young person a serious felony. Since a twelve-year-old is below the age of consent, the intention of the parties is legally irrelevant.) Such an offense—at least the discovery and prosecution of it—was extremely rare, perhaps unprecedented in recent village history. But the fact that serious crime was unusual in the immigrant community was immaterial in the minds of some.

The local press and some of its readers tried Ramirez before he had his day in court. The initial headline in the *Suffolk Times* read "Cops: Illegal Alien Raped Girl in Greenport" (quickly revised to read "Cops: Greenport Man Charged with Raping Girl, 12"), and comments about the news report jumped from the nature of the offense to presumed attributes of the offender. "It's time to crack down on illegals," wrote a former village official (a man also known for tirades in other contexts). Another contributor added, "The reality is that the east end has been overrun with illegals and within the last few years, their presence is known more and more due to their criminal behavior." General outrage that the newspaper identified Ramirez in the story as "a former soccer standout at Greenport High School" suggested that those readers could view him only as a rapist.

Ramirez's crime also had powerful effects on Greenport's teenagers. At the high school, a rumor flew around that, in addition to the offense that was the reason for his arrest, Erick had sexually assaulted three students and a teacher. Speculation about the targets in the form of finger-pointing put several young women on edge. Edgar, as a Salvadoran tenth-grader in his second year at the school, became aware of simmering antagonisms toward male Hispanic students. When asked if he had American friends, his eyes widened at the naïveté of the questioner. "Not now," he said. "They [white male students] make awful comments—not directly, because if they did the other guys from El Salvador would want to take them outside." In this charged atmosphere, he worried that fights might break out.

The incident exposed not-so-latent suspicions among local whites about their Hispanic neighbors and fostered misinformation about their criminality. Those reactions, in turn, illustrate the ambiguity that hovers over law enforcement in a community where longtime residents want to be tolerant of immigrants but also see them as the Other. Determining whether the new people can be counted on to play by the rules is complicated by the fact that so many arrive already marked with the stain of their illegal entry. They live very private lives, for the most part, and the mystery of how they behave and what the justice system can do about it adds to the confusion. Acceptance requires understanding, but for some Greenport residents, that is too much to ask for when it comes to enforcing the criminal law.

◆ ◆ ◆

For most immigrants, the arm of the law is particularly long, and a single swipe of that arm can wipe out—for both individuals and families—an American future. Since federal immigration policy took a lurch to the right in 1996, even green card holders can be deported (the official term is "removed") for crimes as minor as shoplifting or marijuana possession.[1] Immigration offenses—unlawful presence in the country, illegal entry (apprehension at or near the border), illegal reentry (a felony)—are also grounds for removal. Recent data suggest that more than 80 percent of filings in immigration courts are seeking removal orders for these latter offenses.[2] The Obama White House has vowed to give priority for deportation to noncitizens convicted of serious, violent crimes, and federal prosecutors have discretion over whom to charge within a schedule of crimes.[3] Nonetheless, even a traffic violation can put you in the sights of the Department of Homeland Security as a "criminal alien." A 2014 New York Times analysis of ten years of deportations found that only 20 percent were based on serious crime, with the largest increase for traffic violations (including driving while intoxicated—DWI) by undocumented immigrants.[4] And an analysis of immigrant detainers ordered by the federal Immigration and Customs Enforcement (ICE) agency in New York State found an increase in the number of "holds" since the new guidelines for prioritizing serious criminal charges were issued.[5] Even in New York City, considered something of a sanctuary for immigrants, the vast majority of deportation orders in fiscal year 2014 were for immigration offenses.[6] So it is not surprising that whether it is the flashing light of a police car viewed in the rearview mirror, an arrest for a minor matter, or the frown of a judge, contacts with law enforcement, no matter how trivial, cast a long shadow over the lives of noncitizens.

Deportations have risen during the Obama years (though they were dropping by late 2014), and it is likely that his administration will set an American record—over two million removals at last count—through the immigration courts. (Many thousands more are turned back at the country's borders—"returned" in immigration parlance—which is not considered an official deportation.) Internal removals have increasingly relied on assistance from local law enforcement. For a time, that assistance was physical: in one program, jail personnel helped to find inmates who could be deported; in another, police accompanied immigration officers on workplace and home raids. But in 2008 the federal government added to those efforts an efficient way to identify deportable migrants electronically. Secure Communities—a program rolled out around the country over several years but rejected by many mayors and governors—ensured that fingerprints taken by police at the time of arrest and sent to the FBI (standard practice for many years) would go from there to the Department of Homeland Security (DHS) to be matched against the almost 100 million records in its IDENT system. If a match indicated grounds for deportation, ICE ordered the police to detain the arrestee pending a criminal proceeding and possible subsequent removal. By mid-2014 forty-two million arrests had been submitted to DHS, of which two million matched federal records; 375,000 people were deported as a result.

Compared with some other parts of the country (many southern states and California), immigrants in New York State are not deported in great numbers relative to the population. But between 2011, when the county joined the program, and 2014, Suffolk County had a larger percentage of matches that resulted in deportation than either Nassau, the other Long Island county, or Westchester, a large suburban county also in the New York metropolitan area.[7] At first glance, one could conclude from the federal report on these removals that 74.9 percent were for criminal convictions. But closer examination suggests that, reflecting the national picture, almost four-fifths of Suffolk County's 790 deportations were for minor offenses or immigration violations. Only 160 deportees had been convicted of "aggravated felonies," what the federal government designates as Level 1 crimes—for instance, rape, robbery, aggravated assault, and drug crimes serious enough to warrant a prison sentence of more than a year. Although it appears that 264 had committed the least serious crimes—offenses punishable by less than a year's imprisonment—the number may include some of the 168 Level 2 offenders (a category often used for repeat misdemeanors) who had been picked up for drug possession or too many speeding tickets. Immigration offenses of various kinds were the cause of 198 deportations.

In Greenport, deportations are rare. One Guatemalan family with two members who have repeated traffic offenses and drunk driving arrests seems perpetually threatened, but the men in question have been getting off with brief jail stays. The word on the street is that if you have a DWI arrest and an outstanding warrant for reentering the country after being deported, you will be deported again. Gang involvement will get you removed with dispatch. But immigration offenses without criminal charges are usually disregarded. In 2013 a raid on several 7–11 convenience stores, including the one in Greenport, yielded arrests for the owners for fraud, identity theft, and harboring undocumented workers. It was the rare instance in which the workers were considered victims; the storeowners had supplied them with false IDs, kept them as virtual prisoners in nearby housing, and stolen their wages. The workers were not arrested or deported.

Although the odd raid or arrest does not directly threaten most Greenport immigrants, each is widely publicized, reminding residents that their hold on security in the United States is tenuous. Almost any offense can become a "crime of moral turpitude," that catch-all in immigration law that honors a judge's individual discretion in deciding which conduct justifies exclusion from the country or rejection of an application for permanent residency or citizenship. For most of Greenport's Hispanics, the process of enforcing immigration laws is mysterious. Sometimes people just disappear, and no one but the immediate family knows whether it is because they were discovered and deported or because they left town for other reasons.

Even law enforcement personnel may be ignorant of the final disposition of the arrest of an immigrant.

◆ ◆ ◆

Like other residents, Greenport's immigrants occasionally commit crimes less serious than the Ramirez rape. According to Southold Police Chief Martin Flatley—Southold Town provides police services to the village—DWI is the most common offense. Since the department does not keep records that reveal the demographics of DWI arrests, it is impossible to know whether immigrant residents are more likely to drink and drive than the locals. Sociological research is divided on whether Hispanics in the United States are responsible for a disproportionate number of DWI cases; early studies that came to this conclusion have been undercut by more recent findings that suggest diversity among different national groups.[8] The police blotter in the local paper suggests that on the North Fork, Latino immigrants are not disproportionately represented among arrestees.

It is a different story when it comes to other traffic offenses, the second most common source of encounters between Hispanic immigrants and the police. For those who are undocumented, the fine incurred from driving without a license is a cost of doing business. Prohibited from getting driver's licenses, they see paying such tickets as a necessity forced on them by the requirements of their daily lives: the need to get to and from work, the limited availability of public transportation, and their status as legal outsiders. Driving without a current registration or insurance is a more serious matter, and many immigrants have devised a solution. They rely on other immigrants who are legal residents or native-born friends to purchase and insure vehicles that they can then drive and pay for. Occasionally this system fails when an insurance company decides there is something fishy about the owner of five or six cars who has only a family of four, including two children.

Many crimes by and against immigrants go unreported. Victims are often reluctant to go to the police, either because they are afraid to expose their immigration status, because they won't be able to communicate in English, or because traditions of solving problems within families or networks of trusted compatriots are strong. What happens in the community stays in the community, though rumors of assaults and thefts circulate. Members of Salvadoran gangs are said to hang out in an abandoned shed by the railroad and in a local cemetery, preying on immigrant and native-born residents alike and trying to recruit young Hispanic men. Domestic violence is common, women say, but rarely reported. It is not just lack of trust in the police. "Women are too scared of being deported or of losing their children—and even if that doesn't happen, it could affect you in the future," says one woman whose husband grabbed her by the throat and threatened to kill her. "Better to handle it within the family." When a domestic violence incident is reported to police, the informant is usually a friend or relative of the victim, not the woman herself. Social workers at The Retreat, an East End organization that provides services, including a residence, for victims, say that women from the North Fork—Hispanic and otherwise—do request their help. But some women in Greenport say victim services are impractical for them because they require giving up time from work and children to attend counseling sessions and interviews.

Whether and how cultural influences shape the commission of crimes by Latino immigrants on the North Fork is another of the questions obscured by lives lived in the shadows. On the one hand, those who have been here for a few years convey local mores to the newcomers. On the other, attitudes like machismo are deeply embedded. Sometimes American laws seem irrelevant or foolish to the immigrants. In at least some of their countries, there is greater tolerance of public drunkenness, for instance, and romantic relationships between post-adolescent men and young girls are more acceptable. In any case, the United States protects at least a few foreign-born women from violence and abuse with a special nonimmigrant visa if they assist law enforcement in apprehending abusers. And American law comes down hard on undocumented immigrants who commit serious felonies. Erick Ramirez will probably spend several years in prison and then be deported.

The extent to which immigrants are victimized—by the native-born or by each other—is even more difficult to pin down than the prevalence of criminal behavior among them. The local police department does not keep statistics on the demographics of complainants or of those who report crimes. In a rare report on crimes against Hispanics, the police chief of Riverhead, the county seat, attributed twenty robberies of Hispanic men in 2013 and 2014 to the vulnerability of undocumented immigrants without bank accounts who carry large amounts of cash on their person.[9] Underreporting is inevitable when so many people have a powerful incentive to remain invisible. "A major issue with Hispanics is their lack of trust in the police," notes Southold's Chief

Flatley. "So many are here illegally; they're not going to take the chance that we might report them."

For immigrants with long memories, that supposition seems credible. In 2007 a series of raids in Nassau and Suffolk Counties set back police-community relations on Long Island by several years. Justified as part of Operation Community Shield, a national antigang initiative, the raids were hailed by Suffolk County police officials but deplored by civil liberties groups and immigrant support organizations. Greenport's raid was particularly egregious. It took place before dawn and arrested eleven men, only one of whom had a criminal record, a recent Greenport High School graduate indicted for assault. The police had assisted in both planning and executing the raid, leading immigration officers to where the targets supposedly lived—information that, in a few cases, turned out to be wrong. Several of the arrested men were deported, although none had gang associations or outstanding warrants. Many simply disappeared, sent to detention facilities around the country. Two months after the raid, *New York Times* reporters were unable to locate four of them.[10]

Fear of deportation is not the only deterrent from contacting law enforcement when it is needed. Some immigrants remember police in their countries of origin who were brutal and corrupt. They may acknowledge that American cops are less likely to be either, but media reports of conflict between police and minorities in the United States must make them wary. Although the hesitation to call on local police for assistance and protection is understandable, the veil of silence may have the perverse effect of feeding anti-immigrant views: if the immigrants' only known transactions with law enforcement are their arrests for liquor-related crimes and traffic offenses, they can't be seen as victims deserving of help, only as perpetrators.

◆ ◆ ◆

Greenport no longer has its own police department. This is a good thing. A generation ago the village force of nine officers was so corrupt and lawless that a referendum to eliminate the unit passed by a vote of 617 to 339 and turned over policing to the Town of Southold (which includes the Village of Greenport). The scandal was a bonanza for the local press and even found its way across the pond. The *Daily Mirror* of London crowed, "A town's entire police force, rated the worst in the world, is set to be sacked."[11]

Abolishing the department was an appropriate response to a long-running disgrace. (Turning over policing to Southold also cut taxes, providing cash reimbursements for residents of at least $200.) A year-long grand jury investigation had found, in the words of the Suffolk County district attorney, that the department was run "in a grossly unprofessional manner" with "no specific procedures for handling even routine matters, including how to handle evidence, narcotics, contraband, weapons, crime scenes, crime reporting."[12] More than fifty witnesses had entertained the grand jury with lurid stories of errant officers—one who drank on duty and hung out with drug abusers, another who had sex on the police chief's desk. The department ran much as it did when Greenport was a bootlegger's haven during Prohibition, with officers permitted to flush seized drugs (those that weren't appropriated for personal use) down the toilet.

Policing today is vastly improved. As of December 2014 the Southold department had fifty-two officers and fifteen civilian employees who cover the ten hamlets of the town plus the incorporated Village of Greenport. Officers' cars patrol the beaches and downtown Greenport streets (all two of them) and occasionally cruise down residential streets. In interviews, immigrants describe a wide range of police behavior—from helpful to indifferent to mean—but do not report brutality or corruption. They resent the occasional sweep to corral unlicensed drivers, somewhat cynically seeing it as an income-generating exercise.

Police in Greenport are aware of immigrants' fears. In such a small town, they may know the likely immigration status of many, but they never ask. Sometimes they even defend the immigrants against native bias. Maria Rivera tells of a minor accident in which an American woman hit her car from behind. When a policeman arrived at the scene, the woman tried to deflect attention from her responsibility by saying, "You have to check; maybe this is an illegal person, not a licensed driver." The officer merely laughed; Maria's license and registration were valid, and he was not going to be drawn into such suspicions.

Sofia has experienced police services from another perspective. At several times, she has needed help in dealing with the medical problems of Robert, her oldest son, and the police have always been there to provide it. On one occasion, one of the senior officers on the force drove her son Robert fifty miles to the hospital in Stony Brook, where there was no bed for him, and then back to Brookhaven Medical Center. At every point, he called Sofia to keep her informed.

Not all experiences are so positive. Greenport's Hispanic residents consistently report ethnic profiling on the road. Sofia remembers the day that she came out of her apartment with her boyfriend and got in her car parked (legally) at the curb. An officer was sitting in his patrol car across the street. He followed them until they stopped about half a mile away at the 7–11, where he asked Sofia's boyfriend for his license. The only possible basis for the stop was Gabriel's brown skin.

Profiling is frustrating. But most immigrants are sanguine about it, too. "The police are stricter with us," says Sofia matter-of-factly. And a Guatemalan landscaper who drives an elderly truck chuckles as he says, "When they [police] see a Spanish face, they stop you. But it isn't our country, and we just have to put up with it." Perhaps resentment is tempered by an understanding of the enforcement role that defines police work. In general, the immigrants are less forgiving of discrimination on the job or in their neighborhoods.

That law enforcement is a fundamentally clean and professional operation does not mean it always treats the new arrivals with sensitivity. In August 2009 an argument broke out between two Hispanic couples sharing an apartment in the village. As it escalated, one of the tenants called the landlord, the former celebrity chef Eberhard Müller, who lived in nearby Cutchogue. When he and his wife, who operate a large produce farm, arrived at the house, Müller broke down the door of the couple the caller had complained about and, according to them, twisted the arm of Graciela Gomez. (It is unclear whether his fury was motivated by the argument or by the arrears in rent that he maintained Graciela and her boyfriend, José, owed.) When the police arrived, Müller persuaded them that this was a landlord-tenant dispute, and they left without taking a statement from the presumed victims or asking if they wished to press charges. Uncertain of their remedies, the couple waited three days until, encouraged by social workers who had seen Graciela's bruise, they went to the police station to report the incident and file a complaint. There they tried, with limited success, to explain in English what had happened. Although the police appeared initially reluctant to bring a charge against Müller—Satur Farms is, after all, a big economic presence in the area—he was subsequently arrested. Reluctant to call Graciela's injury an assault, the prosecutor charged Müller with harassment. When the case came to court, Graciela was interviewed in Spanish, and her account differed slightly from the story as she had told it in English at the police station. Müller denied having touched her and the charge was dropped. The judge did issue a thirty-day order of protection for Graciela, but she and her boyfriend were taking no chances and fled from their apartment immediately (perhaps because they did indeed owe back rent but also as a precaution against further assault).

This situation was a perfect blizzard of misunderstandings about criminal justice relations with immigrants. The lack of Spanish-speaking officers on the scene or at the precinct, the failure to record the victims' account at the scene, the indifference of the prosecutor—they all bespeak a system unbalanced in favor of the native-born and privileged. Whatever the equities involved, Graciela and José were at the mercy of both the complexities faced by police and courts and the failure of resources and incentives to deal with them. Four years later, Graciela was involved in a fracas with a housemate who insulted and threatened her. When told she ought to go to the police about it, she demurred. "They won't do anything," she said, recalling her previous experience.

With just a few cases like this, it is easy to see why Chief Flatley says, "The Hispanic community isn't burdening us with calls." Finally, in 2014 a native Spanish-speaker joined the police force, but he is supplemented by only two American cops who speak some Spanish. (Officer Witzke majored in it in college and speaks it well; as a result, his beat is Greenport.) The officers must police residents whose backgrounds and cultures are unfamiliar, and if their experience with immigrants is limited to enforcement, as opposed to protection, they may feel some hostility. It's not a problem that is easily solved. And ethnic identification is no guarantee of sensitivity; Latino officers may treat Latino residents just as their colleagues do.

Class barriers impede the protective aspect of policing also. That most of Greenport's immigrants are poor and do not easily negotiate what others consider routine business transactions adds another layer of distance between the white, mostly male, American officers and the Hispanic residents they must serve. A frustrated Guatemalan woman tells of a time a few years ago when someone stole items from cars on the street near her apartment—but only from the cars of the Hispanics. "The police came," she said. "But they just told us to call our insurance." They were indifferent to both the bias of the crime and the barriers to making effective insurance claims.

◆ ◆ ◆

The Southold Town Justice Court, which handles most charges involving Greenport residents, lacks the tension and the gravitas of urban courts. Both civil and criminal matters are heard on Fridays, the only day the criminal court is in session. Most defendants sit with their lawyers, waiting. At the elevated bar, the central characters—what scholars call the courtroom work group of prosecutor, public defender, and judge—huddle to finalize the day's schedule. It's a matter of backing and filling as they postpone one matter, request documents for another, and call for a missing party. When the action finally begins, it's not very intense. Parking tickets are paid, DWIs are reprimanded and fined, and a speeder is sentenced to community service. Even as bearer of bad news, the judge is kindly: he warns one drug offender that another conviction will get him deported. A small flurry of interest accompanies the arraignment of the only person brought to the court in handcuffs—a skinny, middle-aged black man whose dazed expression and shirt askew provide a partial explanation for his crime: he robbed a Greenport bank and was caught less than an hour later, at a house on Second Street with the stolen money and the garb he had worn for the stickup—a colorful hat festooned with fake dreadlocks.

For most immigrants, court appearances do not involve high drama. Traffic offenses are handled with relative lenience in both the Southold town court and the county court in Riverhead. Judges generally ask defendants for their side of the story, and immigrants think they are fair. An element of theater does prevail, however. Judges fine defendants for unlicensed driving and rebuke them in full knowledge that the person standing before them will go out and do it again—immediately. The absurdity of the charade reaches its peak when the judge tells the defendant, usually a working adult, to take the bus (one county route that arrives once an hour) instead.

Defendants with more serious charges—only a very few each year—are arraigned at the Southold court but detained at the county jail and tried and sentenced at the Riverhead court. At that point, the threat of deportation becomes real. The criminal court may try the case, impose the sentence, and then turn the defendant over to ICE for immigration detention and deportation. Or local law enforcement may expedite matters, referring the defendant to immigration authorities without a criminal disposition. Rare cases can bypass immigration courts and come before federal magistrates and judges. Whatever the jurisdictional outcome, the immigrant who has committed a felony—and sometimes just an immigration offense—will often disappear into the system, heading for the exit from America.

◆ ◆ ◆

Much of the recent national debate over immigration has centered on questions of enforcement. While fears of racial mixing or loss of national identity may be at the core of antagonism toward immigrants, some Americans' greatest concern—at least on the surface—is that they are committing crimes that endanger communities. In addition, there is indignation that people with no right to do so enter the country or stay after their permission has expired. For those who associate immigration with criminality, the logical response is to come down hard on the miscreants in our midst and to harden the borders that have enabled entry.

A policy that views immigrants as deviants, however, is an increasingly hard sell. Both scholars and criminal justice professionals are finding *lower* crime rates in immigrant communities. Harvard sociology professor Robert Sampson and his colleagues studied violent acts in 180 neighborhoods of Chicago and found that "immigrants appear in general to be less violent than people born in America, particularly when they live in neighborhoods with high numbers of other immigrants."[13] They concluded that immigration might actually be "protective" for people in such neighborhoods. And nationally, the huge drop of the 1990s and 2000s in both property and violent crime has coincided with an unprecedented surge in immigration. In 2012 the foreign-born made up almost 40 percent of the population of New York City, now considered one of the safest big cities in the country.

Tiny Greenport, too, is far safer than it was a generation ago, before its immigrants arrived. Just ask old-timers who lived through the drugs and decay of the 1970s. That doesn't mean, of course, that the village is peaceful because the immigrants came. But conceding that their presence coincides with growth and stability undercuts other doubts the native-born may have about the effects of immigration. The criminal law—even when it is manifested only by the rules of the road, which immigrants admittedly violate—lends legitimacy to keeping a distance from the Other. The law-abiding are on one side of a line, and miscreants are on the other. But if immigrants rarely commit serious offenses and Greenport remains a relatively crime-free environment, it would be reasonable to expect that the line would blur, making way for increased integration.

The trouble with this argument is that immigration policy maintains the boundary between the new arrivals and the native-born and fosters ambiguity about how law enforcement should treat immigrants, even those who are legally in the country. If undocumented residents were permitted to get drivers' licenses, traffic offenses would plummet (and perhaps traffic accidents, too, as the DMV would have evaluated drivers' skills). If working men from Mexico, El Salvador, and Guatemala were allowed to visit their families at home and return, they might be less lonely and susceptible to drunkenness and its consequences. Domestic violence has complex causes and might not be reduced by authorizing immigrants or by allowing them greater mobility. But greater opportunity to move out of poverty might reduce tensions at home and prevent some abuse. Even if it didn't, victims would be more likely to turn to law enforcement for help if they were not frightened by the prospect—unlikely but not impossible—of being deported or having their children taken away. So relaxing the restrictions of immigration policy for Greenport's undocumented population could actually contribute to a safer village.

As it stands, law enforcement personnel on the North Fork are hard put to know how to treat immigrants humanely and, at the same time, maintain order. The criminal law has given them standards that require, even in homogeneous white communities, interpretations and judgments that are sometimes complex. Now their task is even harder: police must take into account cultural influences on the behavior of those they are supposed to serve and protect, and judges must consider a different set of consequences for those they sanction. Perhaps most important—directly for police, indirectly for judges—they must serve an additional master, the Department of Homeland Security.

Since the 1990s the federal government has increasingly looked to police and criminal courts to participate in immigration enforcement. First came the Criminal Alien Program—a product of the Immigration Reform and Control Act of 1986—that identifies deportable foreign-born prisoners in federal and state institutions and in local jails. Then came Delegation of Immigration Authority Section 287(g), usually just referred to as 287(g), which permits police to "enter into a partnership with ICE . . . in order to receive delegated authority for immigration enforcement within their jurisdictions"—in other words, to help immigration personnel conduct raids.[14] With Secure Communities, the most recent program, an electronic match of an arrestee's fingerprints with IDENT records in Washington was sufficient to justify detaining an immigrant (legal residents as well as the undocumented) until he or she was turned over to ICE, whether before serving a sentence for a crime or as a supplement to it. Police departments were not permitted to make their own decisions about when detention for immigration enforcement was appropriate, further complicating their relationships with immigrant communities.

Secure Communities went too far. State legislatures and courts began to rebel as immigration detention exceeded constitutionally permitted criminal procedure. After a three-year battle by California activists, that state's Trust Act took effect in 2014, prohibiting local jails from detaining immigrants at the request of ICE for low-level offenses. New York City passed local laws, effective in 2013, permitting the sheriffs and police department to refuse ICE holds in many cases, joining Miami, Washington, DC, and many other cities and counties that had adopted similar policies. The movement to reject federal enforcement policy came to the eastern end of Long Island, too. In October 2014 the Suffolk county executive announced that law enforcement agencies would cooperate with detainer requests only when supported by a judge's warrant. In the past, Chief Flatley had felt he had no choice when it came to ICE holds: "You can't say no when a federal agency calls," he said. Now he would have the county behind him if he said no. And perhaps in Southold's hamlets and Greenport Village, the new directive would boost his credibility and that of his officers as protectors of immigrants.

A federal court got into the act too. A magistrate judge in Oregon ruled that a county, in refusing to allow an immigrant defendant to post bail and detaining her after she served her sentence for a minor offense, violated her Fourth Amendment right against unreasonable seizure.[15] The ICE hold sent to local police was only a request—not mandatory—the court said, and did not, by itself, constitute probable cause of an offense. After this judgment was published, sheriffs in seven Oregon counties announced that they would no longer honor ICE hold requests.

The White House was in a tough spot. Through both legislative and judicial action, state and local governments were willing to defy federal policy. In late 2014 President Obama responded by deciding to end Secure Communities. No longer would local jails become conduits for merging criminal justice and immigration enforcement. Federal agents could still screen fingerprints and order detainers in local jails but only for felons convicted of serious crimes or people who endangered national security. "We'll keep focusing our enforcement on actual threats to our security—felons, not families; criminals, not children; gang members, not a mom who's working hard to provide for her kids. We'll prioritize," the president said.[16]

Perhaps the tide is turning in directions that will improve law enforcement relations with immigrants. Ten states and the District of Columbia now permit adults, regardless of immigration status, to get driver's licenses. Two New York state senators are pushing for the state to do the same, echoing New York City's mayor Bill de Blasio, who says that immigrants' needs to drive are "urgent."[17] And nationally, the president's new executive action to extend DACA and to defer deportation for the parents of American citizens or legal permanent residents, DAPA, will lift some of the shadow that hangs over millions of families.

Greenport's Hispanic community may benefit from more than the pushback against harsh immigration enforcement policies. As gangs—the primarily black Bloods as well as the Hispanic MS-13 and Eighteenth Street groups—have established a presence in the North Fork, victimizing Central Americans, police, public officials, and educators have rallied to take steps to curb their influence. Spurred by a gang dispute that erupted in a Greenport park and ended with a shooting in Southold in late 2014, community meetings have focused on ways to protect the village in general and children in particular, including immigrant children who might be targets for gang recruitment. Chief Flatley has announced that the newly hired Spanish-speaking policeman, who is Ecuadorean, will be assigned to patrol in Greenport. And the Guardian Angels, a volunteer organization, visits the village on Saturdays to meet with potential victims and recruits and provide information about gang activities to law enforcement and the public.[18]

Easing immigration enforcement and fostering communication between the ethnic groups in town promotes law enforcement's binary task—to maintain order while also controlling crime. Immigration policy has muddied the waters by criminalizing immigrants and thereby conflating the elements of service and coercion that are at the heart of ensuring public safety. Reversing that effect and taking note of immigrants' fears can go at least some distance toward building the trust that promotes community harmony.

Deferred and Delivered

Although Conchita Cardoza loves her job and credits it with awakening her ambition to become a nurse, she is well aware that in doing it she is flouting American law. She has a fake Social Security number, obtained through the network that supplies such benefits. She was careful to ascertain that it was the number of someone who was no longer alive—using fraudulent documents becomes the more serious offense of identity theft if they belong to a living owner—and she did not hide her deception. She sighs. "I told my boss the truth from the beginning." Although she can chuckle about the insecurity of being undocumented and the risks of run-ins with local law enforcement or immigration authorities that could get her deported, she feels vulnerable. "I worry all the time," she says. "It never goes away."

Working at the Greenport pharmacy in 2012, she stands behind a slightly raised checkout counter where she can see out past the customers in front of her to the rows of vitamins and shaving supplies and the walkers and toilet seats ranked along the back wall. It's a view she cherishes. "I like working with patients, learning about medicine, dealing with customers and residents—that's my field," she says with a smile. Plump and pretty at age twenty-six, she has been at the pharmacy for almost five years. She schmoozes with the Spanish-speaking customers, on whom the business depends, and her boss is grateful.

Immigration policy has defined her young life for more than a decade. She has defied it, been threatened by it, and benefited from it. At least she has companions in her struggles; three brothers also came to the North Fork. They have faced many tests together—multiple journeys from their town in the mountains northeast of Guatemala City, struggles to get an American high school education, and medical problems. As a group, they embody the spirit and the ambitions of the "DREAMers," young people who came to the United States without authorization as children and who now demand the right to remain and the protection of their families from deportation.[1] Whether they will prevail in this quest remains to be seen.

◆ ◆ ◆

Actually, Conchita and her brothers—one older, two younger—are exceptions to the rule that DREAMers arrive in the United States with parents or related adults. Their parents preceded them by four years and were ambivalent about their coming. Parental nerves, however, were beside the point; by the time they were teenagers they were ready to set out on their own. By her own account, Conchita's decision was almost a compulsion. Although she was aware of the poverty around her—"In Guatemala you could eat meat only once a week," she notes—her desire to leave her country was born of intense curiosity rather than of material need. Throughout her childhood she had witnessed aunts and uncles departing for Los Angeles and New York, sending back support for other family members to join them. Her parents had emigrated too, then returned to Guatemala and built a house but left again, lured once more by the prospect of greater opportunity abroad. Although economic motivations had driven them, they were not, by Guatemalan standards, poor. When her parents offered Conchita, at fourteen, the choice of an elaborate party for her *quinceañera* or financing for a coyote to escort her to the border, she did not hesitate. "I wanted to know what was so interesting about the US," she says. "It became a challenge."

Challenge, indeed. She set out five times before successfully entering the country. Getting across Mexico posed many threats. On one occasion, traveling with a brother and an uncle, she was thrown in jail for two days. On another trip, when she and a brother were hopping the infamous train "La Bestia" (the beast), they needed escorts with machetes to avoid thieves lying in wait along the tracks. Whenever they were caught in Mexico, the police "took everything we had—money, shoes, jewelry." She shudders as she remembers the time at the US border when three masked, armed men demanded their money. They didn't have much. "I thought they were going to kill us." She lost track of what was lawful and just. Inured to breaking the law to get across Mexico, she says that "everyone stole," especially the coyotes, to whom they paid as much as $8,000 each time. At least she was never assaulted or raped, experiences reported to be common among women making the journey.[2]

Each time her odyssey failed, Conchita returned home to San José del Golfo, went back to school and waited a few months for the next opportunity. On her sixth try, accompanied by her older brother, she made it into Arizona. Thieves stole their food and water there, too, but at least they were within striking distance of their destination. Smeared with garlic to ward off snakes, they walked in the desert for ten hours until they were picked up by coyotes who took them to Alabama, where a family friend drove them to Greenport. Eight months later her two younger brothers also made the trip. Asked how they dealt with their ordeal emotionally, Conchita said, "We give support to each other."

◆ ◆ ◆

They needed that. The culture, the weather, even the holidays seemed alien, and Conchita missed her aunt, who had been like a mother to her. Relationships with their parents, whom they no longer knew well, were complicated. Like many immigrant parents, the Cardozas expected that Conchita and her older brother would go right to work to pay them back for the expenses of the coyotes and to help with the two younger brothers who followed. Tensions at home led to parental separation; the children were left to fend for themselves, a household of adolescents—the youngest was twelve; the oldest, eighteen—living alone in Greenport.

But these were serious young people. They found succor in teachers and employers. Their parents worked for a Southold woman who insisted that they must get an education and registered them at the local high school. Thinking of the school administrators' reception of them, Victor, the middle brother, chuckles ruefully: "I think they thought we would drop out or make trouble," he says. Hispanic students were still a rarity in Southold in early 2004. With only four children in the ESL class, the arrival of the Cardozas doubled the school's Hispanic presence. "They didn't know what to do with us," Conchita remembers. But Mr. Myers, the ESL teacher, spoke a little Spanish, smiled a lot, and "made us feel comfortable." For the first year, Conchita sat in the content classes—earth science, world history—understanding nothing and not doing the homework. But she clung to the dictionary that a librarian gave her, and her English improved. "They made us repeat ninth grade in 2005, but we passed in the second year." In 2008 she and Victor finished high school, and by 2010 all four had graduated. "We were famous in Southold," Conchita says, with pride. They are still in touch with some teachers who helped them.

It had been, however, a lonely journey. Conchita had not made friends. She could not speak her native language with her classmates, and she found the American girls aloof and sometimes condescending. This was Southold, after all, "where there are a lot of rich people," she notes. She also had to work—first in the home of the woman who had brought her to school and then in a candy store in a nearby town. Once she became a high school graduate, her job at the Greenport drugstore broadened her horizons. Two of her brothers had lupus, and her concern for them combined with her exposure to the tasks of the pharmacy to convince her that in health care she would find her niche.

But barriers loomed. The well-regarded nursing school at Suffolk County Community College seemed too distant an aspiration: the prerequisites were daunting, the waiting list for admission was formidable, and, as an undocumented applicant, Conchita would not be eligible for financial aid. Even if she could surmount these obstacles, she would have to confront the reality that certification as a practical or registered nurse was possible only if her presence in the country were legal. Perhaps in the short term it would be better to train to be a nursing assistant. It would be good preparation for that next step she hoped would be possible one day, and the US Department of Labor called nursing assistance a "Bright Outlook" occupation, likely to be much in demand in the next decade. But even learning to bathe patients and take blood pressure in a Certified Nursing Assistant (CNA) program would require state certification with proof of legal residence, and Conchita was not prepared to take her deception that far.

So she would stay at the pharmacy, where she felt underpaid and occasionally had to put up with customers who said, "I don't understand what you are saying. Is there an American who works here?" (Her English is excellent, though not perfect.) She tried to be patient and appreciate the good things in her life. Living and sharing expenses with two of her brothers enabled them to live in a comfortable house in Riverhead. Her mother, from whom she had been estranged, now visited and brought food to her children, of whom she was very proud. Despite the lack of a driver's license, Conchita owned a car, which she had registered and insured in the name of someone "with papers." (She and Victor say that "all the Spanish do it this way.") She had had no confrontations with immigration officials.

◆ ◆ ◆

In 2012 President Obama announced Deferred Action for Childhood Arrivals (DACA), which would forestall the deportation of young people between the ages of sixteen and thirty who had come to the United States before they turned sixteen and who met educational and other requirements. For a two-year period (renewable for another two years) individual participants would not be shadowed by the worries that had been Conchita's constant companion. The program conveyed a reprieve, not a right, but for likely beneficiaries it was hard to see it that way, since a successful applicant receives a work permit (officially an employment authorization document, or EAD), effectively an invitation to apply for a legitimate Social Security card. States could decide to issue driver's licenses to DACA beneficiaries, and many did. Not surprisingly, young people who qualified saw the acceptance of their applications as an affirmation of their identity as potential Americans and a vote of confidence in their futures.

As soon as friends told her about the program, Conchita thought she was eligible. She had arrived a few months before her sixteenth birthday and had successfully completed high school. A letter from her first landlord proved that she had been in the country on June 15, 2007 (the cut-off date chosen to ensure that an applicant had made at least a five-year commitment to the United States), and teachers' letters and medical records demonstrated the "continuous presence" in the country necessary to qualify. She had recently been pulled over for speeding, but the fine she had to pay did not count as the kind of criminal conviction that would exclude her. She was unlikely to be a threat to national security or public safety. Palpably excited, she hired a lawyer and shared with her friend Yasmina at the pharmacy the agony of waiting.

On the one hand, Conchita seemed like the perfect candidate. In his announcement of the program, the president emphasized the contributions that young, undocumented migrants are making to the country, whether through their work, their plans to get higher education, or their service in the military. Support for Conchita's ambition to become a nurse and perhaps go even further in the medical field would be an investment in human capital, a long-term benefit to a sector that makes up one-sixth of our economy.

Obama also spoke, however, of suspending deportation as a matter of justice. The new policy was a recognition that those brought by their parents to the United States as children were too young to have made the decision to migrate and should therefore not have to bear responsibility for an illegal migration. Would Conchita's case be morally justifiable, given that she came of her own volition and not in the company of her parents? As a legal matter, would there be a record of her five failed attempts to reach the United States that might exclude her from the eligible population?

The Department of Homeland Security, charged with implementing DACA, did not keep her waiting long. It acknowledged her application promptly and confirmed that it was complete. Within two months she had submitted her fingerprints to the government, which either didn't know or didn't care that she had been apprehended in Mexico. Generous of spirit, she was thrilled for Yasmina, who was approved for the program ahead of her. Six months after mailing her application, Conchita had her Social Security card and was preparing for her driver's test. She foresaw a world of new opportunities opening before her.

◆ ◆ ◆

The reality of that world is more complex than she may have understood. The DACA permit is only, as the president noted, a "temporary and stopgap measure," not a legal step along the fabled path to citizenship. The program could theoretically be terminated by a future president, though by then it would probably have taken on the aura of inevitability that usually accompanies benefit programs. More immediately, the employment for which Conchita was newly qualified did not catapult her into comfortable middle-class status. To be sure, she could now command higher pay at the pharmacy, and soon she left that job, lured away by options unavailable to her when she was without papers. But she found that working in a less protected environment had its disadvantages too—"I missed the drugstore," she said in surprise—and she still did not have full-time employment or health insurance.

The first job in her new status was at Peconic Landing, the high-end retirement community just outside the village. But her hopes to learn about health services there were dashed when she was assigned to do prep work in the kitchen. "I didn't get to talk to the residents, and the schedule was terrible," she says. Having never had benefits or taxes deducted from her pay, she was startled to find that she was taking home less money than when working at the pharmacy. Next she took a job in the vitamin department at Whole Foods. She liked the work and the pay was better, but full-time employment many miles from home, just as she was starting her CNA course in a local nursing home, was exhausting. She was learning about the world of lawful work and also about the consequences of being removed from the shadows. A year after getting her DACA permit she had her eye on a job at Stony Brook Hospital, where she said she could make twenty dollars an hour as a nursing assistant. Farther down the road, when she can travel legally, she would like to return to Guatemala. Not to live but to provide short-term help where there are few doctors and fewer nurses— "Maybe at least to give vitamins to the kids," she says, caught up short by her own daring. Giddy about new challenges and opportunities, she says, "All this is happening because I have a Social Security number; they use it to check everything, criminal record as well as immigration status."

Conchita had reason to pay close attention to criminal record checks. She had been arrested at least twice for driving without a license, submitting to the embarrassing courtroom lecture of the judge and paying the pesky fines ($300–$500) that were the cost of commuting, unlicensed, among her several part-time jobs and her home. Her legal guilt might come back to haunt her some day, she knew. But her delight at finally getting a driver's license—she had been driving for more than seven years— was primarily the triumph of having solved a budgetary problem.

Their advocates often note that immigrants are voiceless—even those in the country legally, but especially the undocumented. Fear of exposure and its material consequences—detention, deportation—muzzle even the boldest young people. Conchita felt liberated from that voicelessness as soon as she had her DACA permit. She remembers a moment just before she left her job at the drugstore: "My boss yelled at me, and I was not afraid of him anymore. Before, I took everything—extra work. I wouldn't have the chance to go somewhere else. That day I felt strong, so I could talk back to him. I don't need this any more."

She is also relieved to be a legal driver and car owner, and her new status has given her confidence on the road. Recently she was pulled over for speeding on the Long Island Expressway, going sixty-five in a fifty-five-mile zone. Suspecting ethnic profiling, she gave the police officer her license and registration but didn't leave it at that. "I was not afraid to ask him, why are you stopping me. Others were going sixty-five, too." She laughs. "He looked at my record and came back to the car. He said, 'I'm going to do something nice for you, so tomorrow you can do something nice for someone else.' And he let me go." The pride in her voice speaks to deeper feelings. As welcome as the newly acquired material benefits of the DACA program are, the right to challenge the officer—something she would never have done in her unauthorized past—is an even greater prize.

◆ ◆ ◆

As Conchita revels in her new freedoms to work and drive and move about in public legally, she is planning an even larger future. She loves this country; her best American experience, she says, is "getting to know different kinds of people." She embraces the greater diversity here and approves of a society that is "more liberal" than what she knew at home. Although she deplores it "when people treat you different because you look different," she wants to be a citizen and wishes she had time to join an organization advocating for immigration reform.

But it is far from clear that DACA will lead to citizenship or even a green card. Washington's battles over immigration seem unlikely to be resolved in the near future, as Republicans and Democrats have widely divergent views on what constitutes reform. DACA is probably politically unassailable, with more than a million young people approved or eligible in 2013 and another 400,000 likely to age into eligibility by 2022.[3] And New York State is among the most welcoming of jurisdictions: as a DACA participant, Conchita will be eligible for Medicaid. But she is impatient, active, and ambitious—not someone who will be satisfied with just renewing her "temporary and stopgap measure" every two years. When and if young people take to the streets to demand more permanent inclusion in the American polity, she will certainly be among them.

PART VII

Working Lives

Where There's a Will, There's a Job (or Two)

When Ricardo arrived in the United States from Guatemala in 2007, he went first to Los Angeles. Although he had family and friends there, the network did not protect him from unemployment. "For new people there were no opportunities, no work," he says. For fifteen days he collected bottles for four dollars an hour, after which he quit in disgust, only to discover that the available job in a T-shirt factory paid him only twenty dollars for two days' work. Then a miracle occurred. He phoned a friend from home who had left two months earlier to go to New York—specifically, to Greenport. The friend told him there was plenty of work in the village, paying nine to twelve dollars an hour, and that he would send Ricardo the money to travel east. After four days in the back of a van, Ricardo arrived in Greenport at 9 AM. By noon that day he was at work with a landscaper, a job he obtained through a friend of the friend who had rescued him.

Was this a typical experience for a newly arrived, undocumented immigrant? No—but it was not atypical either. Manuel and Juanita Pinzón, middle-class immigrants from Colombia, found work immediately through family members who preceded them. It was menial but it was a start. Some find work in their chosen field—when they have a chosen field. Hilarino Sanchez, who had studied textiles in Mexico and, during his odyssey from Mexico to Greenport, operated an embroidery machine in a Queens factory, soon went to work at W. J. Mills & Co., Sailmakers ("Everything Canvas").

So, for newcomers eager to work, Greenport in the early years of the twenty-first century was and is a land of opportunity. Unlike many other communities on Long Island and all over the country, day laborers hanging out on busy street corners awaiting the call to dig ditches or wield a hammer are only an occasional sight. But the jobs available to Greenport's immigrants—both documented and *sin papeles*—follow the national pattern of being concentrated in a narrow range of occupations—construction and landscaping for the men, domestic work for the women, and, for both sexes, whatever is needed in restaurant kitchens. And, although this work generally pays better than the minimum wage ($8 per hour in 2014 in New York State, rising to $8.75 in 2015 and $9 in 2016), it can be considered real opportunity only in contrast to what the workers could have found in their countries of origin. The jobs available to immigrants usually do not provide a comfortable, sustainable livelihood, especially when the worker is sending remittances home to family members.

Greenport's low-wage labor pool of immigrant workers is also a huge opportunity for the village. It is the human infrastructure of much economic activity, staffing the kitchens of modest delis and elegant seafood meccas, supplying the supermarket with workers to keep a sharp eye on the freshness of the produce, shoring up old buildings to house both second-home owners and yet more immigrants. The amenities of Greenport in 2014 are, in part, artifacts of the immigrant flow of the past twenty years. What was a decaying community a generation ago has become vibrant once again, with a Latino working class replacing the descendants of European immigrants.

Scholars and union organizers, observing labor conditions in Europe and Asia as well as in the United States, would characterize most employment opportunity for Greenport immigrants as "precarious work." Temporary or part-time, lacking benefits, and not covered by unions, precarious work has shifted the risks and responsibilities of employment from bosses to workers.[1] Global competition, technological development, and the growth of free-market ideology have ushered in employers' expectations of more flexibility (i.e., less commitment) in arrangements with their workers, in both formal and informal sectors. Workers must fend for themselves if they are injured or need time off; pensions are for the elite or the (increasingly rare) unionized. Having work no longer means having a job. Firms that formerly relied on employees now turn to independent contractors, workers not protected by the National Labor Relations Act or Fair Labor Standards Act. It's a trend that affects middle-class people but is particularly difficult for low-wage workers. For Greenport's undocumented and other working-class immigrants, it's the norm.

Your work may be precarious, in part, because it is seasonal. If you are a landscaper, you will be working eighty-hour weeks outdoors from May through October and not at all during the winter months. As a dishwasher or line cook in a restaurant, you may work on weekends all year but full-time only when the tourists are in town during the summer months. It's the lucky women who clean houses or hotel rooms after the school year begins and families are no longer in Greenport on vacation. One of the reasons that Edgar could not attend high school regularly in the spring is that he was working to save money to take him through the lean winter months when he would have no work but would still be paying rent.

Greenport's immigrants are also vulnerable to the national trend of in-sourcing, moving jobs from a high-cost area to one where labor is cheaper, usually the South. Gabriel, Sofia's boyfriend, installed windows and doors for ten years and became very skilled at it. But in 2013 the company was sold and moved to South Carolina, leaving him unemployed. While Americans encounter this kind of problem too, Gabriel's alternatives were fewer than for similarly situated workers who are citizens. They did not include other businesses of the same kind, partly because the community is small but also because his work was relatively specialized, and as an undocumented Mexican, he could not move up to a supervisory or white-collar position.

Not all work for Greenport immigrants is precarious. Because the village and surrounding communities are growing, some construction jobs are long term, with a variety of occupational challenges that provide workers with a modest career ladder. In addition, even unauthorized Hispanic immigrants are starting modest businesses. Luisa's Magic Scissors is the latest in a small chain of Long Island barbershops, and Rinconcito Hispano has been serving *pupusas* (with cheese and beans, shredded meat, or the delicate *loroco*, a vegetable flown in from San Salvador) since 2000. Most visible is "the Spanish store" on Front Street, which sells everything from videotapes to avocados and Mexican *crema* and serves as a depository for remittances being sent home. Even being undocumented does not keep some people from success-ful entrepreneurship. Jorge, a landscaper from Guatemala who sometimes takes his wife and two small children with him when he prunes and mows for a sympathetic client, employs his brother and a couple of friends during the summer season. He has done well enough to have acquired a snappy little convertible to supplement the ancient truck that hauls mulch and compost.

Employment opportunity for immigrants all over the country often relies on family relationships or networks of friends and neighbors who previously came from one's home country. An ethnic enclave—either a residential concentration of immigrants of the same cultural and geographic background or an occupational grouping, with employers like Jorge who share that background—may be the answer to the search for work. Both beneficial and constraining, the enclave is an oasis for recent arrivals who would otherwise be adrift.[2] But it can also trap the worker—or, more important, the next generation of American-born children—in a web of family members and countrymen and -women that is difficult to escape. The ethnic enclave then becomes a barrier for integration into the wider world. Current immigration policy, in punishing both employer and employee, hardens the barrier. Workers such as Javier and Edgar, both of whom were profiled earlier, are likely to remain undocumented even if meaningful immigration reform can get past a recalcitrant Congress—and may be relegated to the ethnic enclave for life.

◆ ◆ ◆

Grateful for the opportunity to support themselves under any conditions, most Greenport immigrants have learned to live with precariousness. At least for those who are undocumented, there are no benefits—no unemployment insurance, workers' compensation, health insurance (with the rare exception of an employee using a false Social Security number in a job where the boss insures the workers), or paid sick or vacation days. (It should be noted that only people who are legally present in the United States may receive Social Security benefits; payments withheld for the undocumented worker will go back into its trust fund.) For those with work permits or green cards, conditions are better; and for citizens, better still. Maria Rivera's green card entitles her to generous benefits from the retirement community where she still cleans the residents' units, and her husband, a citizen since 2001, has health insurance from his paving company. But they are the exceptions. When citizens assert that immigrants are taking jobs away from them, they don't mean the work that most Greenport's immigrants do, which does not provide even the basic security that Americans feel entitled to.

To a certain extent, working conditions for low-wage jobs in Greenport and the surrounding towns are similar for immigrants and the native-born. Pruning vines in a North Fork field is hot and tiring for anyone who does it, and construction jobs are equally dangerous for all workers. Furthermore, most labor laws that regulate wages and working hours, overtime pay and breaks, apply to all workers, whether undocumented or documented immigrants or American citizens. Discrimination among workers on the basis of ethnicity, gender, pregnancy, and so forth, is prohibited.

But on the eastern end of Long Island, as elsewhere, the legal rights of immigrants as workers—especially if those workers are undocumented—are largely theoretical. Undocumented labor is essentially a black market, not reported by employers, not taxed to workers. Violations of the minimum wage go unenforced; for many workers, overtime pay is an alien concept. Unions are nonexistent. In 2013 the National Employment Law Project conducted a survey of 4,387 low-wage workers in Chicago, Los Angeles, and New York and found that 41 percent of those who were documented and 74 percent of those who were undocumented were not receiving information from their employers about their pay or their tax deductions.[3] While hard data on the experiences of workers living in tiny Greenport are unavailable, anecdotal evidence suggests that a similar survey would yield similar results.

Although most of the employers of Greenport's immigrants pay construction workers and landscapers $12–$20 an hour, well above the minimum wage, they also sometimes engage in wage theft. If the workers know little English or arithmetic, they may not know when they are being cheated. Edgar says he was paid $109 for twenty-six hours of landscaping work; his Salvadoran education didn't enable him to calculate the hourly rate quickly enough to protest. In addition, he didn't know that he had rights to a minimum wage and to overtime pay. Another barrier to exercising those rights is that many workers don't keep adequate records to prove the hours they worked and the pay they were promised.

Trying to exercise labor rights can be dangerous; occasionally bosses threaten, implicitly or explicitly, to report a complaining worker to ICE. It's largely an empty threat, as employers know that such a report would invite inquiry into their labor practices, including the hiring of undocumented workers. Nevertheless, most workers would rather not take the risk of exposing themselves. Jorge, the landscaper, tells of sizable masonry job that he did in a neighboring hamlet where the owner of the house, after complimenting him several times on the work when it was under way, refused to pay him the agreed-upon price on completion, saying the work was inferior. Jorge could have gone to Sister Margaret or to a local lawyer to take the homeowner to court, but he chalked it up to experience. Mostly he has worked for "good people," he says.

Supporting their children, whether in the United States or at home, is a powerful incentive for the foreign-born to go to work in difficult and dangerous conditions, but it's not the only one. Sometimes the motivation is simple survival, or paying the coyote, or caring for an aging parent. As Greenport's immigrants remain in the United States and become more aware of the greater opportunities here, their objectives can change. At twenty, Ricardo came to the United States on a lark. "How cool to go to the US," he says; his principal aim was to earn enough money to buy a motorcycle. But then he met Gaby, and his world turned. Now twenty-eight, he has a wife and a baby and has lost all interest in motorcycles. He is one of the lucky ones, with a job as a pizza maker, up from being a prep worker and then a line cook. Undeterred by his illegal status and unafraid of discovery and deportation—"I'm nobody; they are not looking for me," he says—he has taught himself computer repair and is studying for the Test Assessing Secondary Completion (TASC), the successor to the GED examination.

As Ricardo and Hilarino adjusted to American values and dreams, they began to plan for bigger things—doing what economists call investing in human capital, but in different ways. Ricardo was hungry to learn, for his own personal enrichment and for material benefits he and his family might later enjoy. Hilarino, on the other hand, invested more directly in his son, with a passionate conviction that a bright boy born in America can do and become almost anything. When he first arrived and was working seventy-two-hour weeks in Queens, New York, and sleeping on the floor of a one-bedroom apartment he shared with eleven other men, he cared only about the money he was making, he says. But when his son, Jonathan, was born in 1994, his perspective changed.

> I didn't care anymore about the money except for what it could do for my son. . . . I didn't want him to have the same life. I didn't have anything to give him in the future, just to make him study. I talked to him like an adult. He went to school in English, and I saw that he was smart. I taught him to write, draw, count, know about money, math, the alphabet. When he went to kindergarten he knew numbers and his name. I was working at night, and when I went to work I left him homework. In the morning, he would say, "Papi, here is my homework." I put all my time into teaching him.

Jonathan is now majoring in sociology at Cornell University.

◆ ◆ ◆

By definition, benefiting from an abundance of cheap labor is exploitation. It is doubly so when both the presence of the laborers and the act of hiring them are illegal. In enacting sanctions against employers of this labor pool—an aspect of the 1986 Immigration Reform and Control Act—the federal government actually handed them a new tool of exploitation and weakened the workers' ability to assert what rights they had. Weak or nonexistent enforcement of employer sanctions in the policy's early years gave bosses a club to hold over their workers' heads, the threat of largely fictional crackdowns that could discipline them. But exploitation is not the same as abuse. While there are bosses who milk the opportunities for mistreatment, Greenport immigrants say that, in most occupations, cruel or uncaring behavior is rare. Employers, in turn, often express great respect for the Hispanics they hire. Many are grateful for what they see as competent work performed by people with a strong work ethic. Particularly in construction, where pay is highest and work tenure tends to be longer than in restaurant or landscaping jobs, it is possible to get on-the-job training that builds skills; some bosses give their most capable men (in this sector, it is all men) considerable authority on complicated projects. It doesn't make up for the lack of job security, but the appreciation that employers express helps create relative stability.

One American builder, who employs a Guatemalan crew with a Hispanic supervisor (a typical kind of enclave employment), says that his clients compliment him on the workers' competence. Because many residential buildings in Guatemala are made of concrete, the members of his crew—some of whom have been working for him for more than a decade—have experience with that kind of construction. All of them are undocumented, including the supervisor. Several had plans to return to Guatemala but have now concluded that it is an unrealistic dream, that their children growing up at home need the financial support that can be provided only by remittances sent from the United States. During the economic downturn from 2008 to 2011 they had very little work, but this employer continued to pay on a part-time basis. "I told them, 'I can carry you during this hard time, but please try to find full-time job,' and they did," he says.

The beneficent boss cannot offer the protections of a union, but paternalism is better than neglect. One local contractor who has both native-born workers and immigrants—most with work visas—embraces the role. "I tell them we are a family; there is a grand patriarch—me—and it goes down from there. If you stay long enough and do good work, you will get to the top of the family." He hires year-round and full-time; one of his workers has been with him for fourteen years. The Guatemalan members of his crew are "well-educated and efficient," he says, with enough English to speak with clients. The unauthorized workers earn less than the permanent residents and citizens because "there is more of a risk," and no one gets benefits. But this employer also compensates his men according to the complexity of the job they are doing and says that sometimes the immigrants are the highest earners.

It is in the kitchens where immigrants are most likely to be treated badly. Restaurant work—loosely defined to include jobs in delis and coffee shops and excluding the more desirable positions of waiter and bus person—exposes the worst of the exploitation made possible by immigration policy. In this sector, almost everyone is undocumented and therefore particularly vulnerable. Pay for dishwashers and prep workers is low in even the best of situations (not just for immigrants) and workers frequently report being cheated out of wages and tips. Only those with green cards are likely to protest. In one case, a Greenport worker successfully sued his boss for $10,000 of unpaid wages, much of it for overtime. He admits that he would not have gone to court had he not become a permanent resident a few years earlier. Laboring in food services also subjects workers to verbal abuse and arbitrary dismissal. "The boss is bipolar," laments one young woman, reinforcing the stereotype of the temperamental chef. Both native-born and immigrants suffer from this behavior, but it is harder for the latter—especially the undocumented—to walk away because they are less likely to find decent alternative employment.

In the past, a few Greenport employers have helped unauthorized immigrants obtain green cards. The sponsorship process for all but highly trained professional workers is lengthy and tedious; if you are at the bottom of the occupational ladder, it is probable that you will never be approved. The employer must offer a permanent job and make a convincing case for why an American worker is not available to do it. The petition filed with the Department of Labor must demonstrate the need for the employee and his or her qualifications for the job—most likely, for Greenport immigrants, in the EB-3 category for skilled and unskilled workers. Even if your petition is approved, you are merely getting in the line of others applying under that category. Only when the "priority date" is current—meaning that there is no wait—may the worker apply for "adjustment of status" and receive the precious green card.

For many years the line has been so long and the number of permanent residencies granted so tiny that the process has become an exercise in futility. Getting to the front of the line will never happen.

North Fork employers in the economically essential sectors of agriculture, viniculture, and construction are in a bind if they wish to hire the native-born for low-skill jobs. By the 1990s many young Americans had moved away or into cleaner, more lucrative occupations. Farmers and builders turned to the flood of immigrants for their low- and semi-skilled positions. Between 2000 and 2010 Hispanics in the largest town—Riverhead—rose from 9 percent to more than 25 percent of the population, and many were young, strong arrivals eager for any job available.[4] They were primarily undocumented, willing to work without benefits and for wages that most Americans would reject. The threat of employer sanctions for hiring unauthorized workers was largely toothless. Immigration policy empowered the employers.

But more recently it has hobbled them. For one thing, the federal government has become more vigilant in monitoring employers' use of immigrant workers, fining and occasionally raiding enterprises where documents provided at the time of hiring do not identify the worker as legally present in the country. In 2010 the trend to conduct audits of immigrant hiring—sometimes called silent immigration raids—came to Greenport. In the East End world of seasonal and low-paid work, jobs at the Peconic Landing retirement community at the edge of the village were a great opportunity. Housekeepers there, the women who cleaned residents' apartments and provided other small personal services, could count on decent pay and humane treatment; the company even provided health insurance. But at least a dozen of them lost their jobs when the company was notified that tax-withholding information for them did not match federal records. The consequences for the employer of retaining the workers were potentially dire—not just a modest fine (up to a hundred dollars per employee) but criminal penalties for violating tax and immigration laws. For the housekeepers, the termination was disastrous. Many were already struggling to make ends meet; several had children to support, one with newborn triplets. The most common employment alternative was domestic work in private homes—off the books without benefits and, in some cases, lasting only while the summer season supported a large labor force.

Farmers and vintners are also mindful of the increased enforcement of employer sanctions if they hire unauthorized workers, and they are more likely than in the past to check documentation of new hires. Theoretically, they could use the national guestworker program—H2-A, Temporary Agricultural Workers—to hire migrants legally, but they rarely do. The program authorizes employers to employ an unlimited number of foreign workers for up to three years, but they must pay a wage set by the government ($10.91 per hour in 2013) plus room and board and the cost of round-trip transportation for the worker. "It's cumbersome, expensive, and farmers do not want to deal with that type of program," the executive director of the Long Island Farm Bureau told the *Suffolk Times*.[5] So, as in California and other western states, North Fork farmers are facing a serious labor shortage, modifying what they grow and when and, in at least one case, letting crops wilt on the ground because there is no one to pick them. Like employers in other sectors, some throw caution to the winds and hire from the available pool of unauthorized workers.

Strategies for evading employer sanctions can be elaborate, but ultimately they all rely on cash. Generating that cash can be simple or complicated. Employers may simply withdraw it from their business accounts, but that risks tipping off an auditor. To avoid using a bank, some bosses give workers cash payments made by clients or customers and endorse to the workers the checks they have received. Employers also cash checks for each other for a fee, constituting an informal, private banking system. All of these latter methods add income tax evasion to the violation of immigration law.

◆ ◆ ◆

For some of Greenport's immigrants, just getting to this peaceful place and finding work is enough reward for the agonizing dislocations of leaving home. An added benefit may be the comforts of family, that is, finding relatives who are here and sending money to those who are not. Without complaint, they live with the knowledge that immigration status (and often their minimal schooling) sharply limits their occupational futures; the upgrade will have to wait for the next generation, whether for children born here as American citizens or those being supported at home. Other people, however, come with dreams of economic betterment, whether through additional education, steps up the rungs of a career ladder, or both. Given the confines of immigration law for most of Greenport's immigrants—even permanent residents are vulnerable to deportation, after all—upward mobility is unlikely. But a few people do achieve it. When they do, it is usually because a change in immigration status has supplemented their talents and drive.

It stands to reason that as the immigrants learn English and pick up the skills needed in various sectors, they will move away from the jobs they held when they arrived. With dismay, East End farmers can attest to this, even when the workers are undocumented; they expect only a worsening situation as more people gain legal status. But the barriers to moving very far without the encouragement of legalization are great. Javier's dead-end job working with his brother as an assistant barber is an example; the work is much less oppressive than what this teenager had been doing in hot kitchens and greenhouses but will not open up opportunities for him to refine his skills or learn new ones.

Acceptance into the DACA program, however, does just that. Conchita's trajectory was clear from the moment she received her work permit and Social Security number (this time, a legitimate one). Where she previously had a minimum-wage job at the local pharmacy, she now works in the vitamin section at Whole Foods, which pays better and gives her time off to attend her Certified Nursing Assistant program. She will soon be on the way to becoming a registered nurse, enrolled in the Suffolk County Community College program. Even when an improvement in immigration status doesn't give the recipient a new life, as it did for Conchita, it can boost a worker's value. Blanca and Rosa Lopez, ages fifteen and twenty-one, are students in Greenport, contributing to their Salvadoran household with part-time housecleaning jobs. In the early days of this family's migration north, one by one, most members were undocumented. But then the earthquakes hit El Salvador, making its nationals eligible for Temporary Protected Status (TPS), a category for countries beset by natural disasters, epidemics, or civil war. When their father was given TPS, the Lopez girls benefited too; they have work permits and the possibility for travel outside the United States. "Because of that we now have good jobs; it's still housekeeping, but they pay us more," they said triumphantly. TPS gives protected individuals the chance to apply for permanent residence, and this family has acted upon that possibility. Several members now have green cards, and a few have become citizens.

Conchita, Rosa, and Blanca are all looking forward, confident of their acceptance as Americans now that they have received work permits. But immigration decisions at both the institutional and individual level can be fickle and unpredictable. TPS status and DACA approval are not immigrant visas, and there is no guarantee of the political will necessary to convert them into permanent residencies. While they may permit approved applicants to receive Medicaid and other medical benefits, that permission is state policy, and a recipient who moves out of New York may become ineligible, just like those without papers.

Consider the fickle finger of fate as it wags at Ricardo, the Pinzón family, and Hilarino, the immigrants who found employment opportunity at the beginning of this chapter. All except Hilarino remain unauthorized, in employment limbo, although, as parents of American-born children, they may receive temporary work permits thorough the new Deferred Action for Parental Accountability program. As of early 2015 their contributions to Greenport's economy were stuck in second gear. (As Aviva Chomsky notes, "Undocumentedness has everything to do with work and the economy."[6]) Ricardo has moved up from his restaurant positions as dishwasher and prep cook to that of pizza maker, to be sure, but only in the winter when business is slow. Despite enrolling in an online culinary school and "learning a lot about grains, meat, fish, and how to keep your tools in good shape," his restaurant life has not changed much. He still has no benefits and no authority. The door has closed for employment-based visas, and even if it hadn't he would most certainly not be eligible. Pizza cooks in the United States are a dime a dozen. Even if his boss were willing to sponsor him to apply for an available visa, his petition could not credibly assert that Ricardo was performing tasks that he couldn't find an American to perform. Ricardo would like to open his own restaurant some day; "If I save I can buy my own place in the future," he says. But how realistic is that when the law prevents the contractual and bureaucratic negotiations necessary to do such a thing?

Manuel Pinzón has also advanced in his work, which, along with Juanita's contributions from her job at DiAngela Leather, now gives his sons a middle-class life. But he is constantly juggling the limitations of an undocumented business, a situation that would be extremely precarious if he did not have family to help him shield it from official scrutiny. Although she likes her job at the store, Juanita, too, is constrained by immigration policy; although she long ago received word that she was eligible for a work permit, it has never come and those permits are no longer granted. Without major legislative change at the national level, she and Manuel have little recourse to better jobs. Their sons will have to justify the sacrifices they have made—assuming, of course, that the DACA permits that now give them professional opportunity do not fall victim to political assault.

Like Ricardo and Manuel, Hilarino has proved himself, by any measure, as very productive. He has become became an indispensable part of one of Greenport's oldest and most important businesses, designing canvas products—cushions, awnings, accessories for boats. "I never stopped doing the job until it was finished," he says of the eight years he worked for Bill Mills before applying for his green card. He was also very lucky. Mills was willing to fill out reams of paperwork, expose the operations of his business to the federal government, and guarantee future employment to Hilarino so he could be on the way to citizenship. An experienced, well-connected lawyer oversaw the process, which Hilarino fronted with $11,000 of savings. Now that his American future is assured, Hilarino is working on a second career in video production. He shot a *quinceañera* in 2013 and first-communion ceremonies at Saint Agnes Catholic Church a year later; he says he would like to make videos showing what immigrant life is like. Before applying for citizenship in 2016, he wants to improve his English, which is already adequate. Asked how the green card had changed his life, he expressed relief that he now had a driver's license and the chance to travel. Beyond that, permanent residency has released his American Dream. "The greatest advantage will be in the future," he says.

The contrasting situations of these workers—Hilarino, on the one hand, and Ricardo and the Pinzóns on the other—seem very arbitrary. Differently talented but equally hardworking, they are all exponents of the (sometimes mythical) American work ethic. Manuel's persistence has enabled him to give jobs to at least three other people. Both Hilarino and Ricardo maintain that a forty-hour workweek is not enough; "The pay is good, but it doesn't occupy me for enough hours," says Hilarino. "Spanish people want to work more than Americans do." Ricardo's description of his approach to the boss who has promoted him is typical: "I said to him, 'Why don't you teach me to be a pizza maker? You always hire troublemakers, lazy guys who are working just to make money, not to make something better for the restaurant.'" These ambitions are good for Greenport and good for the country. That the immigration system doesn't reward them is a national shame.

◆ ◆ ◆

A running argument underlying immigration policymaking is whether immigrants displace native-born workers, taking jobs they would otherwise do. Advocates for immigrants contend that Americans don't want the low-skilled and sometimes backbreaking jobs that most of the recently arrived are willing to do. Supporters of restricting immigration, however, argue either that this position is simply wrong—that the native-born occupy many job categories where immigrants compete—or that if the jobs that immigrants take were better paid, Americans would fill them. Employment of immigrants depresses the wage scale, argues Harvard professor George Borjas. As employers benefit from the lower pay they can give to immigrants, low-income citizens, particularly African Americans and Hispanic Americans, suffer. "What this is, is a huge redistribution of wealth away from workers who compete with immigrants to those who employ them," he maintains.[7]

The scholarly literature provides some support for all these arguments but also concludes that generalizing about the effects of immigrant employment is futile. So much depends on the location of the work, the ethnic identity of immigrant workers, the nature of the jobs to be done, and the route followed to find work—employer network, ethnic enclave, kinship group. In Greenport, however, the pattern is clear. Although many jobs are seasonal, when the immigrants are working they earn just enough in low-skilled jobs to cast doubt on the argument that if those jobs were better paid Americans would take them. At fifteen to twenty dollars per hour for landscaping work and housecleaning, a worker cannot live munificently, but many are making do, despite lacking the benefits of the social safety net available to citizens. Few of Greenport's native-born residents do these jobs. In fact, one might argue that the availability of immigrant workers at the lowest wage levels—in what some economists call secondary labor market jobs—enables at least some formerly working-class Greenporters to move up in supervisory roles. The immigrants' productivity spurs investment and consumption. Borjas may be right that immigration depresses wages, but in Greenport the effect is modest and may benefit local small businesses. Even as we acknowledge that employing unauthorized immigrants is exploitation, at least in the short term and in the small communities of the North Fork, everybody gains.

Sacrifice and Success

When Patty Carlos (née Acero) came from Bogotá, Colombia, to Long Island in 1983, it was on a lark, a college student's summer adventure, legitimized by taking an English course at Stony Brook University. She planned to return to her university, but romance and athletics intervened. "I fell in love—with my future husband but also with volleyball," she says with a chuckle. "I played for three years. I had to be a full-time student to be on the team, so I finished and graduated with a psychology degree from Stony Brook."

In a sport that prizes height—two-thirds of the Americans on the 2012 Olympic women's volleyball team were over six feet tall—Patty was an anomaly. Not only the shortest woman on the team, "I am maybe still the shortest," she says. At just five feet she couldn't block, but "I was fast and good on defense, good serve." Her energy and enterprise on the court carried over to larger precincts. Within three years of her college graduation in 1986, she and her husband had started a successful business importing leather goods from Colombia. Wholesale evolved into retail, and her business still contributes to the success of three of the siblings (out of seven) who followed her to Greenport. Thinking of the nineteen members of her extended family who have arrived in Greenport in the last two decades, her niece Nathalie says, "Patty was the reason so many of us ended up there." "That little girl is a big person," says her sister-in-law Mireya.

By any measure, Patty's family has made a successful transition to American life. Two brothers own small businesses, and one sister-in-law's dress shop is a jewel in the small crown of Main Street stores. If you shop at Di Angela Leather, Patty's enterprise, another sister and sister-in-law will help you find purses or shoes or tasteful costume jewelry. The older members of the next generation—most of whom came as small children to the United States—are starting careers in business, journalism, nursing, education, and fitness, while the young ones are excelling in Greenport schools. Nathalie has both a bachelor's and a master's degree from Harvard.

Despite their middle-class origins and relatively easy access to the United States—with one exception, no one had to swim a river or walk for days across a desert to get here—the Acero-Pinzón family is deeply affected by being what immigration policy scholars call "mixed-status"—that is, including both citizens and noncitizens. This family is mixed, indeed; it consists of both native-born and naturalized adults, US-born and naturalized children, one legal permanent resident, and unauthorized adults and children. Four of the young people who were brought to the United States before the age of sixteen have received Social Security numbers and work permits as beneficiaries of President Obama's DACA program—temporary, renewable permission (not legalization) enabling them to work, attend school and move freely around the country for two years.

Notwithstanding that the threat of deportation is remote for anyone in the family, the undocumented status of five members—as well as the uncertain prospects for the young people with DACA approvals—takes its toll. Their range of educational opportunities is narrower than for those who are legally present in the country. Career ladders are shorter, trapping workers in jobs for which they are overqualified. Health insurance is prohibited for the adults. Licenses that open doors to greater freedom, whether for driving or for professional advancement, are unobtainable without deception. Bank loans are out of the question. And there are the shadows of illegal status: the secrets that children must keep from their friends at school, the anxiety of wondering whether the police officer who has stopped you for a minor infraction will accept your international driver's license, the worry that an accident or illness or legal dispute will expose you to bureaucracies unwilling or unable to protect you.

◆ ◆ ◆

Some of Greenport's nineteenth-century European immigrant families resulted from one member—usually a young male—coming to the

New World to test the waters, with the intention of sending for others if conditions were propitious. For today's Latino immigrants, that process is far less common. An exploratory journey requires resources that most do not have. Tourist visas are often denied even to an applicant with family legally resident in the village, and even if they are granted, travel costs may be prohibitive. To make the overland journey these days without permission to enter the country is fraught with dangers; it is arduous and expensive at best, not to be undertaken lightly. Rather than being the anchor of the migration chain, most arrivals these days are following it, linked to family members or friends who came a decade or two ago.

So the usual odyssey of a family from Mexico or Central or South America is a long-drawn-out process full of obstacles and risks. The brave (or foolhardy) adventurer who made the initial journey cannot easily return home to collect his wife and children, as he might have done a century ago. Having recourse to a smuggler who may or may not be reliable is usually a less daunting prospect than escorting a family from the home country.

But not always. The Acero-Pinzón family is an exception to these generalizations. Once Patty settled on the North Fork and became a citizen and business owner, she was able to sponsor family members who worked in the same sector—leather goods—and help them naturalize. Several came as tourists with the intention of checking out the possibilities for long-term residence here. For many years she ran a one-woman hostel for at least a dozen of her close relatives testing the waters. Several then returned home to settle their affairs and make a permanent move. They were more mobile than most Latinos arriving in Greenport because they could easily get tourist visas and they were middle class.

Mireya and Gustavo Acero were among the first to arrive. As immigrants with family ties and occupational opportunities, they benefited from the relatively relaxed travel visa policies pre–September 11 and from sheer good luck. As a result, they have had little difficulty finding work, educating their three sons, and becoming citizens.

For them and for others in the family who migrated, hard times in Colombia were the catalyst. In the late 1990s the economy, which had been relatively robust, began to contract and by the end of the decade was in a deep recession. The peso's value had capsized, a real estate bubble had burst, and the country was shaken by both guerillas on the left and paramilitary groups on the right. Then as now, corruption at every level of government was rampant.[1] Foreign investors, wary of political instability and the influence of the drug lords, were pulling out of the country. They reduced their investments in Colombia's three stock markets by more than 35 percent between mid-1998 and a year later.[2]

Their country's agonies affected Mireya and Gustavo directly and personally. In Bogotá they were part-owners of a leather goods factory, where Gustavo was the production manager and Mireya helped out when she was not occupied with raising their three sons, Gustavo, Edgar, and Diego. But it was losing money, and they reluctantly sold their share to a brother. Their savings were evaporating; "Money was tight and so was hope," says Mireya. Equally worrisome was what they perceived as threats to their children. As a family, they liked to visit friends and relatives around the country but were afraid that guerillas would snatch their teenage sons and conscript them into the political wars. So they decided to see whether they could make a new life in the United States. It would be a one-year adventure. "If it doesn't work, we can come back and start again," Mireya and Gustavo told their sons. So, with their six-month renewable permits (allowed with a five-year multiple-use tourist visa), they arrived at Kennedy Airport in March 2000.

Their decision to stay was forced upon them long before their year of exploration ended. From the beginning they knew that becoming authorized to remain was a lengthy and complex process, so they consulted several lawyers. The one who seemed most knowledgeable suggested that Patty, whose business was not only successful but also closely related to the family business in Colombia, sponsor her brother's visa by filing an application for a labor certification that would enable him to work for her in the United States. She would have to persuade the US Labor Department that she had searched without success for qualified American employees before turning to Gustavo. And they would have to file immediately, before their six-month permit expired.

There was a problem, however. To be eligible for that visa, they would have to go home to Colombia and wait for it to be issued. Joining the line of supplicants waiting around the world, however, would mean that it would be many years before they could return. But there was an alternative, a mini-amnesty called Section 245i of the Immigration and Nationality Act, which allowed people who had already applied for green cards to legalize their status by paying a thousand dollars. But there was a catch: this program was available only to undocumented applicants. So Gustavo and Mireya, rejecting the option of renewing their tourist visa, depended on a perverse irony of immigration policy and allowed their permit to expire so that they could be eligible for this route to permanent residency. In December 2000 Congress passed and President Bill Clinton signed an omnibus budget bill that included a three-month extension of the Legal Immigration Family Equity Act. Although the Aceros were now undocumented—and would remain so for almost two years until their work permits arrived—they had taken the first step to regularize their situation. They became naturalized citizens in 2012.

Along the way, there were still hurdles. When, in 2004, they became legal permanent residents, holders of the precious green card, their youngest son was inadvertently omitted. The lawyer had assumed that Diego would be incorporated automatically because he was under fourteen. That was incorrect, and he had to apply separately, which he did. But by the time he graduated from high school, he was still waiting for his residency permit. The family was in a bind because he had been offered a full scholarship to attend Stony Brook University, contingent on legal residency. Despite assurances that the green card was on its way, it still hadn't arrived on the last day when he could accept the award. So his family held its collective breath and wrote "yes" on the form. Three days later the green card arrived.

Although Patty's helping hand smoothed the way for Mireya and Gustavo, they had to work very hard to survive. Gustavo's training as an industrial engineer did not take him far in his new land, so initially he worked in construction and later in environmental cleanup. At one point Mireya worked three jobs: from six to eight in the morning she cleaned O'Mally's Steak House, then put in several hours helping Patty at Di Angela Leather, and ended her day busing tables at another restaurant. At first she knew no English and was terrified that patrons or customers would ask questions she couldn't answer. But she got help from American colleagues, and she and Gustavo took evening English classes at Suffolk County Community College in Riverhead, twenty miles from Greenport. ("If I don't learn the language I am going to be someone who doesn't belong to this community," she says.) Soon she began to think about opening a small store. Colombia was a good source for her inventory of lingerie and leather goods. At first the store was in a tiny annex in Patty's building, but a year later Mireya moved to her present location and opened Simply

Beautiful Boutique. She has done well enough so that Gustavo may leave his current job doing maintenance work at the elegant Peconic Landing retirement community on the edge of Greenport to help her expand.

Flush with American passports, businesses, and careers, this branch of the Acero-Pinzón family has grasped the American Dream. Although they remain devoted to Colombian food and music and artistic traditions, they are unlikely to return to their homeland except as vacationers. They see their country as still too violent to give their children a secure future. Besides, they are signed, sealed, and committed to the United States. Several years ago the Acero brothers went on holiday together to Colombia, and while there Gustavo Jr., now in his thirties, renewed his acquaintance with a young woman he hadn't seen since they were both children. Facilitated by Gustavo's new freedom to travel back and forth, international courtship followed, and in 2011 Paola Ayala came to New York to marry and join the Colombian diaspora.

◆ ◆ ◆

For Mireya and Gustavo, the path to a comfortable life in the new country was relatively smooth. But each had a brother for whom that was not the case. For them, more than a decade after they migrated, the path is still stony. Although they are educated people, their undocumented status sharply limits their opportunities and those of their children. Not coincidentally, both arrived after the terrorist disaster of September 11, 2001, when immigration policy became inextricably linked with the war on terrorism. The political view that "border security is national security," as Senator John Cornyn put it in 2006, has dominated congressional consideration of immigration reform ever since. It even affects the availability of tourist visas from countries never thought to be sources of terrorism, and it has put a virtual hold on the issuance of work visas. Pablo Acero and Manuel Pinzón were caught in this bind.

But in this close-knit family, the migration chain was very strong. Both brothers followed their siblings, despite the uncertainties. Although he has been on the North Fork for more than a decade without papers and, therefore, working at a job for which he is overqualified, Manuel has no regrets. Faced with an untenable situation in Colombia, he endured a difficult odyssey to find a new life for his family. His three sons, Pablo, Andres, and Angel, reward him amply for that choice. "They know our story, and they appreciate it," he says. "They know that we made the best decisions for them and that we support them totally."

That story began, as it did for Mireya and Gustavo, with economic hardship. Neighbors who met during college, Manuel and his wife, Juanita, grew up in Colombia's substantial middle class. As young adults, they had reasonable expectations of comfortable lives and rewarding careers in Bogotá. Juanita had studied architecture; Manuel, business. For fifteen years he had worked for a large shoe company with stores all over the country, donning a suit and tie each morning to go to his job as a junior executive. But in the 1990s the recession forced the company to close stores and lay off employees, and Manuel was one of them. Initially confident of finding work through friends and professional contacts, he realized that, especially in a downward economy, good jobs in Colombia were available only with *palanca*—political and economic influence, the pull that comes with knowing powerful people. Others around him were suffering also; some left for Spain, which they found to be poor and unwelcoming. The recession dragged on and on, with unemployment close to 20 percent. Juanita kept her job in an architectural firm, but after three years they had run through their savings. By this time Manuel had been unemployed for so long that he thought he would never be hired. "The door had closed," he says.

He was fortunate to have his sister Mireya in Greenport, as well as a five-year tourist visa that could be used for a succession of six-month travel permits. Mireya's suggestion that he come to look for work there was what he needed. It was an exploration he would undertake alone: perhaps it would amount to nothing, but he would give it a try. After the humiliations of the previous years he was ready to work at any job he could find. And he started out with a rosy view of the United States. "I thought this was a blessed country with many opportunities, a minimum of corruption, and respect for law," he says.

That was in mid-2001. He had just arrived when the terrorists attacked the twin towers, and shortly thereafter immigrant enforcement intensified. But living in a quiet rural spot and not being a young Muslim man, he was not rounded up or interrogated about his immigration status. For about six months he washed dishes twelve hours a day at a local restaurant, and by the time he went home to Colombia at the end of the year he had a plan. He would follow the time-honored tradition of millions of migrant workers: he would work in the United States and return home to visit his family when he could.

But the plan did not work out. One night when he was tucking his oldest son in bed, the boy began to cry and begged his father not to leave the family again. And Juanita was firm in preferring to keep the family together and go back to Greenport with him. (They had no difficulty getting tourist visas for the children, since the parents already had them.) Within two months, they had sold their apartment, along with other possessions, and packed five large suitcases with what remained. Leaving was particularly hard for Juanita, whose sister had just died.

Manuel grimaces when he recollects the first two years. He and Juanita were forty when they arrived—not old, but not full of the energy of youth, either. Even to them, starting a new life in a new country seemed a bit crazy. "Everything was a shock—the culture, the food, the environment," says Manuel. "We were used to the city, and this place was so small. We found a little house—ugly, dirty, falling down—on Main Street. The move was particularly hard for Andres, who was eight and knew no English. The first four months of his school—oh my God!" Manuel went to work in a nearby delicatessen (a place where the boss was known for exploiting immigrants), and Juanita joined Mireya at O'Mally's, chopping vegetables.

Even where a family is undocumented, human capital matters in getting ahead. Manuel and Juanita could move out of their menial jobs because they learned quickly and had skills that were transferable to more lucrative and more rewarding pursuits. Another big boost came from having helpful family nearby. After the first year Gustavo, who then had a job with a contractor, found work there for his brother-in-law even though Manuel didn't know how to clean a paintbrush. Another year passed, and Manuel was able to start his own business, though he professes to have remained ignorant about how to do it. "I had no tools, no ladders, nothing. I didn't know how to set a price for a job." Ten years later his handsome maroon truck, with the services—house painting, power washing, and staining—advertised on the side, is a common sight around town. He has three permanent employees—also immigrants—and some part-time help. A leading North Fork citizen recently praised his "meticulousness and professionalism" in the local paper.[3] Juanita now works at Di Angela

Leather, where she waits on customers in English and helps in buying leather and accessories for the store. They live in a small but comfortable house on a pond at the edge of town.

◆ ◆ ◆

Manuel and Juanita are able to accommodate to their undocumented condition in ways that are available to few. They are knowledgeable enough about negotiating the world to be able to open bank accounts, get library cards, and establish identities that will document their contributions to the United States if and when they can gain legal residency status. And they benefit from a support system that includes legal citizens. Family members can register their cars, apply for professional licenses that will cover them, and insure their employees.

But accommodation comes at a price. Neither of them is free to step out from behind the family shield. Furthermore, they are always aware that a strategy of avoidance defines their lives. The strategy has risks. Although Manuel has had only two minor medical situations that took him to the local hospital—and in each case, he was able to pay for his treatment out-of-pocket in installments—he does not have health insurance to protect him against a future, more serious problem. If he and Juanita want to fly domestically, they must rely on their Colombian passports and risk the possibility that they will be questioned about the basis for their presence in the United States—and, of course, they cannot leave the country for any reason. (Pablo Acero, the younger brother of Gustavo who also arrived after the watershed of September 11, lacked the Pinzón confidence when a family reunion in Florida took place in early 2014, so he and his wife and children drove instead of flying.) Juanita yearns to see her family, but they must come to her; for her, the highlight of the 2013 Christmas season was that her brother came from Colombia for a visit, the first time she had seen him in ten years.

The children of the undocumented branches of this family bear the limitations imposed on them by immigration policy (and their parents' decisions to defy it) lightly. Coming to a new country probably put the greatest demands on Gustavo Jr., who had just graduated from high school when his family immigrated. With only minimal English, he and his parents decided that he should attend the Greenport High School for a year before attempting an American college. It is a testament to his fortitude and to his Colombian private school education that he was able to pass the New York State Regents exams and graduate after that year, as the only Spanish-speaking student in the twelfth grade. He and his next youngest brother—and later, the older daughter of his uncle Pablo, along with Manuel and Juanita's two older sons—all started higher education at Suffolk County Community College. Tuition was low, but the choice of a public two-year institution was also necessitated by the families' undocumented status, which was a barrier to admission at most four-year colleges and a source of frustration to these college-ready young people. By the time Gustavo's youngest son, Diego, was ready for college, his family was "legal." A soccer star in both high school and college, he graduated in 2010 with a psychology major from Stony Brook, a research university at the top of the New York State university system with a strong reputation for preparing undergraduate students for elite professional schools.

For the sons of Manuel and Juanita, immigration policy still limits expectations, at least for now. The branches of the New York State and New York City university systems where Pablo and Andres study charge them only in-state tuition, a benefit available in only sixteen states as of early 2014.[4] Their undocumented status renders them ineligible, however, for either state or federal financial aid, not even in the form of loans or work-study assignments. (A few states—Minnesota and California, notably—make state grants available to undocumented students, but New York has rejected such a proposal.) Although both are authorized to work as recipients of DACA permits, it is unclear whether that program will be renewed under a different president, and in any case, it does not convey the status of a green card or even a student visa. Pablo will soon graduate from Baruch College, a branch of the City University of New York known for its business programs, and he is interning with a Wall Street firm. But for the time being, a change in his status is not in the cards. As he looks for a permanent job at a time when even well-prepared college graduates are having difficulty finding and keeping good jobs, he is at a competitive disadvantage.

◆ ◆ ◆

Young, childless people come to the United States with a wide variety of memories, impulses, and images in mind. Like Rigoberta, they may be fleeing violence or threats of violence; like Javier, they may be yearning for renewed connection with a parent; or like Edgar, they may want a future more appealing than feeding the chickens and taking the cheese to market. But migrants who are parents all share an abiding concern: they want a tangible improvement in their children's lives.

It may be a primary motive or one that lurks beneath the immediate instinct for survival. It also manifests itself differently for different immigrants: the father who comes alone and sends remittances to ensure that his children are warm and dry, eating well, growing up in conditions that will support a life in the home country; the mother whose principal concern is saving enough money to enable her children to follow her to the new land; the family who decides that they will sink or swim together and arrives with children who are immediately launched on their new American lives.

Choosing the latter route imposed significant burdens on the children of the Acero-Pinzón clan. The initial language barrier was frustrating, and immigration policies denied them opportunities available to other young people. But these obstacles beyond their control have not defeated them. On the Acero side, all three of Mireya and Gustavo's sons have budding professional careers—Gustavo as a graphic designer, Edgar as a sports journalist in Los Angeles, and Diego as a traveling nurse, interning in hospitals around the country and studying to become a nurse practitioner. Nathalie Galindo, daughter of Clara and niece of Gustavo and Patty, has lived up to the most ambitious family expectations with her degrees from Harvard. Despite the handicap of still being without visas or green cards, the Pinzón sons, Pablo and Andres, seem destined for success in business. The accomplishments of these young people continually validate their parents' choice to endure the hardships of leaving the home they loved but rejected. And both the Aceros' and the Pinzóns' offspring reciprocate their parents' support of them. Edgar Acero wrote on the Baruch College website the year he graduated that the person he most admired was his father, and Pablo Pinzón, who described the trip from Colombia as an "odyssey [that] changed my life," also credited it with teaching him to be "strong and responsible."

What of the youngest migrants of this clan?

Angel came to Greenport with Manuel and Juanita when he was not yet two, so he knows Colombia only through photographs and the efforts his parents have made to connect him to Colombian culture. "I have been brought up here, adapted to the culture; I'm used to how everything is," he says. A twiggy fourteen-year-old, he is taller than his father and brothers. He says he feels both Colombian and American, equally interested in soccer and basketball. His first exposure to English came when he attended the local Head Start program, and later he needed help to catch up with his American peers. He repeated first grade—"I didn't read as well as I should"—and spent three years in the ESL class. He likes school, though, and assumes he will go to college. His favorite subjects are math and science, and he is now on the high honor roll in the Greenport junior high school.

Three grades above him is his cousin Valentina. (Technically, they are not cousins—her father is Angel's aunt's brother-in law—but these families are so intertwined that it hardly matters.) She too is a top student, poised and articulate, enrolled in the AP global history course as a tenth grader and proud of her accomplishments. "My teacher said I got out of ESL faster than anyone," she chuckles. Having arrived in Greenport at age seven, she remembers her family's challenges, although she is careful to not to exaggerate their effect on her. "I don't remember it being hard. My parents took care of everything. My sister was fifteen and did really well, but it was way harder for her than for me," she says. She notes that her sister, Vanessa, graduated second in her Greenport High School class but couldn't go to private college and couldn't get financial aid because of her immigration status. "I am very lucky. I haven't had to struggle," she says.

Both of these teenagers assume that they will have comfortable American lives as they mature. Valentina—along with her sister and Angel's two older brothers—is a beneficiary of the DACA program, and Angel will "age into" eligibility when he turns fifteen. They anticipate immigration reform that will include them, and they look forward to being able to visit their home country. With many American friends and support from family, school, and community, they enjoy a level of integration not often seen among Greenport's Latinos.

It is easy to conclude that the present successes and future bright prospects for the Pinzóns and Aceros rest primarily on strong family ties. Bonds are undeniably strong and are continually reinforced. In February 2014 one of Patty's nephews (not a Greenport resident) got married, and the entire clan, almost fifty strong, met in Florida for the wedding. Anticipating the visit of Juanita's brother's family during the 2013 Christmas vacation, Angel looked forward to showing the cousins he had known only through photos and phone calls the wonders of New York City. And the advantages of the migration chain, where the earliest to immigrate lend a hand (and more) to the later arrivals, extend well beyond family celebrations. Valentina remembers very few adjustment problems. "It was pretty comfortable for me," she says. "When I got here my cousins were already in school, and they spoke perfect English."

But a close family is not the only advantage that these young people and their parents have as they become integrated into US society. Among Greenport's Mexicans and Central Americans, family ties are also strong. The Colombians benefit from their class position. It enables them to mix with the native-born more easily than most other Greenport immigrants. It's not just that the adults arrived with more education and at least a bit of savings to tide them over while they launched their new lives. They are also closer to many local citizens in a social hierarchy defined by ethnicity and race. For many observers, Colombia seems to be closer to Western Europe than to Latin America and Colombians to occupy a higher plane than, say, Guatemalans or Salvadorans. Manuel Pinzón points out that physical appearance matters. "Most Americans don't think we are Hispanics. They think my wife and I are Italian or from Spain. Because of their physical aspect—short and dark—Americans can discriminate against those from Central America."

Angel and Valentina and their older cousins and siblings are less likely to face discrimination. Beyond their ethnic advantage, they are smart and good-looking and conscientious; they fit right in. As he looks to the future of the young, Manuel is optimistic. "Here, with two languages and a good education, I think my sons can find good jobs without *palanca.*"

PART VIII

What Next?

The New American

Physically, Maria Rivera conforms to the stereotype of the middle-aged Mexican woman. She is short and solid, with a mass of black curls and a warm smile. But everything else about her defies stereotypes of any kind. She is a seeker, a leader, waiting for a chance to be a political presence. She sees herself as half American, with American values and American energy.

From the beginning, images of America and its promise shaped her life. Her aunt and uncle had migrated to the United States in the early 1960s, seeking a better life in New York City and hoping to bring their children north. At the time there were not many Mexicans in the city and few people to help them with English. They ate cat food when they arrived, because they knew the words "tuna fish," which they saw on the cans. But they adjusted quickly, and in 1965 Maria's aunt convinced her sister to bring her baby—Maria—to be baptized in Saint Patrick's Cathedral. After a six-month stay, Maria and her mother returned to Mexico City, but the die was cast. Soon afterward Maria's cousins joined their parents in New York, and throughout her childhood the family held out the prospect of more trips to New York, the rich, exciting metropolis where anything was possible.

This was an era when many immigrant families—even those of the working class—lived at least a part of their lives in both the country where they were born and the country where they settled. Especially if they were from nearby Mexico, migrants could take vacations "at home" and thereby expose their children to their traditions and rituals and preserve family ties more generally. Participating in a local festival or religious pilgrimage would give Americanized children rich experience that would boost their self-confidence as they faced discrimination or deprivation in the United States. A returning migrant could see and stay in the fine house his remittances had paid for. Transnational lives could affect communities as well as the families left behind. From their American homes, migrants could fund economic development projects in their hometowns and even influence local elections.[1]

While Maria's family did not have all the advantages of easy transnationalism, border and visa control were not such hurdles then as they are now, and some relatives went back and forth, at least occasionally. When Maria turned fifteen her *quinceañera* gift was a trip to New York. Once more she came with her mother—somewhat ambivalent at leaving her friends and her school. Arriving in New York City, she enrolled in the local junior high school, where she felt completely out of place. In Mexico City, there were uniforms and rules, but her classmates in Queens acted with a kind of freedom that she found frightening. "Teenagers have liberty to do whatever they want. I see them kissing or touching in the corners at school. That is very surprising to me." It was a harsh introduction to sexualized American youth. The school was in a large building with an elevator, which suggested terrifying possibilities. "Sometimes the kids stop the elevator in the middle and do stupid things and it's very bad for me." She shudders. The last straw was when the school sent home a notice that Maria would be given birth control pills unless her mother signed a rejection form and waived any claim against the school if her daughter got pregnant. Shortly afterward, Maria went home to Mexico "because I am so nervous and I don't feel happy here."

But the pull of the north was still powerful. In the wake of the financial collapse of 1982 in Mexico, Maria's mother heeded her sister's plea: It's better here, even if you are working in a sweatshop in the garment district. And Maria was soon to follow.

◆ ◆ ◆

When Maria returned to Mexico City, it was to work. The family had fallen on hard times; her parents had separated, and there was no money for school. Arriving from the United States, she enrolled in a vocational program, at the urging of her father, to become an industrial mechanic. She had wanted to work in a hospital, but, as she says, "In Mexico, the parents often decide what you will be." She hated her studies, and after a year she quit. But the next move introduced her to work she loved and still pursues: she found a part-time job in a hospital, giving shots to children.

But then disaster struck—literally. The economic crisis that had propelled her mother to seek work in the United States was beginning to ease in September 1985, when the worst earthquake of the century occurred in Mexico City. A second quake the next day compounded the harm, leveling weakened structures. Estimates of lives lost range upward from ten thousand. Over fifty thousand buildings suffered mild to severe damage. The greatest harm was concentrated in an area with many hospitals, where more than nine hundred patients, doctors, nurses, and medical students died.[2] Almost half of the public sector beds in the city were lost; several hospitals—Maria's among them—simply collapsed. Her job was gone.

The transnational lives of her family offered a solution. From New York, her mother assured her that she would find work there and sent her money for a plane ticket. Her father invented a deceit that worked: Maria applied for and received a ten-year work visa with the support of her father's boss, alleging that she would be traveling for his company. This precious document meant that she never had to cross the US-Mexico border on the ground, with its physical and legal hazards. It also enabled her to return to Mexico to see her family and escort two nephews back to the United States.

That benefit, however, did not provide her with a good job, and it didn't advance what she had hoped would be a medical career. The day after she arrived in New York—at her mother's house on the western end of Long Island—she went to work. "It was a bad experience," she says. She vividly recalls the indignities. As a live-in housekeeper, she had to cook breakfast for her employers. They asked her to set the table with a paper plate on the side. "When they finish eating, the things they don't want to eat they put on that plate and give it to me for eating. I only worked there for one week." A subsequent job on the assembly line of a factory that made light switches and plugs was much better, but in 1994 the company moved south, leaving her jobless once again. For a time, she took care of her young son Danny and the Mexican nephews while her mother and a sister worked. As the children grew up, she returned to housecleaning. By then her visa had expired. Without a high school education, legal residency, or a good command of English, she did not have many choices.

Her life improved when she married and moved to Greenport. Her husband Max was a former soldier from El Salvador who became a citizen in 2001. That year they had a son, also named Max, now in junior high school. But even after Maria got her green card in 2010, she was still cleaning houses, although now her job was housekeeping at Peconic Landing, which provided her with good benefits and a comfortable work environment. Domestic work is hard on a forty-nine-year-old body, "very physical," she sighs. "I have to carry the vacuum, supplies, in and out of residents' houses or apartments four times a day. The vacuum is heavy and I'm very tired when I get home. My body will not support me for another ten years." Sometimes Maria jokes with her best friend, also a housekeeper: "You want to be working here many, many years, cleaning the house with a cane?" "This is a country of opportunities," she says. "But it's not easy."

She still dreams of work that will bring her closer to the medical field she had yearned for thirty years ago in Mexico. A local training program to become a certified nursing assistant and provide home care beckons. Maria feels very strongly about caring for the elderly, which she associates with the spirit of home. Spanish culture gives you heart and feelings, she says; people don't send their mothers to the nursing home. In this respect, she is on guard to protect against American influences on her children. "Little Max said once, 'When you are old, I am going to send you to a nursing home.' I was horrified. This is not the Spanish way." She told Max she wanted him to take care of her and pointed out that when they took a teddy bear Max had made to a nursing home resident, the woman clung to it. Max revised his plan; he said that when he grew up, he would have a house with a wide staircase to the second floor that would accommodate a wheelchair. Maria was greatly relieved.

◆ ◆ ◆

Esquipulas is a small city in southeastern Guatemala, a pilgrimage destination for hundreds of thousands of Central Americans every year. Housed in a huge white basilica, the attraction is a wooden crucifix called the Black Christ. In 1595 Spanish priests commissioned it from a local sculptor who chose balsam wood either to match the skin color of the indigenous people (the explanation on tourist brochures) or to portray the dried blood encrusted on Christ's body after the beating he endured before his crucifixion (the ecclesiastical explanation). By now the color has darkened to the color of black coffee. Miracles attributed to the statue began with the visit of the bishop of Guatemala in the mid-eighteenth century, according to local lore, though there is no specific miracle that first drew the faithful to it. Recognizing the draw of a sacred icon, clerical authorities replaced the modest thatched chapel that initially housed the statue with the church that stands today. Despite the lack of a founding miracle, the faithful come to thank the Lord for a benefit received—a sailor returned from the sea or child healed—or to request deliverance from a current woe. Although the Black Christ is celebrated in Esquipulas all year, the rest of the Latino world—including Central Americans in American communities—honors the statue on or around January 15.

Greenport draws Guatemalans from all over the North Fork for the Festival of Esquipulas. In 2012 Maria was a vigorous presence at the celebration held at Saint Agnes Parish, even though she isn't Guatemalan. She performed the traditional dances, dressed in the vivid attire of the Guatemalan women who arrived for the party, and dished up beans for the tostadas of the celebratory meal. She was in a good mood; she told everyone who would listen that her older son Danny would be finished with his navy boot camp in a couple of weeks and that he aspired to be a Navy SEAL—undaunted when she heard how much competition there would be for the elite squad.

It was a testament to what is most important in her life—her church, her commitment to Hispanic traditions and connections, and her family. Asked why she celebrates Esquipulas in addition to helping organize the Mexican feast of Guadalupe, she says, "I don't have lines. No matter whether you are from a different country, you all speak Spanish and try to help each other. Here, you have to meet different kinds of people from different countries. You can make a life that is similar, sometimes different in little aspects but in general the same." That perspective helps to compensate for what she misses from home—the close family when everyone came to the huge dinners her mother made on Sunday. "Migration can break families apart," she says, so you have to make a family here.

Neither material nor educational deprivation gets in the way of Maria's defense of the rights and interests of her family. In 2009 her husband Max was working for a paving company that could no longer afford to provide health insurance for its workers. He had a gastrointestinal disorder, and his doctor told him he needed to have a colonoscopy. Maria was frantic, determined to get him medical care. Her limited education slowed her down but did not defeat her. Initially she signed up for a discount service that promoted itself as health insurance for undocumented immigrants who wouldn't be eligible for most plans. This didn't make sense: her husband wasn't undocumented (although, at the time, she was) and many important benefits were not included in the discount plan. She didn't understand the difference between this service and real insurance. But she was tireless in pursuing a solution, asking everyone she knew for information about alternatives. She finally found out that, since her husband's hours had been reduced due to the economic downturn, he and her sons would qualify for New York's Family Health Plus for families with incomes too high for Medicaid.[3] Making her way through the thicket of bureaucratic brambles that can deter even people with advanced degrees, she was indignant that it was the Great Recession that made her family eligible for public health insurance. They worked hard, after all; it felt as though they were being punished for that.

One day in 2009 Maria's second son, Max, then eight, did not want to go to school (in Southold, not Greenport), and Maria noticed a scratch on his face. After coaxing from him the story of how another child had attacked him because he refused to hand over his milk, Maria determined to speak to the school principal. When she arrived at his office, a social worker tried to deflect her by saying they didn't have translators to help her. She didn't need a translator; she needed to convey her concern directly to the principal. "I don't want someone else to tell him what happened because if you change one word, two words, it can make a difference." She told the social worker she had taken the day off from work—which wasn't true—and would sit outside the principal's office until he had time for her. She prevailed. "I talk to the principal, and I tell him my son don't want to come to school any more, he's giving me a hard time in the morning, he's not a bad kid, and I want to go to my job and not worry about my son. I said, I just want you to be watching what happens at lunchtime." She also threatened to go to the police if another such thing occurred.

For Maria, this was not an act of boldness. It was just standing up for someone she cares about, something she did even when undocumented. To hold people to account for what they say and do is a guiding principle. When a receptionist at the local hospital treated her rudely, she complained and got an apology. She holds everyone to the same standard, troubled as much by fellow Hispanics who take more than they need from the Saint Agnes soup kitchen as by people in authority who treat immigrants "like a mouse or a cat—a very small animal." When the Southold school social worker, who was Latina, tried to keep her from speaking with the school principal, "I say to her, 'You have to help the Hispanic people. If you don't do that, they don't trust anybody.'" During Maria's first months in New York City as an adult, she sometimes got lost in the subway system. She saw many people she assumed were Hispanic, but when she asked for help, some said, "Oh no, I speak English," which she did not believe and found appalling.

◆ ◆ ◆

When the US Citizenship and Immigration Services called Maria in for an interview in response to her application for a marriage-based green card, she was told to bring someone to help her with English as well as all documents relevant to proving the legitimacy of her marriage. She knew that she would be quizzed about her relationship with Max, and she was prepared. Sure enough, the officer asked her about the marks on her husband's body, his favorite foods, and so on. Maria is not easily intimidated and perhaps her belief in herself helped her case. She told the officer she didn't need a translator and gave him her album with wedding pictures and the birth certificate of little Max. When he asked to put the album in his file, she refused. "I said I wanted to keep it, that he could take anything else." Perhaps because her husband had a post office box at an address different from their apartment, the officer took Max aside and questioned him much more aggressively. He withstood scrutiny, however, and in 2010 Maria became a legal permanent resident. Asked how she felt when she got the news, she said, "They gave me wings to fly."

Those wings have carried her to new worlds. No longer forced to work off the books, she got a new job with benefits; her health insurance covered consultation for a bout with tendonitis, and the copay was only ten dollars for the medicine she needed. In the past she had never driven; now she took the county bus to a driver's education class twenty-five miles away until she got her license. Beyond her new legal status, her green card gave her a new identity. Her life changed "360 degrees," she says. "I think you grow up when you get your permit to work. Now people talk to you with respect." She had always been active at Saint Agnes, reading scripture to the congregation in the Saturday night Spanish service; now she served on the parish council. Her pursuit of the education she has missed was less successful. Trying to study for her GED, she found the practice essays very demanding—she still wrestles with the past tenses in English—and has postponed that challenge.

These days her crusade is to become a citizen. It has been more than three years since she got her green card, so she is eligible to apply. She is studying for the civics test by going over sample questions with young Max. The ceremony has particular meaning for her as she remembers the process of getting citizenship for her husband. He had fled El Salvador during its civil war and was detained at the US-Mexico border for three months, after which he was granted Temporary Protected Status and then asylum. "When he got his citizenship, I couldn't be with him. I am so glad he can be with me."

◆ ◆ ◆

Maria and her husband have bought a house in Greenport—a small, comfortable house on a quiet corner, the fulfillment of a long-held dream. It's a place in which she can bring the past and present together and chart the expected future. Although Maria frets about the expenses of homeownership, she also feels confident that she's launched on a good American life. Her husband now has a job with a successful paving company, and her sons are thriving—Danny, in the navy, is the father of a baby girl, and Max is always on the honor roll. It gives her satisfaction to remember her earlier life and contrast it with the present. "When I was little, sometimes I had only black coffee in my belly, but my son has all the food and clothes he needs."

Other relatives have done well too: cousins with professional careers in the United States as well as a nephew who returned to Mexico after American high school, married a doctor, and now teaches English in a university there. She laughs at the memory of what he was like as a toddler when she had to tie him to a sofa to keep an eye on him while she cleaned the house. He was her favorite, and she is proud of his accomplishments, seeing them as an endorsement of her family's strategy of living transnationally in the battle against poverty. "He broke the chain," she says, "with a successful life and a career in Mexico."

Although family triumphs are foremost for the moment, Maria is also thinking about the larger community of which she is a part. As a citizen, she looks forward to voting and joining with others to exercise the power of the collective voice. "I am expecting that voting will give Spanish people many more opportunities," she says. She is optimistic that immigration reform is coming and sees a multilingual future in which, even as Hispanics master English, more and more Americans will be learning Spanish. "If everybody gets papers, it will make a big difference—in this country and in their countries, too." It's a confident vision of an integrated nation.

CHAPTER 11

A Small-Town Model?

In some respects, Greenport may be unique—its history of boom and bust, its shifting demographics over two hundred years, its fusion of the influences of sea and soil. But its waves of immigrants reflect the patterns of American development quite precisely. The Protestants who crossed Long Island Sound from New Haven were participants in the colonial empire building that defined the New World of the seventeenth century. Portuguese adventurers defied traditional restrictions of place to get off the whaling ship, arriving in Greenport in the mid-nineteenth century much as, a few decades later, Chinese and Irish laborers populated new settlements in the westward push propelled by the opening of the transcontinental railroad. The products of Italian craftsmen and Polish farmers who came to the North Fork at the turn of the twentieth century housed and fed the denizens of New York as it and other cities became the great industrial maw that heralded the American Century. Finally, nowadays Greenport's Latino immigrants and their children are drops in the "golden stream"—Andrew Carnegie's characterization of those who came a century ago—that flows through the country, spreading beyond the southwestern border into cities and small towns previously unacquainted with Spanish language and cultures. Once again, immigrants are redefining national character and direction. As Latino arrivals have helped revitalize Greenport, so they have breathed new life into Ulysses, Kansas; Dalton, Georgia; Beardstown, Illinois; St. James, Minnesota; and Denison, Iowa, to name just a few.

Can this energy be sustained, bringing economic health to other small communities? What would it take for immigrants, in tandem with American hosts, to bring prosperity to small towns that have suffered a century-long slump? And how can Greenport, initially successful at absorbing today's immigrants, nourish that accomplishment in ways that foster true integration?

It is beyond the scope of this book to make predictions about how economic growth (or the lack of it) will affect today's immigrants or how immigration policy will evolve to improve (or not) the lives of people who are now waiting for some form of greater inclusion in the American polity. Those large forces will shape the future for both immigrants and the native-born in small towns, as they shaped the way those towns lost population in the past and the ways in which they revived, if they did. Local decisions and actions will also have an effect, however. Efforts at economic recovery that benefits from rural immigration and fosters integration are still relatively new and tend to be clustered in the Midwest, where the decline of agriculture has forced the hand of municipal leaders. So it is hazardous to make generalizations about what works. But a few themes characterize the successes of small towns that have recovered from dark times and accommodated recent immigration.

Investment in infrastructure is one. It can stem outmigration, attract visitors, and provide local jobs. Perry, Iowa, population 7,702 in 2010 (one-third Hispanic, most thought to be immigrants) is one of several Iowa towns that have taken this route. With a recently renovated bank and hotel and an industrial park that includes a hog-processing plant employing more than a thousand workers, it has also established the Van Kirk Career Academy to supplement its branch of Des Moines Area Community College. Independence, Oregon, population 8,650 in 2012 (35 percent Hispanic, 10 percent estimated to be immigrants), was designated an All-America City in 2014, based in part on the success of a ten-year program of economic development. As agricultural revenue sagged, the town galvanized residents to plan and rebuild the business district. "The consensus was that small communities live and die with their downtowns," wrote the planning director in the All-America City Award application.[1]

These communities have realized that fitting their new working class into economic recovery requires conscious effort and planning. Acknowledging a shortage of housing for the immigrants, Perry's comprehensive plan calls for redevelopment of "diverse housing" (a euphemism for low-cost housing?) and, looking about twenty years down the road, annexing land for longer-term growth.[2] To move beyond its downtown revitalization projects, Independence undertook a planning process that involved more than a thousand residents (over 10 percent of the population) in surveys and meetings. With support from the federal stimulus package and the Workforce Investment Act, young workers took jobs building parks, ball fields, and a bike path, which boosted local employment.

Residents and officials have not always welcomed the arrival of immigrants in smaller communities. Resistance has usually taken the form of citizen complaints to the media and sporadic trash talk in neighborhood watering holes. In Hazelton, Pennsylvania, however, the mayor pushed through a local law that would have fined landlords a thousand dollars for renting to undocumented immigrants and revoked business licenses of employers who hired them. The ordinance was struck down by the Court of Appeals for the Third Circuit as infringing on federal authority to regulate immigration enforcement, but it had spawned similar legislation elsewhere and served as a reminder that demographic transformation requires tolerance, calm, and respect for the Constitution.[3]

What can Greenport take from these experiences and others like them? Perhaps it is important to start with an awareness of some advantages the village enjoys as it confronts the next stage of development with an immigrant population (including, importantly, the American-born children) that seems likely to remain. Unlike Perry, Iowa, it has multifamily housing available for low-income tenants, if only it can control overcrowding and keep rentals reasonably priced. Unlike many towns in the Midwest, the schools are not closing, a sign of the aging of the population and the job loss and local depression that follow. Unlike the Iowa and Minnesota towns that rely on agribusiness behemoths like Tyson Foods, Greenport's employers are small businesses that operate in a number of sectors; if one fails or relocates, the local economy is not held hostage. And unlike Hazelton or Maricopa County, Arizona (where Sheriff Joe Arpaio has, until recently, reigned supreme), overtly anti-immigrant hostility is rare.

But Greenport has also not engaged in the kind of strategic planning that has brought economic success to some revitalized small towns. How can the village retain its vitality and charm in the face of real estate speculation that, driving up house prices, threatens to turn it into another homogeneous, exurban outpost for affluent New Yorkers? What kind of economic development could supplement the amenities that bring visitors in the warm months but leave locals—immigrants and native-born alike—without work in the cold ones? Where are the jobs that provide upward mobility for immigrants and their children, fostering entrepreneurship that supports middle-class people of whatever origin?

One key to successful revitalization is building on what you already have. Perry has focused on creating walking and biking trails that connect with an existing regional system; Independence developed an amphitheater and a greenway along the Willamette River. Greenport has resources aplenty to develop for a winter economy. With some municipal energy and a willingness to take a few financial risks, businesses that preserve and market the produce and seafood of nearby farms and waterways could take off. Initiatives to manage wastewater runoff on the North Fork have already attracted attention from the federal government; it's a promising area for job development. But growth that would buttress the core economy of a town now so dependent on tourism and leisure requires deep community engagement to come up with a plan.

Such a commitment assumes a spirit of inclusion on the part of the planners. That spirit dominates in some arenas in Greenport, but not in others. Employers who are grateful for the labor of their immigrant workers may not be so happy to have them living across the street. Teachers who work tirelessly to perfect the English of their students and get them college-ready may be less willing to promote the interests of adults whose language and culture they don't understand. Future social relations in Greenport may be a test of what sociologists call the contact hypothesis, which holds that under the right conditions, antagonisms between groups can lessen as a result of personal acquaintance.[4]

The right conditions are hard to find. Police, for example, do not predictably become less racially antagonistic as they interact with people of a different race. Some of the most positive conclusions, however, have come from the study of attitudes toward homosexuals, where the experience of people becoming acquainted with gays—or discovering that people they already knew were homosexual—dissolved previous bias.[5] Another right condition often cited as a prerequisite for establishing friendly contact between groups is the possibility of cooperation in an important activity. Sharing military goals, black and white soldiers can serve together; concern for the welfare of children can bring parents of different races and classes together in a school. By and large—there are exceptions, of course—whites and Latinos in Greenport do not, as yet, have equal social and economic status. But they do cooperate in many spheres, and the contact can lead to mutual acceptance and respect, and occasionally friendship.

Sister Margaret—ever the realist, despite her religious role—thinks there will be no real integration in Greenport until Latino and Anglo families are going to dinner in each other's houses—in the next generation, she thinks. Another indisputable sign will be frequent intermarriage. (Not incidentally, in Ulysses, Kansas, one of the midwestern towns being transformed by Hispanic migration, thirteen of the 102 babies born in 2010 had one white and one Hispanic parent.[6]) It would be nice to think that real integration of Greenport's Latinos would happen sooner than Sister Margaret predicts. But congressional unwillingness to act decisively on immigration reform and uncertainty about the economic fortunes of both the country and the village are forces that undercut progress toward this goal. Even in such a tiny community, acceptance of such a different demographic future requires a congeries of forces: private and public vision, the fiscal capacity to implement the vision, human commitment to change, and a large dose of luck. The combination is a daunting challenge.

NOTES

CHAPTER 1 — HOLA, GREENPORT

1. Minneapolis Foundation, "A New Age of Immigrants: Making Immigration Work for Minnesota," August 2010, 30.

2. "Heartland Hispanics Bolstering Local Economies," CBN News, April 2, 2013, http://www.cbn.com/cbnnews/us/2013/April/Heartland-Hispanics-Bolstering-Local-Economies/.

3. For a discussion of the prospects of immigration as a remedy for the decline of some small towns, see Patrick J. Carr, Daniel T. Lichter, and Maria J. Kefalas, "Can Immigration Save Small-Town America? Hispanic Boomtowns and the Uneasy Path to Renewal," *Annals of the American Academy of Political and Social Science* 641 (2012): 38–57.

4. Suffolk County Comprehensive Plan 2035, vol. 1, chap. 2, August 2011, http://www.suffolkcountyny.gov/Portals/0/planning/CompPlan/v011/V011EXESUMRE8182011.pdf.

5. "At Gateway to Hamptons the Ku Klux Klan Advertises for New Members," *New York Times*, August 29, 2014.

6. Southern Poverty Law Center, "Climate of Fear: Latino Immigrants in Suffolk County, New York," 2009, http://www.splcenter.org/get-informed/publications/climate-of-fear-latino-immigrants-in-suffolk-county-ny.

7. Extrapolated from FBI Uniform Crime Reports, "Hate Crime Statistics 2011," http://www.fbi.gov/about-us/cjis/ucr/hate-crime/2011/narratives/incidents-and-offenses.

8. Michael Savage, *The Savage Nation* (radio program), July 5, 2007.

9. *Henderson v. Mayor of New York City*, 92 U.S. 259, 260 (1875).

10. Robert P. Jones et al., "What Americans Want from Immigration Reform in 2014," Public Religion Research Institute and The Brookings Institution, 2014, http://www.brookings.edu/~/media/research/files/reports/2014/06/10-immigration-reform-survey/finalimmigrationsurvey-(2).pdf.

11. *Suffolk Times*, September 15, 2012.

12. "Village Needs Enforcement, Not New Code Provisions," *Suffolk Times*, June 24, 2010.

13. Quoted in Kitty Colavita, "Mexican Immigration to the USA: The Contradictions of Border Control," in *The Cambridge Survey of World Migration*, ed. Robin Cohen (Cambridge: Cambridge University Press, 1995), 236.

14. Andrew Carnegie, *Triumphant Democracy; or, Fifty Years March of the Republic* (New York: Charles Scribner & Sons, 1886), 34–35.

15. Quoted in David Nasaw, *Andrew Carnegie* (New York: Penguin Press, 2006), 342.

PROFILE — LOST AND FOUND

1. "Bush to Press Free Trade in a Place Where Young Children Still Cut the Cane," *New York Times*, March 12, 2007.

2. Laurance Wolff and Martin Gurría, "Money Counts: Projecting Education Expenditures in Latin America and the Caribbean to the Year 2015," UNESCO Institute for Statistics, 2005, http://www.uis.unesco.org/Library/Documents/wp05-en.pdf.

3. "Guatemala," CIA World Factbook, 2014, https://www.cia.gov/library/publications/the-world-factbook/geos/gt.html.

CHAPTER 2 — THE EUROPEAN LEGACY

1. "The Indian Archeology of Long Island," Garvies Point Museum and Preserve, http://www.garviespointmuseum.com/indian-archaeology-long-island.php#3.

2. Epher Whitaker, *A History of Southold, Long Island: Its First Century* (privately printed, 1881), 39.

3. Antonia Booth, "A Brief Account of Southold's History," Southold, NY, http://ny-southold.civicplus.com/index.aspx?nid=159.

4. *Southold Town Records*, 3 vols. (Riverhead, NY: S. W. Green's Son, 1882), 1:154.

5. 1658 Deposition of Thomas Osman (copy), *Southold Town, 1636–1939* (commemorative book, 1939), 8.

6. Donald M. Bayles, "Hashamomuck and Arshamomaque," 2011, unpublished essay, Southold Free Library.

7. Whitaker, *History of Southold*, 27, points out that some of the men who supposedly took this voyage were "scarcely born in 1640."

8. Booth, "Brief Account."

9. Edward Rodolphus Lambert, *History of the Colony of New Haven: Before and After the Union with Connecticut* (New Haven, CT: Hitchcock and Stafford, 1838), 185.

10. Richard Ellis, *Men and Whales* (New York: Knopf, 1991), 99.

11. Eric J. Dolin, *Leviathan: The History of Whaling in America* (New York: Norton, 2007), 47.

12. Ibid.

13. Augustus Griffin, *The Diaries of Augustus Griffin, 1792–1852*, ed. Fredrica Wachsberger (Orient, NY: Oysterponds Historical Society, 2004), 138.

14. Ibid., 262.

15. Dolin, *Leviathan*, 44 (table 2).

16. Ibid., 223.

17. Wesley Logan Baker, *Study of the 1658 and 1686 Depositions of Thomas Osman and Early History of Hashamomuck in the Town of Southold, Long Island, N.Y.* (n.p., 1969). Database online provided by Generations Network, Provo, UT, 2005. http://search

.ancestry.com/search/db.aspx?dbid=20847.

18. *Southold Town Records*, 1:98n.

19. Ibid., 422–423.

20. Antonia Booth and Mark Terry, "Ardent Spirits and Brickmaking in Southold, Part I," *Peconic Bay Shopper*, November 2009, 15.

21. US Immigration and Naturalization Service, Statistical Yearbook of the Immigration and Naturalization Service, 2001, table 2.

22. See Booth and Terry, "Ardent Spirits and Brickmaking in Southold, Part II," *Peconic Bay Shopper*, December 2009, 1–9, for a detailed account of the growth of local brickmaking in the late nineteenth century.

23. *Long Island Traveler*, July 15, 1887.

CHAPTER 3 — BOOM, BUST, AND BACK AGAIN

1. Elsie Knapp Corwin, *Greenport, Yesterday and Today: The Diary of a Country Newspaper* (Greenport, NY: Suffolk Times, 1972), 22–23.

2. Epher Whitaker, *Whitaker's Southold: Being a Substantial Reproduction of the History of Southold, L.I.; Its First Century* (Princeton, NJ: Princeton University Press, 1931), 177.

3. "Statistics and Speculations Concerning the Pacific Railroad," *Putnam's Magazine*, September 1853, reprinted in *Putnam's Magazine: Original Papers on Literature, Science, Art, and National Interests*, vol. 2 (New York: G. P. Putnam, 1858), 271, https://books.google .com/books?id=og5BAQAAMAAJ&pg=PA692&dq="Statistics+and+Speculations +Concerning+the+Pacific+Railroad,"&hl=en&sa=X&ei=n4qcVISzNJWTsQTj _YH4DQ&ved=0CB8Q6AEwAA#v=onepage&q="Statistics%20and%20Speculations %20Concerning%20the%20Pacific%20Railroad%2C"&f=false.

4. Whitaker, *Whitaker's Southold*, 177.

5. Walt Whitman, "East Long Island." Reprinted from the *Brooklyn Daily Eagle*, June 27, 1846, in Walt Whitman and Emory Holloway, *The Uncollected Poetry and Prose of Walt Whitman: With Various Early Manuscripts V1*, vol. 1 (Garden City, NY: Doubleday Page, 1921), 118.

6. David S. Reynolds, *Walt Whitman's America* (New York: Knopf, 1995), 342.

7. Ibid., 70–73.

8. Aristide Zolberg, *A Nation by Design: Immigration Policy in the Fashioning of America* (Cambridge, MA: Harvard University Press, 2006), 126.

9. Benjamin Franklin Thompson, *History of Long Island: Containing an Account of the Discovery and Settlement; with Other Important and Interesting Matters to the Present Time* (New York: E. French, 1839), 252.

10. Patrick J. Blessing, "Irish Immigrants to America," *Irish Studies* 4 (1985): 11–38.

11. *Suffolk Times*, October 10, 1930.

12. *Suffolk Times*, April 24, 1936.

13. *Long Island Traveler*, March 8, 1889.

14. Rosalind Case Newell, *Rose Remembers* (Mattituck, NY: Amereon, 2008), 134.

15. Geoffrey K. Fleming and Amy Kasuga Folk, *Hotels and Inns of Long Island's North Fork* (Charleston, SC: History Press, 2009), 117.

16. *Yearbook of Immigration Statistics: 2011*, Legal Permanent Residents, table 1, US

Department of Homeland Security, Office of Immigration Statistics, 2012, https://www
.dhs.gov/sites/default/files/publications/immigration-statistics/yearbook/2011/ois_yb
_2011.pdf.

CHAPTER 4 — MIGRATION FROM WITHIN

1. Isabel Wilkerson, *The Warmth of Other Suns* (New York: Random House, 2010), 536.

2. David S. Reynolds, *Walt Whitman's America* (New York: Knopf, 1995), 20.

3. Steve Wick, *Heaven and Earth* (New York: St. Martin's Press, 1996), 50.

4. Grania Bolton Marcus, *Discovering the African-American Experience in Suffolk County, 1620–1860* (Mattituck, NY: Amereon House, 1988), 14.

5. Ibid., 79.

6. Ira Berlin, *Many Thousands Gone: The First Two Centuries of Slavery in North America* (Cambridge, MA: Harvard University Press, 1998), 230–231.

7. Vivienne Kruger, "Born to Run: The Slave Family in Early New York, 1626 to 1827" (PhD diss., Columbia University, 1985).

8. Augustus Griffin, *The Diaries of Augustus Griffin 1792–1852*, ed. Fredrica Wachsberger (Orient, NY: Oysterponds Historical Society, 2004).

9. Dorothy Mealy, "Missing Life: A Matter of Talk," 1990, unpublished document available at Floyd Memorial Library, Greenport, NY (quoting Epher Whitaker, "The Christian at Work," March 6, 1879, an unpublished essay in the Brooklyn Historical Society archives).

10. Ira Berlin and Leslie M. Harris, eds., *Slavery in New York* (New York: New Press, 2005), 4.

11. Antonia Booth, "Wayland Jefferson, Southold's First Town Historian," in *Trawling My Town: Glimpses of Southold Past and Present* (Southold, NY: Academy Printing Services, 2012), 6.

12. Eric Foner, *Reconstruction: America's Unfinished Revolution* (New York: HarperCollins, 1989), 36.

13. Antonia Booth, "Local History of the KKK," *Peconic Bay Shopper*, July 2009, 6.

14. "Racial Problems Discussed," *Suffolk Times*, March 17, 1967

15. "When Whites Just Don't Get It, Part 4," *New York Times*, November 15, 2014.

CHAPTER 5 — IS DEMOGRAPHICS DESTINY?

1. US Bureau of the Census, 1960 Census of Population, New York, vol. 1, 19, table 7.

2. US Bureau of the Census, 1940 Census of Population, New York, vol. 1, 720, table 4.

3. Ibid., 326, table 22.

4. US Bureau of the Census, 1970 Census of Housing, New York, vol. 1, 132, table 27.

5. US Bureau of the Census, 1980 Census of Population, New York, General Population Characteristics, 567, table 42.

6. US Bureau of the Census, Profile of General Demographic Characteristics: 2000, Greenport Village, New York. table DP-1.

7. "A View from Main Street," keynote address of Dave Kapell, public launch of the Long Island Index, January 23, 2008, 3 (unpublished document in the author's possession).

8. See Hagedorn Foundation, "Census Analysis: Greenport Village," 2007 (unpublished

document in the author's possession). The 2000 census counted 353 Hispanics; the private census six years later estimated that there were 730, based on a sample of 19 percent of the households in Greenport Village. The margin of error for the survey was ±5.0 percent, with a 95 percent confidence level.

9. US Department of Homeland Security, *2011 Yearbook of Immigration Statistics*, 92, table 34, http://www.dhs.gov/sites/default/files/publications/immigration -statistics/yearbook/2011/ois_yb_2011.pdf.

10. US Bureau of the Census, Profile of General Population and Housing Characteristics: 2010, Greenport Village, New York, table DP-1. Hispanics constituted 746 residents out of 2,197.

11. Migration Policy Institute Data Hub, "Foreign-Born Population by Country of Birth, 2000, 2006–2011," http://www.migrationinformation.org/datahub/. Nationally, Mexican immigration increased by 28 percent, Salvadoran by 49 percent, Hondurans by 85 percent, and Guatemalans by 73 percent. It should be noted that not all Hispanics in Greenport are foreign-born. The private census taken in 2006 estimated that 24 percent were born in the United States, which probably reflected the Puerto Ricans surveyed and the children of recent immigrants.

12. Migration Information Source, "Central American Immigrants in the United States," March 2013, http://www.migrationpolicy.org/article/central-american -immigrants-united-states.

13. US Bureau of the Census, Profile of General Population and Housing Characteristics: 2010, Southold CDP, New York, table DP-1. In Greenport, 52.4 percent of housing units were rentals; in Southold, 16 percent.

14. For a synthesis of work on labor market segmentation, see Gilles Saint-Paul, *Dual Labor Markets: A Macroeconomic Perspective* (Cambridge, MA: MIT Press, 1996).

15. "Ethnicity and Jobs on Long Island," *Newsday*, http://data.newsday.com/long -island/data/jobs/ethnicity/.

16. Kenneth Hudson, "The New Labor Market Segmentation: Labor Market Dualism in the New Economy," *Social Science Research* 36 (2007): 286–312.

17. US Bureau of the Census, Median Income in the Past 12 Months, 2007–2011, American Community Survey Estimates, table S1903. These figures have large margins of error and should therefore be regarded cautiously as estimates. They indicate, however, trends and general comparisons that can be valuable for understanding the demography.

CHAPTER 6 — SCHOOLING NEW CITIZENS

1. *Long Island Traveler*, February 20, 1931.The department's report noted that farmworkers' pay ranged from $3.50 per day in the Northeastern states to just over $1.00 in the Deep South. In 1934 the local Potato Institute recommended a daily wage for potato workers of $2.55.

2. "Grandmothers of Greenport," unpublished transcript of a performance of recollections, 2005.

3. "Greenport School against Discrimination," *County Review*, February 17, 1949, 19.

4. The birth rate for foreign-born women in that period declined by 22 percent; for US-born women, by 11 percent. Pew Research Center, "U.S. Birth Rate Falls to a

Record Low; Decline Is Greatest among Immigrants," November 29, 2012, http://www.pewsocialtrends.org/2012/11/29/u-s-birth-rate-falls-to-a-record-low-decline-is-greatest-among-immigrants/.

5. Unless otherwise noted, data presented in the following paragraphs come from New York State report cards of 1998–1999 to 2012–2013 that can be found at https://reportcards.nysed.gov/.

6. Since the overwhelming majority of immigrant children in Greenport are of Hispanic descent and vice versa, I am treating the category of "Hispanic or Latino" in the state data as a proxy for immigrant children.

7. For information about the National Blue Ribbon Schools program, see http://www2.ed.gov/programs/nclbbrs/index.html.

8. The American Community Survey School District Demographic-Economic Dataset reports median household income of the Southold district to be $76,953 and of Greenport as $51,513, based on 2011 five-year estimates. See table E062 for both districts at http://proximityone.com/sd11dp3.htm.

9. Interestingly, disadvantaged students were 98.1 percent proficient in English and math, while a slightly smaller percentage of nondisadvantaged students (95 percent) were proficient. Presumably a number of these disadvantaged students who performed well were immigrants or the children of immigrants.

10. Education Law Center/Rutgers Graduate School of Education, "Is School Funding Fair? A National Report Card," http://www.schoolfundingfairness.org/National_Report_Card_2012.pdf.

11. Steve Billmyer, "New York Schools Ranked by Spending per Pupil," May 20, 2014, http://www.syracuse.com/news/index.ssf/2014/05/new_york_state_schools_ranked_by_spending_per_pupil_look_up_compare_any_district.html.

12. British Council, "How Young Children Learn English as Another Language," n.d., http://learnenglishkids.britishcouncil.org/en/parents/articles/how-young-children-learn-english-another-language.

13. Nancy S. Landale, R. Salvador Oropesa, and Cristina Bradatan, "Hispanic Families in the United States: Family Structure and Process in an Era of Family Change," *Hispanics and the Future of America*, ed. Marta Tienda and Faith Mitchell (Washington, DC: National Academies Press, 2006), chapter 5.

PROFILE — EDGAR AND THE BLUE MOSQUE

1. "El Salvador," CIA World Factbook, https://www.cia.gov/library/publications/the-world-factbook/geos/es.html.

2. "Immigrant Deaths Soar in South Texas," *My San Antonio*, December 30, 2012, http://www.mysanantonio.com/news/local_news/article/Border-woes-no-longer-just-on-the-border-4155003.php.

3. U.S. Customs and Border Protection, "Falfurrias Station," http://www.cbp.gov/border-security/along-us-borders/border-patrol-sectors/rio-grande-valley-sector-texas/falfurrias-station.

4. TRAC Immigration, Syracuse University, "Nature of Charge in New Filings Seeking Removal Orders through October 2014," http://trac.syr.edu/phptools/immigration/charges/apprep_newfiling_charge.php.

CHAPTER 7 — HOUSING OR HOUSES?

1. Greenport Zoning Board of Appeals, minutes of meeting, August 21, 2013. Material in the next four paragraphs comes from this source.

2. Gregory M. Maney and Margaret Abraham, "Whose Backyard? Boundary Making in NIMBY Opposition to Immigrant Services," *Social Justice* 35 (2008): 66–82.

3. US Department of Commerce, Bureau of the Census, 1860 United States Federal Census for David Graham, schedule 1, Free Inhabitants of the Town of Southold, 69.

4. Ruth Graham, "Boardinghouses: Where the City Was Born," *Boston Globe*, January 13, 2013.

5. Geoffrey K. Fleming and Amy Kasuga Folk, *Hotels and Inns of Long Island's North Fork* (Charleston, SC: History Press, 2009), chapter 4.

6. Regional Plan Association, "Long Island's Rental Housing Crisis," September 2013, http://www.rpa.org/article/long-islands-rental-housing-crisis.

7. US Department of Commerce, Bureau of the Census, 1940, Housing, vol. 1—Small Areas, part 2, New York, table 5.

8. These data are taken from ibid. and extrapolated from US Department of Commerce, Bureau of the Census, 1960, Census of Housing, vol. 1—States and Small Areas, New York, tables 25, 26, and 27.

9. Village of Greenport Code, chap. 150-8 R-2, http://www.ecode360.com/10977367.

10. Ibid., chap. 103, http://www.ecode360.com/28815627.

11. Greenport Board of Trustees, minutes of meeting, July 23, 2012.

12. *Berman v. Parker*, 348 U.S. 26, 33 (1954).

13. *Village of Belle Terre v. Boraas*, 416 U.S. 1 (1974).

14. See NYS Department of State, Office of General Counsel, Legal Memorandum LU05, "Definition of 'Family' in Zoning Law and Building Codes," http://www.dos.ny.gov/cnsl/lu05.htm.

15. Greenport Board of Trustees, minutes of meeting, July 23, 2012.

16. Partnership for a New Economy, "Immigration and the Revival of American Cities: From Preserving Manufacturing Jobs to Strengthening the Housing Market," 11, http://www.renewoureconomy.org/issues/american-cities/.

17. Long Island Index, "Housing Affordability in Greenport," http://longislandindexmaps.org/?zoom=5&x=1435485.35359&y=345805.37045&code=30576&tab=tabAffordability&panel=PctAffordable09&satellite=false&landuse=true&mainlayers=9%2C12%2C27%2C28%2C34%2C35%2C36%2C37%2C38%2C39%2C88&labellayers=18%2C90%2C91%2C92%2C93%2C94%2C97%2C98%2C99%2C100%2C101%2C103%2C104%2C114.

18. "With Rental Demand Soaring, Poor Are Feeling Squeezed," *New York Times*, December 9, 2013.

19. David Kapell, "It May Take a Village," *Newsday*, February 21, 2004.

20. "Annexation Plan Stirs Debate," *New York Times*, April 11, 2004.

21. Ada Louise Huxtable, "Housing, the American Myth," *New York Times*, April 21, 1969.

PROFILE — SOFIA'S QUEST

1. Robert V. Kemper and Anya Peterson Royce, "Mexican Urbanization since 1821: A Macro-Historical Approach," *Urban Anthropology* 8 (1979): 274.

2. US Bureau of the Census, Total Hispanic Population by Selected Subgroups, New York City and Boroughs, 2010, table SF1-P8 NYC, http://www.nyc.gov/html/dcp/pdf/census/census2010/t_sf1_p8_nyc.pdf.

3. Guillermo Vuletín, "Measuring the Informal Economy in Latin America and the Caribbean," IMF working paper, 2008, https://www.imf.org/external/pubs/ft/wp/2008/wp08102.pdf.

4. Mexico Voices Blogspot, "Using New Metric, INEGI Finds 60% of Workers in Informal Economy." December 12, 2012, http://mexicovoices.blogspot.com/2012/12/using-new-metric-inegi-finds-60-percent.html.

5. "Ambulantes, un Desafio," *El Universal*, January 26, 2006, http://www.eluniversal.com.mx/nacion/134456.html.

6. US Department of State, "2010 Human Rights Report: Mexico," http://www.state.gov/j/drl/rls/hrrpt/2010/wha/154512.htm; Mary Faith Mount-Cors, "Special Education in Mexico," in *Bridging Spanish Language Barriers in Southern Schools* (Chapel Hill, NC: UNC School of Education, 2007), http://www.learnnc.org/lp/editions/brdglangbarriers/1911.

CHAPTER 8 — COBBLED CARE

1. Emergency Medical Treatment and Labor Act, 42 USC §1395dd.

2. American College of Emergency Physicians, "Costs of Emergency Care Fact Sheet," http://newsroom.acep.org/index.php?s=20301&item=29928.

3. S. Collins et al., "The Income Divide in Health Care: How the Affordable Care Act Will Help Restore Fairness to the U.S. Health System," Commonwealth Fund, February 2012, http://www.commonwealthfund.org/publications/issue-briefs/2012/feb/income-divide.

4. For a list of aggravated felonies, see 8 USC §1101(a)(43).

5. "Alexander Hamilton on the Naturalization of Foreigners," *Population and Development Review* 36 (2010): 177–182.

6. Aristide Zolberg, *A Nation by Design: Immigration Policy in the Fashioning of America* (Cambridge, MA: Harvard University Press, 2006), 138.

7. For the early language of the doctrine, see An Act to Regulate Immigration, 47th Cong., August 3, 1882, sec. 2, http://library.uwb.edu/guides/usimmigration/22%20stat%20214.pdf. The list of today's excludable conditions is in sec. 212 (8 USC §1182), http://www.law.cornell.edu/uscode/text/8/1182.

8. For the early legislation, see An Act to Regulate Immigration. For current policy, see USCIS, "Public Charge Fact Sheet," http://www.uscis.gov/news/fact-sheets/public-charge-fact-sheet.

9. Brian K. Bruen et al., "No Evidence that Primary Care Physicians Offer Less Care to Medicaid, Community Health Center, or Uninsured Patients," *Health Affairs* 32 (September 2013): 1624–1630.

10. Michael D. Tanner, "War on Poverty at 50—Despite Trillions Spent, Poverty Won," Fox News, January 8, 2014. http://www.foxnews.com/opinion/2014/01/08/war-on-poverty-at-50-despite-trillions-spent-poverty-won/.

11. Lyndon Baines Johnson, State of the Union address (January 8, 1964), http://millercenter.org/president/speeches/detail/3382. "Paul Ryan: 'Dump' War on Poverty

Programs for New Approach," January 25, 2014, http://www.newsmax.com/Newsfront/paul-ryan-war-poverty-growth/2014/01/25/d/549018.

12. US Department of Health and Human Services, Health Resources and Services Administration, "Health Center Data," 2013, http://bphc.hrsa.gov/healthcenterdatastatistics/index.html.

13. See, for general information and standards, NCQA, "Patient-Centered Medical Home," http://www.ncqa.org/Programs/Recognition/Practices/PatientCenteredMedicalHomePCMH.aspx.

14. See Children's Defense Fund, "Profile of America's Uninsured Children, 2010," http://www.childrensdefense.org/child-research-data-publications/data/profile-of-americas-uninsured-children-2010.html.

15. Olivia Golden and Karina Fortuny, "Improving the Lives of Young Children: Meeting Parents' Health and Mental Health Needs through Medicaid and CHIP so Children Can Thrive," Urban Institute, March 17, 2011, http://www.urban.org/publications/412315.html.

16. "Obamacare: The Rest of the Story," *New York Times*, October 13, 2013.

17. Atul Gawande, *The Checklist Manifesto* (New York: Henry Holt, 2009), 79.

18. Stony Brook School of Medicine, "Translating Research and Transforming Medicine: The Stony Brook University School of Medicine Strategic Plan 2011–2015," 2, http://www.stonybrook.edu/sb/plans/SOM.pdf.

19. "Cowboys and Pit Crews," *New Yorker*, May 26, 2011.

PROFILE — AN ACCIDENTAL NURSE

1. "In Guatemala, Officers' Killings Echo Dirty War," *New York Times*, March 5, 2007.

2. US Department of State, "Guatemala 2013 Crime and Safety Report," OSAC, https://www.osac.gov/Pages/ContentReportDetails.aspx?cid=13878.

3. Guatemalan Human Rights Commission, "Three Thousand and Counting: A Report on Violence against Women in Guatemala," September 2007, http://www.ghrc-usa.org/resources/publications/.pdf.

4. "Women Crossing the U.S. Border Face Sexual Assault with Little Protection," *PBS NewsHour*, March 31, 2014, http://www.pbs.org/newshour/updates/facing-risk-rape-migrant-women-prepare-birth-control/.

CHAPTER 9 — LEGAL LIMBO

1. Illegal Immigration Reform and Immigrant Responsibility Act of 1996, Pub. L. 104–208, http://www.uscis.gov/iframe/ilink/docView/PUBLAW/HTML/PUBLAW/0-0-0-10948.html.

2. Transactional Records Access Clearinghouse (TRAC), Syracuse University, "Nature of Charge in New Filings Seeking Removal Orders through February 2014," http://trac.syr.edu/phptools/immigration/charges/apprep_newfiling_charge.php.

3. TRAC, "ICE Criminal Offense Level Business Rules," http://trac.syr.edu/immigration/reports/330/include/DocumentReleased_13–15734_Criminal_Offense_Level_Business_Rules.pdf.

4. "More Deportations Follow Minor Crimes, Records Show," *New York Times*, April 6, 2014.

5. TRAC, "Targeting of ICE Detainers Varies Widely by State and by Facility," http://trac.syr.edu/immigration/reports/343/.

6. TRAC, "US Deportation Outcomes by Charge," September 10, 2014, http://trac.syr.edu/phptools/immigration/court_backlog/deport_outcome_charge.php.

7. US Immigration and Customs Enforcement, Secure Communities Monthly Statistics through August 31, 2014, http://www.ice.gov/doclib/foia/sc-stats/nationwide_interop_stats-fy2012-to-date.pdf.

8. See "The Hispanic Americans Baseline Alcohol Survey (HABLAS): Rates and Predictors across Hispanic National Groups," NIHPA Author Manuscripts, October 2007, http://www.ncbi.nlm.nih.gov/pmc/articles/PMC2390823/.

9. "Violent Robberies in Riverhead Target Hispanic Men," *Newsday*, July 10, 2014.

10. "Immigrant Workers Caught in Net Cast for Gangs," *New York Times*, November 25, 2007.

11. "Our Towns: After Dismissing a Police Force, a Village Finds No Peace or Order," *New York Times*, June 6, 1995.

12. "Sex, Drugs and Police: Jury Urges End to Force," *New York Times*, October 27, 1994.

13. Robert J. Sampson, "*Rethinking Crime and Immigration*," *Contexts* vol. 7, no. 1 (2008), 30. http://contexts.org/articles/files/2008/01/contexts_winter08_sampson.pdf.

14. US Department of Homeland Security, Delegation of Immigration Authority Section 287(g), Immigration and Nationality Act, February 24, 2014, http://www.ice.gov/news/library/factsheets/287g.htm.

15. *Miranda-Oliveras v. Clackamas County*, No. 3:12-cv-02317-ST (D. Or.), April 11, 2014, http://scholar.google.com/scholar_case?case=7183853698243436215&q=miranda-olivares+v.+clackamas+county&hl=en&as_sdt=6,33&as_vis=1.

16. "Obama, Daring Congress, Acts to Overhaul Immigration," *New York Times*, November 20, 2014.

17. "Give ID Cards to All New Yorkers," *Daily News*, May 15, 2013.

18. "Guardian Angels Patrol Greenport, Say Latino Store Owners Threatened if They Don't Pay Gangs," *Southold Local*, March 12, 2015, http://southoldlocal.com/2015/03/12/guardian-angels-patrol-greenport-say-latino-store-owners-threatened-if-they-dont-pay-gangs/.

PROFILE — DEFERRED AND DELIVERED

1. DREAMers are young undocumented immigrants brought to the United States as children, self-identified as supporters of the Development, Relief, and Education for Alien Minors (DREAM) Act. This federal legislation, introduced into Congress but not enacted, would go farther than the presidential initiative of 2012, DACA, and would provide a path to citizenship for these young people.

2. "Women Crossing the U.S. Border Face Sexual Assault with Little Protection," *PBS NewsHour*, March 31, 2014, http://www.pbs.org/newshour/updates/facing-risk-rape-migrant-women-prepare-birth-control/.

3. Migration Policy Institute, "Deferred Action for Childhood Arrivals at the One-Year Mark," http://www.migrationpolicy.org/research/deferred-action-childhood-arrivals-one-year-mark-profile-currently-eligible-youth-and.

CHAPTER 10 — WHERE THERE'S A WILL, THERE'S A JOB (OR TWO)

1. See Arne L. Kalleberg and Kevin Hewison, "Precarious Work and the Challenge for Asia," *American Behavioral Scientist* 57 (2013): 271–288.

2. See Yu Xie and Margaret Gough, "Ethnic Enclaves and the Earnings of Immigrants," *Demography* 48 (2011): 1293–1315.

3. National Employment Law Project, "Immigration Status and Pay Documentation: Findings from the 2008 Unregulated Work Survey," http://www.nelp.org/page/-/Justice/2013/Fact-Sheet-Immigration-Status-Pay-Documentation.pdf?nocdn=1.

4. US Bureau of the Census, American FactFinder, data from 2010 General Population and Housing Characteristics and 2000 General Demographic Characteristics, http://factfinder2.census.gov/faces/nav/jsf/pages/community_facts.xhtml#none.

5. "Special Report: A Dwindling Work Force for Local Farmers," *Suffolk Times*, September 27, 2013.

6. Aviva Chomsky, *Undocumented: How Immigration Became Illegal* (Boston: Beacon Press, 2014), 151.

7. "Immigrants and the Economics of Hard Work," *New York Times*, April 2, 2006.

PROFILE — SACRIFICE AND SUCCESS

1. Transparency International, which ranks and rates countries according to their levels of corruption, found Colombia to be the 94th most corrupt country (out of 176) in 2013, similar to Greece and India. See http://www.transparency.org/country#COL.

2. "Colombia Devalues Peso by 10% in Emergency Decree," *New York Times*, June 29, 1999.

3. "Gustavson Column: Love and Hate for My Old House," *Suffolk Times*, July 28, 2014.

4. National Immigration Law Center, "Basic Facts about In-State Tuition for Undocumented Immigrant Students," http://www.nilc.org/basic-facts-instate.html.

PROFILE — THE NEW AMERICAN

1. For a rich ethnography of transnationalization between Brooklyn and a village in the Mixteca region of Mexico, see Robert Courtney Smith, *Mexican New York: Transnational Lives of New Immigrants* (Berkeley: University of California Press, 2006).

2. Guillermo Soberón et al., "The Health Care Reform in Mexico: Before and After the 1985 Earthquakes," *American Journal of Public Health* 76 (1986): 675–680.

3. This program has now been folded into the New York State health care exchange under the Affordable Care Act.

CHAPTER 11 — A SMALL-TOWN MODEL?

1. 2014 All-America City Award Application, Independence, OR, 4.

2. Perry Comprehensive Plan 2030 (draft August 21, 2013), 3–4, http://www.perryia.org/uploads/1/0/9/5/10951144/august_draft_web.pdf.

3. *Lozano v. City of Hazelton*, 2013 U.S. App. LEXIS 15256 (3rd Cir. PA, July 26, 2013).

4. The classic statement of this position is Gordon W. Allport, *The Nature of Prejudice* (Cambridge, MA: Perseus Books), 1954.

5. For a comprehensive literature review of this and related issues, see Hugh Donald Forbes, *Ethnic Conflict: Commerce, Culture, and the Contact Hypothesis* (New Haven, CT: Yale University Press), 1997.

6. "Hispanics Reviving Faded Towns on the Plains," *New York Times*, November 13, 2011.

INDEX

accountable care organization (ACO), 150–151

Acero family, 207–219; Diego, 210–211, 216–217; Edgar, 210, 217; Gustavo, 208–217; Gustavo, Jr., 210, 212, 215–217; Mireya, 207–217; Pablo, 212, 215–216. *See also* Carlos, Patty (Acero)

Acero-Pinzón family, 207–219. *See also* Acero family; Pinzón family

Advanced Placement (AP), 63, 71–72, 86, 218

Affordable Care Act, 136, 139, 146–147, 149–151

African Americans, 2–3, 5, 57, 206; discrimination against, 45–50, 65–66, 108; education, 10, 45, 66, 68–70, 84; enslavement, 11, 42–49, 66; in Greenport, 42–50, 54, 59–60; health care, 142, 144; housing, 47–48, 53–54, 101–120; internal migration, 11, 42–46, 49; whalemen, 26, 52

African migrants, 4, 26, 42–44

agriculture, 3, 4, 9, 35–36, 47, 64, 74–75, 123, 140, 201–202, 233. *See also* vineyards

Alcus, Pat, 142

Aldo's Coffee, 51–52

All-America City, 4, 233

Amelia. *See* Rigoberta and family

American-born children of immigrants, 3, 38, 64, 76, 122, 141, 196, 204, 234, 241n11

American identity, perceived threats to, 6, 48, 178

AME Zion Church, 46, 49

anti-immigrant groups, viii, 5–7, 173, 234. *See also* Ku Klux Klan; nativists

anti-immigrant violence, viii, 5–6. *See also* crimes against immigrants

architecture: public, 64–65; residential, 1–2, 28, 36, 53

Asha (housing administrator), 160–161

Ashley. *See* Rigoberta and family

Asian immigrants, 4–5

assimilation, 21–22, 32, 39–40, 65, 74, 105

asylum, 56, 91, 137, 149, 230

attention deficit hyperactivity disorder (ADHD), 122, 128–129

Augusta. *See* Martinez family

Aviles-Nott, Christine, 83–84

Baruch College–The City University of New York (CUNY), 216–217

"beaner-hopping," viii, 6. *See also* anti-immigrant violence

Black Christ. *See* Esquipulas, Guatemala

blacks. *See* African Americans

boarders, 15, 17–18, 94, 104–105, 109, 114

boardinghouses, 29–30, 34–35, 37, 104–105, 107

boatbuilding. *See* shipbuilding

Booth, Antonia, x, 23–24

border security, 92, 169, 178, 212

Borjas, George, 206

Brentwood, NY, 5, 94–95

brickmaking, 22, 28–32, 52, 104

Brookhaven, NY, 5, 45, 174

bunker fish. *See* menhaden

Bureau of Primary Health Care, 144

Burns, Liz, 69–70, 81

business owners. *See* entrepreneurs

Cabral, Erika, 73, 80, 82

California, 91, 169, 180, 202, 216

Cardoza family: Conchita, 11–12, 182–189,

ABOUT THE AUTHOR

DIANA R. GORDON has written widely about politics and criminal justice for academic and general audiences. Her books include, among others, *The Justice Juggernaut: Fighting Crime, Controlling Citizens* and *Transformation and Trouble: Crime, Justice and Participation in Democratic South Africa*. She is professor emerita of political science and criminal justice of The City College of New York and the Graduate Center of the City University of New York. Since her retirement, she has been writing scholarly and popular articles about recent Hispanic immigrants and their contributions to American life. *Village of Immigrants* is her first book about immigration. She lives in Greenport, New York.